MW00469265

Detour Down Desperation Road

Ann Renigar Hiatt, Ph.D.

Copyright © 2017 Ann Renigar Hiatt, Ph.D.
All rights reserved.
ISBN-10: 0-692-89478-0
ISBN-13: 978-0-692-89478-1

For Alex, Alana, and Others

Dedication

This book is dedicated to Jean Small. Thank you, Jean, for being there during a traumatic time in my life.
When I was confused, you listened.
When I doubted, you encouraged.
When I was afraid, you understood.
When I was frantic, you calmed me.
When I was desperate, you helped me make good decisions.
When I was lost, you showed me the way.
When I was in despair, you reminded me of the wonder and beauty in life.
You will live in my heart for the rest of my life. As you requested, everyday I will light a lantern and then let it go.

CONTENTS

Introduction   9

CHAPTER ONE - ANN'S DETOUR

On The Road Again   12
Mountain Top Enlightenment   16
Unwanted Journey   21
Driving North With My Monkey Mind   25
Attention!   34
Analyzing and Committing   39

CHAPTER TWO - FINDING HELP

Learning And Seeking Advice   46
Mom's Legal Plans   50
    Rob's Guardianship   53
    Diane's Disrupted Future   54
Is Mom Driving Safely?   57
    Rob's Surprise   59
Can Mom Continue Driving?   63
Can Mom Pass the Driver's Test?   65

CHAPTER THREE - HONORING EMOTIONS

Mom's Denial   68
    Betsy's Anger   70
    Jack's Turmoil   71

Dan's Acceptance   73

The Doctor's Self-Diagnosis   76

The Gun Collector's Despair   78

Tim's Embarrassment Prompts Silence   81

CHAPTER FOUR

PROCEEDING SLOWLY AND RESPECTING DIGNITY

Changes For Me, Changes For Mom   84

JOBS AND IDENTITIES – "I Have To Be Me"

The Hardware Lady   85

    Claudia - The Public Relations Expert   87

    Jack Wants A Job   89

CONTROLLING FINANCES – "Respect What Is Mine"

    Mom Needs A Little Cash   90

    Ken Frets and Checks   95

    Bill's Great Deal   96

DRIVING WITH DEMENTIA – "I Can Still Do It"

Mom Drives On   98

    Bob's New Toy   99

    Jack Is Late for Work   101

    The Doctor Drives Everywhere   104

ROLES AND TRADITIONS – "I Still Care"   107

Holiday Excursion   108

    The Bucket   110

    Where's Beanie?   112

    Reclusive Betty   115

    Role Reversal   116

CHAPTER FIVE
GRASP THE WHEEL AND HANG ON!
MID-STAGE DEMENTIA

The Road Warrior Struggles 120
Christmas Homecoming 122
Moving Home 125
Problems Solved? 126
All Is Well! Or Is It? 127
Mom Steps Down Again 131
My Day With A Mission 132
Diversion Accomplished 136
IRRATIONALITY AND CONFUSION
  The Doctor Wants To Marry 141
  You Moved Us 143
  Tommy Needs to Go 146
  You Are Not My Boss 149
LIVING IN THE PAST
  Bill's Daily Drive 151
  Jenny Begs To Go Home 153
  Dan Dances 156
  Myra Needs People 158
  The Guys' Table 159
FEAR AND ANXIETY
  Wilma Panics 161
  Stuart's Shadow 163
  Incoming! 165

CHAPTER SIX
ROAD BLOCKS AHEAD!
FROM MID TO LATE-STAGE DEMENTIA

Mom Meets Her Great Granddaughter	169
House Hunting Problems	170
I Don't Know How Much Longer	
I Can Handle It All	172
Finding Assisted Living	174
Move-In Day	177
Mom's Hallucinations	179
HALLUCINATIONS AND DELUSIONS	
Tim's Girlfriend	182
Luke Banishes The Squatters	183
Maggie Flees	186
Karen Grieves	189
SEVERE ANXIETY AND CONFUSION	
I Don't Know You	191
Dan Cannot Sleep	194
Sun-downing Seth	196
Jon Disappears	199

CHAPTER SEVEN – ROUTE CHANGES
CARE CHANGING EVENTS

Mom Cries, "Help"	202
Midnight Turmoil	206
THE Appointment	207

Mom's Psychiatric Evaluation   212
Soul Searching At The Hospital   216
You Are Sending Mom Home?   218
Seeking Validation   222
CARE CHANGING EVENTS
   Leah's Love Prevails   223
   Dan Fears Falling   225
   Bob Begs To Go Home - Beth's
      Dreaded Decision   227
   Marjorie Needs Time   230
   Ida's Recurring Infections   235
   The Doctor Is Down   237
   Curt Falls   239
   Myra Needs Peace and Quiet   241
   Jack's Last Rant   243
   Claudia's Obstinacy   246
   Jon Leaves   247
   Michael's Surprise   248
   Marie's Near Miss   250
   Jane's Ultimate Challenge   253

CHAPTER EIGHT - ACCEPTING AND LETTING GO
MOM HAS A NEW HOME

A Week Of Respite   256
Return To Real Life   261
The Dreaded Visit   263
DAILY LIFE IN MEMORY CARE   268

Hilda's Daughter	269
The Boss	271
Call My Lawyer	273
The Resident Romeo	277
The Interior Decorator	278
Mom's First Trip Out	280
Betsy Thrives	282
Bob Takes Care of Others	283
Kindhearted Dan	285
The Doctor's Eccentricities	285
Mom's Ninetieth Birthday	286
The Party	288
Sweet Excursions	290
Thank You, Stranger	291
Ann's Quandary	293
A Looming, Gigantic Task	294
One Day At A Time	295
Middle of the Night Emergencies	298
Why Are Those People Looking In My Window?	299
Boom!	301
Why Oh Why?	301
Time, Where Did You Go?	302
Hospice	303
Epilogue One	304
Epilogue Two	305
Advice For The Road	306
A Plea	307
Acknowledgements	308
About The Author	309

Introduction

The mental deterioration of a loved one is never a happy story. But for many, it is a reality that must be embraced, faced, and survived. The stories in this book invite you to step into unpredictable situations, thoughts, and emotions of determined, courageous, and loving people as they interact with and care for their loved ones. All of the stories are true and some are funny and will make you chuckle. We never laugh at those who are slowly changing as dementia claims their brains. But as they move from mild to severe dementia, we have to take a few minutes to laugh at situations and ourselves. How can we live if we cannot find meaning and, at times, humor in our challenges?

Without exception, the lives of the caregivers in this book, including me, were forever changed. We came together and poured our hearts out to each other. Because each of us shared a common plight, we empathized, understood, accepted, and encouraged each other.

All too often, caregivers find themselves alone as friends disappear, perhaps because they are uncomfortable and uncertain what to say or do. Unless a person experiences daily life with someone who has Alzheimer's or one of the many other dementias, it is difficult to understand the disease. Loved ones with the disease can no longer engage in meaningful conversations and caregivers sometimes feel as though they are in solitary confinement. After you read, you will have walked a little way in our shoes.

These stories were written over ten years of weekly support group meetings and interviews with caring people in southern communities. Episodes from the lives of nine of the caregivers appear in several chapters and follow their changing challenges as the disease progresses.

The events are true although individuals' names and identifying characteristics were altered to insure privacy. In some instances, dialog was edited or rearranged to better convey behaviors, emotions, and the impact of the events on lives.

CHAPTER ONE

ANN'S DETOUR

On The Road Again

The roar of my tires on the shoulder of the road jolted me. Rational Ann chastised, *wake up! Take a break, walk around, breathe fresh mountain air!* Emotional Ann warned, *if you stop, Mom will fuss.* Rational Ann countered, *better than being scraped off the side of the road!*

The 450-mile sprint lost its novelty last year. The route, curves, speed limits, and hiding places favored by highway patrol officers were branded into my memory and the journey became automatic, much like brushing my teeth. My body was trapped behind the wheel, but my monkey-mind relentlessly jumped around, anticipating my week in North Carolina.

Mom's irrationality and memory loss remained in the back of my mind regardless of my physical location. I knew that her memory was slipping when we moved to Singapore three years ago. As much as I relished all of the new experiences there, Mom's decline festered in my mind like an annoying splinter.

Sixty more miles, time to make the call. "Mom, I am coming down the mountain and will be there in an hour."

"What? Today? I thought you said that you would be here tomorrow."

"Today, Mom. I'm starving. Are you hungry? Let's eat early."

Unless Mom arrived at the cafeteria before it became crowded, she became agitated waiting in the long line. "I am glad you called, I was thinking about warming the food that I brought home yesterday."

"Save that for another day and as soon as I arrive we will go get a hot meal and your favorite pie."

"I'll be ready."

My plans to return to our southern home and resume my career as a professor at the university after we lived in Asia fell apart when Dale accepted a job in Ohio. As always, I supported his decisions and assured him that I could apply for a position at one of the northern universities. But Emotional Ann flinched, *what about Mom?* Daily phone conversations provided little assurance that she still thrived living alone.

My phone rang, Dale was excited. "I just booked our flight to Amsterdam. We leave a week from Thursday."

My heart raced. Dale's company recently expanded and opened an office in The Netherlands. Frequent travel to Europe was part of his new job. Since I had not resumed working, I usually went along on his trips.

I longed to see the explosion of spring color across the tulip fields in Holland. But my nagging problem invaded my thoughts and dampened my enthusiasm. Could I go? As usual, I downplayed my concerns. "That is good news. I just hope I can accomplish my mission here and return to Ohio in time to pack everything."

Dale was silent for a moment and I wondered if he was dreading hauling my over-stuffed suitcase. "Did you tell your Mom about her appointment?"

"No. I didn't want her to cancel it."

"Well, good luck with that, she may refuse to go at the last minute. You can fill me in oh how she is faring later tonight. Don't forget to turn on the water heater as soon as you arrive."

Topping the last hill in Virginia, I began my descent into my home State. On clear days, I gasped at the sight of five tall buildings fifty miles in the distance, monuments against the undulating hills of piedmont

13

North Carolina. The sight was fleeting but filled me with awe and pride. On cloudy days, I gasped anyway. My inner joy soared when I glimpsed my home city. It was the same comforting feeling that flooded me every time I flew over the USA coastline thousands of feet in the air on my way home from foreign lands. I would soon be there.

Before I turned into Mom's driveway, she crossed the lawn to greet me. How did she know that I was approaching at that moment? Her intuitive mind always amazed me. I learned long ago to be careful what I was thinking.

She smiled and hugged me. "Aren't you tired after driving all that way?"

She wore her typical uniform, black slacks and black and white print blouse. Her tinted, dark hair was stark against her pinkish-white skin. Bright red lipstick was her only makeup.

"I'm just glad to be here with you. Are you hungry? If we hurry, we can beat the crowd and avoid a long line."

Before entering her little house, I paused and took one last deep breath of fresh air and then followed her inside to retrieve her purse and jacket. Ugh! The piles were higher but nothing else changed.

Mom selected her favorites at the cafeteria. The menu seldom changed but our mealtime conversations had definitely changed. Discussions of my dreams, plans, and the details of my daily life were too confusing for her and required breaking things down into short, repeated sentences.

Mom looked around. "This chicken and rice is good but the decaf is getting cold. Where is the coffee lady? Why is that man over there staring at me?"

"He probably recognizes you from the hardware store. Everyone in town knows you, Mom"

She asked how Dale was and if I had heard from Alexandra, my daughter. Had Alex called Mom recently? I did not ask. She probably would not remember and if she said 'no,' sad feelings may follow.

"As usual, Dale is focused on his work and Alex is swamped by her graduate classes and working part-time."

My comments were sufficient. I was just too tired to offer repeated explanations of the details of Alex's life. We ate in silence for a few minutes. I was happy that she enjoyed the hot meal and was eating most of it. She looked thinner. Was she losing weight? For the first time in years, we wore the same size clothes. I assured myself that she was not too thin and her arthritic joints were better off.

"What time is it? You should get on the road to the lake before it gets dark. It is not safe for you to drive by yourself at night. Will you get me a takeout box? I can't finish all of this." Her motherly concern for me was still intact and moderated her own needs.

"There is plenty of time but I need to turn on the hot water heater when I arrive. The sun shining on the windows will have warmed the house. It is spring here but we received snow flurries in Ohio two days ago."

"Aren't you afraid of going into that deserted place with all those windows? Someone could be out there peering in at you."

I tightly closed my lips to keep from saying, "*If someone can hang in the tops of the trees while looking in, they have a problem, not me*". Rational Ann scolded, be *ashamed*!

As we drank another cup of decaf, I patiently waited for THE question.

"Will you be coming tomorrow? When can we ride up to the mountains again?"

Ah ha! There it was. She loved our day-trips to the mountains. Riding in my car to the edge of the Blue Ridge was a tradition that she enjoyed every time that I was home for the week.

"Well, why don't we go tomorrow? I will pick you up in the morning and we will have lunch at the Hungry Farmers' Café."

She smiled and sipped her coffee. I resisted the urge to tell her my plans for the day after tomorrow.

Mountain Top Enlightenment

Mom never changes. A simple, "Let's go," and she wastes no time climbing into my car. I discovered years ago that any destination would do, her joy was in the ride. Perhaps that is one reason why she was attracted to my dad. He loved cars and always drove a nice one, even during the depression years. On dates, they whipped around town in his snazzy, dark blue 1937 roadster, window-shoped at new car showrooms, enjoyed ice cream at the Tastee-Freeze, and were regulars at Singleton's, the popular drive-in food and music spot for young adults. Sunday afternoons were special. A fifty-mile trek to the nearby mountains was routine. Roberta snuggled close to R.O. as he skillfully managed the curves with one hand on the wheel and the other arm around her when he wasn't shifting gears. Sometimes, they packed siblings, friends, and picnic baskets into the car.

Mom's long-term memory was still sharp. She loved entertaining me with tales of her early life and dating my dad. I relished every detail of her stories. My memory of Dad was that of a child; he died when I was eleven. She repeated her favorite stories each time I was in town we both enjoyed them over and over.

To please Mom, we were climbing the same mountain that I descended the day before. It was my way of assuaging my guilt and making up for my last absence. My mission every time that I was in town was to get her out of her house and take her to the places she loved. In truth, I also enjoyed our mountain excursions, listening to the sound of my engine purring up the incline, and maneuvering my car around the sharp curves. Practicing my driving skills put a big smile, not a look of horror on Mom's face. I must have inherited a 'need-for-speed' gene. Mom admitted that at times Dad had 'a heavy foot'.

The crisp, sunny spring day was exceptionally pleasant. She loved the expansive views, but then she loved everything about our trips, southern country food, road side produce stands, the ever-changing majesty of the hills, and just being with me. The day was always predictable. She liked visiting the same places every trip.

Our final stop was a quaint clothing store at the top of the mountain. We passed under the parkway as we approached her favorite shop that was owned by a gracious southern lady. Mom respected her and understood the daily toil and challenges of small business ownership. After Dad's death, she kept his small hardware store alive to support us and pay the huge hospital bills that accrued from his long bout with cancer.

As I slowed and turned into a parking space, Mom gathered her purse, jacket, and a bag containing a blouse that she purchased on our previous visit but decided to return. She always found something to take home and sometimes returned it on the next trip.

"It's important to support small businesses. The nice lady that owns this shop works hard and doesn't make a killing." She hopped out of the car. Her steps were quick and lively. Her smile was reason enough for our return visits. *Enjoy your favorite shop, Roberta.*

I paused just inside the door at a rack of dresses, hoping to please Mom by magically finding her vision of the perfect black dress with flared skirt that was no longer fashionable or available. *Relax, Ann, and take your time analyzing each dress on the rack. You will be here for a while.*

Mom headed straight for the friendly owner who smiled as she greeted Mom warmly. The kind lady acknowledged me with a nod and quickly gave her assistant a task before settling down to again hear Mom's life story in a nutshell. Mom's standard, short version focused on the highlights of her forty-year, single-handed *running* of the hardware store. The longer version included her life growing up on a farm during the hard times of the depression. I never reminded her that the lady heard her stories every time we were there. They were her identity, her life, and telling them grounded her.

After I inspected every dress in Mom's size, I finally took pity on the owner and interrupted, holding up a black dress. "Mom, how about this one?"

I realized that it did not fit Mom's notion of the perfect dress that she could keep on hand in case of an emergency, usually another funeral. She no longer wore dresses, favoring pants for every occasion. That fact did not deter her search for the one perfect specimen that was appropriate for any occasion in any weather.

I knew by the look on her face that she thought

the dress was awful, but she said nothing negative. She was always aware of other people's feelings and did not want to insult the owner with disparaging remarks about her inventory.

"Well, keep that one out and see what else you can find." Then, forgetting that we had been there many times, she realized that she had not introduced me and turned back to the owner. "Oh, I am sorry! This is my *mother*, Ann."

I gasped and my eyes widened. What? I waited, but she did not catch or correct the error. I almost overturned a rack of blouses grasping something to hold me up. The owner's weak smile flashed her implied understanding and sympathy.

Many times throughout my life, Mom proclaimed, "I am *your* mother!" That declaration was always followed by whatever I did or said that was unacceptable. The reminder of her status was her way of demanding respect from her only child. Reflecting on this recent change in my title, I needed fresh mountain air. "Mom, I will be right back. I want to check something in the car." I never disappeared without informing her of my destination. Pausing, I knew that her next statement was coming.

"Don't leave me!"

Argh! I never considered that an option and never left her anywhere except safely in her home. Why would she say that? Abandon my Mother? What an unthinkable, ultimate disrespect! Her appeal always frustrated and confounded me.

Once outside, I took deep breaths. My brain needed a good infusion of oxygen. I thought about the mother that I knew so well. My strong, resolute mother, determined to be in control of her life and the way she lived it. Her memory of events long ago was still sharp but she could not remember what she ate for lunch. Keeping track of things, making plans, and carrying them out were no longer possible.

Oh! It hit me like the proverbial 'ton of bricks'. I looked out over the spectacular vista that spread for fifty miles that day and it was suddenly clear. In my mind, *I had become my mother's mother.* There was no ceremony, no formal pronouncement, not even a bolt of lightning. There was just the simple realization that was perhaps an overdue acknowledgement and acceptance of the severity of her mental decline. This was more than normal aging.

The full weight of my new responsibility held me in place as I stared over the majestic vista. There was no choice. She was declining and had no one but me. In her lucid moments, she would never accept me as her mother. But somehow, I had to step up and begin steering her future.

My mind screamed, *"NO! I am not ready! I am not qualified!"* I never believed that I was qualified to raise my *own daughter.* That she became a mature adult was not the result of any deliberate action on my part. It is probably more accurate to say that my daughter raised me, or that we gradually learned the mother-daughter thing as we went along.

My daughter, my baby, will soon graduate as a doctor of psychology and hopes to specialize in child psychology. She loves helping children! This fact amazes me since she was an only child. I always took a low-key approach to motherhood. I was very lenient, chose my battles carefully, and within reason, encouraged her to make her own decisions. Of course, I annoyed her in her teen-aged years. She never forgave me for sharing tales of her adolescent escapades as examples and 'fodder' for my students' thoughts in my lectures at the university.

"Mom! I could have died. I met one of your students and she asked if I was Dr. Ann's daughter. She knew about my party at our house when you and Dad were out of town and my friends built a bonfire on the lawn and burned the yard furniture. What else about me is common knowledge on campus?"

In my opinion, *raising* a child is not even a word that refers to parenting. I think the truth is that we just hang in there, trying to make certain that they don't hurt or kill themselves before they 'reach the top of fool's hill.' That was my grandmother's designation for finally becoming an adult.

The top of fool's hill is where Mom and I are supposed to be now. Ideally, adulthood is that state of being rational, in control, and at the top of the world. It is a place with many vistas and many options. Adult mental deterioration and decline is one of those slow routes back down the hill, characterized by childlike thinking and behaviors and the need for constant supervision. The future flashed before my eyes as I stood there. I had a premonition that I would be anything but *in control.*

Unwanted Journey

"I don't know why I have to come here. This place is just too big. I want to see a doctor on my side of town so that I can drive myself and find a parking space right outside his door."

"Mom, neighborhood doctors have all joined large practices. Few are located in residential communities. Besides, you live in a city that has one of the best medical centers in the country. It makes good sense to see the experts here."

"What will I do if you can't bring me?"

Like most parents, I knew that the best way to respond to her fears was to assure her that everything was all right and that I would take care of her. "Don't worry, I am back from Singapore and will always bring you."

Rational Ann was dubious. *Can you live up to that promise?* I knew myself. My need for travel and novelty took precedence over plodding through daily routines. Trips to Europe were a wonderful feature of my life in Ohio. Plus, careful advance planning and scheduling of my life was not my preferred operational mode.

Mom panicked when she saw Psychiatry over the door of the department we were entering. "What? Why are we going here? I'm not crazy."

Rational Ann prodded me. *Be vigilant, more motherly assurance and soothing required.* "Dr. Stone is a neurologist and his office must be in here. This place is growing. They probably stick doctors everywhere."

Perhaps Mom's panic-struck expression was commonplace. Dr. Stone's staff greeted her warmly and soothed her anxiety. "Of course your daughter can be with you throughout your exam." Whew, no waiting. I had visions of chasing her down the hall as she retreated. She can run fast.

Routine assessments verified her good physical condition. She walked up and down the hall several times while the nurses evaluated her gait. Her balance and coordination seemed normal. A technician administered a series of questions that were obviously memory tests. Some of the questions seemed routine. What day, month, year is it? Mom successfully drew a clock face and inserted the hands and numbers although that task took a while. Occasionally, she glanced inquiringly at me, expecting me to provide the correct response. I looked around and pretended not to notice. Three familiar items, ball, apple, and house were repeated several times, and she was instructed to remember them. Later, she became frustrated when she could not recall the three items.

As the memory test progressed, I could no longer deny her cognitive decline, the proof was happening in front of me. I was glad that this was not one of those days when she was able to function better than normal and *'give a good show.'* Or was I? Yes, it was time. I needed an accurate, expert analysis of her mental status.

Dr. Stone was mild-mannered and pleasant. Mom smiled, shook his hand, and made small talk. He focused directly on Mom's expressions as he asked her questions about her life and daily routines, but glanced at me, checking my non-verbal responses to her answers. In preparation for the visit, I practiced two facial expressions, raised eyebrows and a slight nod conveyed *I agree,* and a frown and pursed lips indicated *no way.*

He paused and contemplated his next words. Then, he dropped the bomb. "I believe that you have some cognitive impairment, possibly vascular dementia or perhaps Alzheimer's."

I gasped. Although I was having nightmares about this possibility, my optimistic spirit kept hope alive. Surely it was low vitamin B-12 or some deficiency that could be easily corrected! I slumped in my chair and quietly mumbled, "Oh, no. Oh, dear." The whole, ugly picture of her future decline flashed before my eyes. I knew that there was no hope, no cure.

Mom interrupted my mental horror show. "Oh, Ann, stop it. It's not that bad, I'm fine. Why, I can still dance the Charleston! I can do everything for myself."

Dr. Stone smiled and agreed that it was very important for her to continue her normal activities, but he added a big qualifier, *for now*. Perhaps Mom did not understand the words Alzheimer's or vascular dementia. I was certain that she did not connect those words with the consequences of the diagnosis. Whatever the reason, this normally fearful, worrywart mother of mine seemed unconcerned.

Dr. Stone prescribed an anti-depressant and Aricept, a dementia medication that may keep the disease from becoming worse for a while. He wanted to conduct additional tests including an MRI of her brain for baseline information.

Mom's normal negativity and resistance revved up. I reassured her that her insurance would pay and that we needed all of the information that we could get. Only part of my statement was correct. In truth, I did not know whether Medicare would pay for the MRI and I doubted that her minimal supplemental insurance would cover the remainder of the bill. It was true that I wanted the MRI to better understand the areas of her brain that were affected. Several years later, I appreciated the existence of the first MRI.

We returned to the car and Mom's thoughts focused on our next adventure. Surprisingly, her short-term memory worked well. She remembered my promise of a delicious, hot meal at a favorite restaurant that, for years, we enjoyed on special occasions. As we drove across town, I silently agonized as she chatted, mostly to herself. She was obviously in a good mood and happily looking forward to dinner.

After we ate, she finally became quiet. "What did that doctor say is wrong with me?"

I reminded her of the Alzheimer's diagnosis, and again she wrinkled her brow and scowled a look of disbelief. "There is nothing wrong with me, I'm healthy as a horse. If it weren't for Old Arthur causing pain in my joints, I could do anything."

Quick flashbacks to her depression over the years since Dad died made me decide that it was unwise to elaborate on a diagnosis that meant nothing to her. To me it meant everything, slow decline and losing her a little at a time. Eventually I would face the ultimate loss that tears apart every daughter's heart, at least those who were lucky enough to experience the unconditional love of a mother.

Driving North With My Monkey Mind

One week after I arrived, I turned off the hot water heater, locked the windows and doors, threw my bags into the trunk, blew a kiss toward the lake, settled into the seat, and tore out of the driveway. Rational Ann chastised me. *Slow down! Watch for hungry, desperate deer.* The lure of young, tender grass in early spring drove them out of the woods and into the sunlight near the roads. If only I could stay and walk along our paths in the woods. The swaying pines and chirping birds often provided answers to my problems in the past.

Our little lake house saved my sanity many times over the years. Building it was a labor of love and the fulfillment of hours of planning and drawing blueprints, a final design project completed in my senior undergraduate year. Dale and I measured, sawed, hammered, and lifted boards into place on weekends. Except for laying the foundation and pouring the cement basement floor, our hands touched every board, nail, and shingle that went into the structure. We wired and plumbed it and were so invested that when Dale lost his job during the recession and my part-time teaching position was cut, we sold our starter house close to our families and moved our ten-year old daughter and everything that we owned across two counties to the lake.

I was in grad school. That was the beginning of my life behind the wheel as a 'road warrior.' From that moment on, work, school, seeing Mom or anyone else, required time on the highway. Through many crises and changes, our small lake house served as home base and was my oasis, my retreat.

After I merged onto the Interstate, our house in Ohio was 440 miles north, six to eight hours of driving, depending on how hard I pushed and how often I stopped. Traffic thinned and I adjusted my seat and focused on driving and the scenery for about two minutes. Emotional Ann was on edge. My monkey mind bounded around in my head. My thoughts drifted to Mom's parting words.

"Don't worry about me, I will be all right. I will miss you, but I enjoy being by myself. I like living alone. I can do as I please."

Dear Mom, the survivor. At thirty-eight, her four-year struggle with the downward spiral of Dad's cancerous demise ended with the loss of the love of her life and cast her into a scary, lonely, world of sadness and uncertainty. Somehow, she summoned strength, trudged up the street to the old store building, placed the open sign on the door, built fires in the pot-bellied stoves, and endured the ups and downs of the hardware business.

Dad's seventy-two-year-old father, Papa, still repaired shoes in the space beside the hardware store. The two businesses were in the same building and connected by a wooden door. If asked, Papa did his best to provide Mom with advice and assistance. Papa suffered through a mental breakdown after his only son was sent to England during World War II. But he opened his shop every morning and repaired shoes or made things from leather and wood. His daily presence assured Mom that she was not totally alone. I can still see her helping him watch for cars and cross the busy street on his way home in the late afternoons.

Over time, she earned enough to pay off thousands of dollars of hospital bills, replace the coal stoves with gas heaters, and pay the household bills. We lived in the small, two-bedroom house that Dad built next door to Papa, Grandma, and Aunt Ruby, Dad's older, unmarried sister. Dad planned the house while he was a medic in Europe and began building it soon after he received his discharge. I was only one year old when we moved from Grandma's spare bedroom into our new home.

My childhood there was 'Ann in paradise.' I played in the combined back yards with neighborhood friends, skated on the sidewalks, dashed in and out of Grandma's for her homemade cornbread, and played 'dress-up' in my Aunt's good clothes and shoes. Dad worked alongside Papa repairing shoes and at night, transformed the old space that was once Papa's neighborhood grocery store into the ideal place for his dream, his hardware store. Mom helped Grandma wash clothes on Mondays, cooked lunch and dinners for Dad and me, and celebrated my birthdays with parties in our backyard. Every Sunday afternoon, we went to Mom's parents' farm, her childhood home. My cousins and I played kick-the-can and outdoor games, but stopped to eat watermelon or homemade ice cream.

Three years after the hardware store opened, Dad began walking with a cane. He had surgery but his pain became worse. His suffering hit me all of a sudden the day as I watched him crawl from the front porch into the house. Another surgery soon followed. His recovery was slow and Mom began working in the hardware store.

She was overwhelmed and desperate during those years that he was bed-ridden and in and out of the hospital. I stayed next door with my grandparents and aunt when a hospital bed was moved into the bedroom and Mom slept in mine. When he was at home, I often sat by his side after school while Mom ran back and forth between our house and the hardware store.

I was eleven years old and scared. IV's and tubes disappeared under the thin white blankets, he was in excruciating pain and could not move. Mom fed him and turned him regularly to avoid bedsores. I don't remember much about those days except that I often ran to a makeshift tree house in the neighbor's yard, climbed the ladder, dangled my legs, and cried. I did not know what to say to him or Mom.

My grandparents and aunt loved me dearly and assured me that he would be all right, but an overall sadness pervaded the whole neighborhood and I tried not to show my distress. When he again entered the hospital, Mom left very early every morning before I went to school, fed him breakfast, returned, opened the hardware store, and then rushed back to the hospital after closing to be by his side in the evenings. Exhausted, she often drove across town after midnight. She slept in a chair beside his bed at the hospital unless a family member or a kind family friend volunteered to sit with him overnight.

I vividly remember being alone in my favorite tree, tears streaming down my face and praying for an end to his suffering. "If he is going to die, let it be soon." Two days later, he did. When my Aunt Margie appeared at my schoolroom door, I stood up, closed my book, inserted it into my book bag and marched out without saying a word.

It was all over and Mom was worn out, physically and emotionally. Her WWII dreams of being a happy, stay-at-home wife and mother were dashed. Even though she took business courses in college and was sharp and capable, the reality and loneliness were as difficult to carry as the buckets of coal that fueled the pot bellied stoves in the old store building.

I tried to make her life easier. I did not forget that I wished him dead, felt responsible, and wanted to take care of her. I helped her after school by organizing, straightening stock, pricing, arranging new items, and reluctantly assisting customers, relying on Mom's presence and guidance.

Mom's doctors prescribed anti-depressants and anti-anxiety medicines. She tried to hide her feelings but she suffered. Her negative, 'glass-half-full' attitude about everything frustrated me. Nothing that I did made much difference. She walked up the street to the store every morning and home every evening, exhausted. She kept Dad's vision exactly as it was the day he could no longer walk around and assist customers.

After the hospital bills were finally paid, she made a few changes to our house, added closets in the attic and wall-to-wall carpeting in the living room, but the furniture that they chose remained in the same locations in the house as when placed there the year that Dad finished the house.

My idyllic childhood ended when the nightmare of Dad's slow demise began. The happy, bright future faded at that time. The passing days produced nothing but uncertainty and unhappiness. Three years after his death, I began my teenage quest to discover me and make my own life. Who was this person called Ann? What did she believe, what did she want, and what did she need? All of a sudden, I understood that my life was ahead of me.

Unfortunately, I was thinking with an adolescent's brain and was in a hurry to experience an adult's life of freedom and adventure. In my mind, Mom was stuck in fear and depression. She pulled inward just as wagon trains circled their wagons for protection. Mom's old-fashioned, Victorian attitudes repulsed me. My belligerence accelerated and I forged ahead alone, a teen in the 1960's.

At that time, my answers came quickly. I needed someone special, someone to love me, someone to believe in me, someone to replace my daddy. My tumultuous journey through those years added to Mom's problems. She did not understand me, and was not prepared. I did not want to upset her, but I could not help myself. I had to move on with my life.

Everyone recognized Mom as the strong, competent woman who knew everything about tools and hardware. Every morning, she moved wheelbarrows, trashcans, and toy wagons outside the front door to announce that she once again welcomed customers. They did not have to remember the name of that gizmo or item that they needed, a short description of the function it served was sufficient for Mom to quickly locate it in her little store of useful items. If a customer needed a handful of 20-penny nails, she fished them out of the bin, dropped them into a paper bag, and weighed them on the old scale. "That will be five cents, please." Only a few people saw through her act and knew that she was functioning, but was depressed and fearful.

Papa died eight years after Dad. Everyone wondered how his sudden death would affect Mom. The loneness in that old building hit her hard but did not change her resolve to remain there. What else could she do in her late forties but continue the same, familiar pattern?

Uncle Bobby and I took over Papa's job of assembling wagons, tricycles, wheelbarrows, anything shipped in pieces that came with instructions, nuts, bolts, and screws. Aunt Mary Frances worked in the store one day each week to give Mom a day off. In my twenties, I softened and better understood how Mom's hard experiences had shaped her attitudes and beliefs. I tried to give up my impossible dream to restore her happy life. The most that I could do was lend a helping hand and spend as much time with her as possible.

I helped Mom in the store after I married and began working and taking college courses. My main contribution was to keep things organized. She tended to pile new stock on top of old without sorting and arranging.

Two years after Alex was born, I taught full-time and took graduate classes. The neat old store became disorganized and her house accumulated clutter on top of more clutter. My eyes warned that a major problem was developing. Her behaviors were more than simply being frugal and mimicking her mother who saved everything useful, including small pieces of string. Mom was a hoarder and was slowly amassing piles of *'stuff.'*

She often kept Alex after school so that I could study and teach classes, and on weekends while Dale and I built the lake house. The trinkets and toys that Mom bought Alex were mixed into everything else in Mom's house. I was grateful for her love and assistance and refrained from commenting about the jumbled mess. Challenging and questioning her behavior was never easy.

"You just don't know how hard it is to be a widow and have no one to depend on but myself. I do a man's job to make a living. I can't afford to just throw things away and buy new ones."

Time passed, and with the loss of our jobs during the recession, we had to choose between our starter home and our project at the lake. To me, the decision was more than just 'where do we want to live?' We loved the lake but how could I move my daughter fifty miles from her grandmother? In my melancholy moments, I often wonder why and how I did it. From then on, Mom's daily life was changed and my guilt resurfaced and compounded.

Mom's accumulation of *stuff* in her house grew exponentially. Rather than walk, she drove her car the short distance to the hardware store and loaded it with items that she 'may need one day.' Her home became a mini-hardware store. Paper bags full of nails, screws, hooks, fishing lures, as well as miscellaneous screwdrivers, hammers, pliers, and much more were everywhere. The attic overflowed and the steps to the attic became impassible. All spaces under furniture were stuffed full, as were the corners of each room. Shovels, rakes, brooms, ladders, and wheelbarrows, were piled within a couple inches of her car in the garage and the small half-basement was full.

I worried. What if she became ill? No one could stay there and care for her. She slowly barricaded herself into an environment that only she could stand or understand. Sometimes, I made an innocuous comment. "Mom, you have to let me help you clean some of this stuff out. I need to run the vacuum and dust for you."

"Oh, no. My house is small and I won't know where anything is located if you move things around. I'll go through things when you are not in town." She never did.

Fortunately, I had my retreat, the lake house. Unfortunately, my refuge was fifty miles from her home and too small for anyone except the three of us. I gladly raced back and forth, desperately needing the time driving to calm down, regroup, think, and prepare for the next day.

Except for visits to her siblings, Mom's social life was limited to brief conversations with customers, neighbors, and people who stopped to say hello at the cafeteria where she ate lunch everyday. Family and neighbors often teased her, "Roberta, have you found yourself a man, yet?"

To my surprise, I learned from Aunt Edith that about fifteen years after Dad died Mom accepted one date with a man. He was a widower and a regular customer at the hardware store. He stopped by often, purchased something, and then lingered a while to talk. Somehow, he convinced her to go out to dinner with him.

He arrived wearing tan slacks, shirt with open collar, and a casual jacket with zipper. They went to a good restaurant, but nothing fancy. After dinner, there was a lengthy discussion. What should they do, where should they go? Mom nixed his suggestion for a movie. Instead, they visited Mom's youngest sister, Margie, and her husband.

Everyone sat in the family room, talked, and Aunt Margie served lemonade and cake. Later, when he took her home, any infatuation that she felt abruptly ended. The nerve of that man! He tried to kiss her goodnight! Not only that, he showed up in beige slacks and a sports shirt. Any serious and responsible man would have worn proper attire, a dark suit, tie, and shined shoes, like my Dad.

After that, Mom never went out with anyone and when asked if she had met anyone interesting, she dismissed the question with a frown. "You cannot find a decent, single man in a hardware store. They are all married and only want a fling."

Attention!

Suddenly, I was jolted as I flew by a highway patrol car hidden in the bushes on the side of the road. How fast was I going? Whew! He did not pull out to stop me. A few unpleasant past experiences taught me to obey the speed limits, especially when traveling across Virginia where the speed limit on the interstate dropped from 70 to 65 miles per hour. I usually stopped for gas in Virginia because it was cheaper and I liked to stretch and breathe the brisk mountain air. The short break bolstered my spirits and soon, I was on the road again, determined not to speed.

Good intentions fell by the wayside on my solitary journeys. The events of the past week hijacked my thoughts. Thanks to the referral from Mom's primary care doctor, we obtained the diagnosis from the psychiatrist. Mom's confusion and short-term memory loss were now serious and impossible to explain away or ignore. I convinced myself before we moved to Singapore that forgetfulness is normal with advancing age. That was wrong. What now? Scientists have been unable to discover the causes of Alzheimer's and there are no cures. The only medications are the ones that may temporarily halt the disease for a short time but have annoying side effects.

I learned years ago that Alzheimer's is one type of dementia and is a debilitating and downward mental spiral, fast for some and slow for others. Vascular dementia sometimes develops slower, over many years. Since I have been noticing Mom's forgetfulness for several years, perhaps her dementia is caused by slow degeneration of the small blood vessels in her brain. Hopefully, further decline will be gradual and she can continue to live alone, and with my help, function until we can find a way to return to North Carolina.

Mom's keen intelligence helped her devise clever habits to combat her memory loss. She attached her keys to her slacks with large safety pins, turned medicine bottles upside down after taking her pills and righted them at bedtime, taped lists of important telephone numbers to the wall, and wrote the date received on each piece of mail. She made daily to-do lists and notes, but never discarded the old ones and scattered them everywhere.

When I was in town, our days together always began with a hot lunch at Mom's favorite cafeteria and in the afternoons we visited her siblings or bought items that she would need during my next absence. She favored canned tuna, soup, peaches, and cookies over the frozen dinners that I stacked in her freezer.

We seldom stayed for long in her dusty, packed house. If we were there for more than a few minutes, my tendency to gather trash and junk mail angered her and raised her anxiety level. She hovered over me and demanded to inspect everything that I threw in the trash. "I'll take care of that after you leave. I need to look through those papers to see if there is anything that I want to keep." Her trashcans remained empty.

I was unsure whether I was relieved or dismayed when I learned that Mom was no longer driving across town to visit her brothers and sister. Mom was fearful and often self-regulated her behavior if she felt threatened. Her sister Margie, remarked, "Bertie, you aren't coming to see us anymore." Instead, she drove the shorter distance to the neighborhood where two of my aunts built homes on the family farm years ago. After we moved to the lake, Mom's Saturday evening event was to visit her sister Edith, and watch Lawrence Welk on Edie's big, color television.

Mom was the middle of seven children. An older brother, Kenneth, married a nurse he met in Europe during the war and settled on the west coast. He died from heart problems in his seventies. The others stayed near their beloved hometown, were healthy, and always welcomed us when we dropped in unannounced. Most of them gave up trying to visit Mom. She discouraged them by pretending that she was not at home, hiding quietly inside until they drove away. She later confessed to me that she was ashamed. "I don't want them to see my house. I have to get things straightened up before I have visitors."

Mom was always very private and, except for her siblings, had few close friends. A dear friend that she met in college died in her forties from the inevitable decline of multiple sclerosis. Mom avoided lengthy conversations with neighbors but always smiled and waved as she hurried by on her way to and from her garage. She was kind and pleasant with strangers, cashiers, and sales ladies. She entertained them with her life story of single-handedly operating the hardware store after her husband died. Her casual friends were appreciated but kept at a distance.

Visits with my aunts and uncles revealed that she deftly covered up her memory loss. How had she managed to conceal that she sometimes forgot birthdays, special events, and even names of her nieces and nephews? After a lengthy debate with myself, I decided that it was important to tell them about Mom's diagnosis. I asked them to alert me if they became aware of any issues or problems that they had previously passed off as normal. They were amazed and totally unaware of Mom's fading memory. I warned them that she had forgotten the diagnosis, and may deny it if mentioned. They promised to call her often and take her out to eat. Uncle Bobby and Aunt Dorothy took her to the mountains when I was out of town.

I requested that her MRI appointment be scheduled two days after our trip to The Netherlands. It would be tough to unpack and drive my jetlagged body south, but I was determined to have that image of her brain before further deterioration. I considered telling Dale that I could not go, but decided that I would make it all happen since my future trips abroad may be limited. Dale would hide his disappointment and 'take care of business' as usual, but my presence provided an excuse for him to enjoy the sights and savor exotic places in the evenings and on weekends.

As I emerged from the tunnel through solid mountain rock that connects Virginia and West Virginia, a little warning bell rang in my head and I became serious about focusing on the road and driving. It was too risky to allow my thoughts to wander. The stretch of highway between Beckley and Charleston, the West Virginia turnpike, was particularly tricky. It crossed my mind that handling my car mimics the way I am managing the sharp curves in my life. At times, I am rational and purposeful, but often switch to emotional, automatic pilot. Unfortunately, I cannot practice life events the way I repeatedly drive the turnpike.

A scenic river snakes its way through Charleston. Clear areas between the tall, black rock cliffs provide spectacular glimpses of the river and the city. To the north of Charleston, the road straightens and I am halfway home. The remaining three and one-half hours of driving provided few challenges.

Dale and I talked on the phone every morning and night when I was in North Carolina. We briefly spoke of Mom's diagnosis, but serious discussion of what it means for us must wait until we sit down face to face. He senses the distress in my voice. My phone rang. It is strange that when I think of him, he often calls.

"Hi, Dear. I just passed through Charleston and traffic is light. I should be home by six. Are you in the mood for Asian food tonight? I am tired of cafeteria meals and crave something totally different."

"Sounds good. I'll meet you at the house, and then we will try that new Chinese restaurant. Be careful and keep your mind on your driving. You cannot solve all of your mother's problems before you get here."

He knew me well and as hard as I tried, my mind continued jumping around. I usually prepared for our trips abroad by listening to recorded foreign language lessons on my long drives, refreshing the French I took in college, Mandarin Chinese in Singapore, and indulging my obsession with Italian. I hoped to be going to Italy soon. Nagging doubts crossed my mind.

Detour Down Desperation Road

What was I going to do? Years ago, when Mom
was younger and mentally and physically able to take
care of herself, it was easy for me to embrace the world
and live life on the edge of whim and opportunity.
Mom's downward spiral with dementia recasts
everything in a different light. The only certainty is that
Dale planned a business trip to Italy. I pressed 'play' but
the melodic sounds of a man and woman conversing in
Italian went unnoticed.

Analyzing and Committing

Mom is a worrier. Am I? I prefer to think of
myself as an analyzer. In fact, my brain tends to over-
analyze. For me, that trait is not accompanied by the
ability to make decisions. Rational Ann insists, b*efore
you decide, you need more information. Do not overlook
something important.* The process could go on
indefinitely, and often drives Dale crazy. Sometimes, if
the issue is critical, he shakes his head, makes the
decision and announces the action needed.
In other ways, we are compatible. Soon after we
met I felt comfortable being with him, we understood
each other. We were both from entrepreneurial
families where we learned many 'do-it-yourself' skills.
We relished challenges and opportunities to learn.
Dale grew up working in his father's small
furniture factory. He sawed and assembled wood
frames, cut and sewed cushions, upholstered, loaded
trucks, and assisted the driver delivering to furniture
stores. When trucks had mechanical problems, his dad
and he repaired them. When the factory needed a new
machine, they did the electrical wiring. While in college,

he took business and accounting courses and worked in the office, managed employees, swept floors, and repaired stopped-up toilets.

Mom raved about how he could do anything. "He reminds me of your dad."

Mom barely scraped by financially but she always found ways to help us get established. She purchased a vintage table and chairs, gave us tools from the hardware store, and bought most of Alex's clothes and toys. She placed a 'Be Back in 20 Minutes' sign on the door of the hardware store and picked Alex up at kindergarten, and later, elementary school. In between customers, they they played 'store.' Two evenings each week, she treated Alex to dinner and they shopped for toys while I took or taught night classes. Then Mom drove her to our house, bathed her, and tucked her in bed. Sometimes it was late before we arrived and Mom drove home in the dark. Alex loved staying with her grandmother on weekends while we built the lake house.

Mom had definite ideas about how things should be done and she often expressed those ideas. Her parents and siblings, except for one, were of the same determined mindsets. However, Mom was usually very diplomatic. After clearly stating her opinions, she always followed with, "But you two do what you think best."

Dale admired her spunk. He was happy for her to go with us on vacations, especially when we rented lake or beach cottages. He seldom complained about family parties and picnics, even though he was challenged to remember names of my many aunts, uncles, and cousins, and forced to play silly parlor games that Mom's generation loved. My cousins joined in the fun, but we frequently 'rolled our eyes' in protest.

He learned early on to avoid the mental stress involved in my efforts to solve Mom's problems. When it came to making decisions that had anything to do with Mom, he knew that he was in way over his head and usually gave up trying. Except for occasional mechanical advice or a repair job that was second nature to him, he managed to save his sanity by ignoring our hesitations and discussions. He knew that changes were needed but was frustrated by our incessant indecision, Mom's inability to act, and my failure to talk her into 'doing the logical thing.'

The dementia diagnosis was an elephant in the room for Dale. "You have to begin making some important changes for your Mom. She is not able to do so on her own."

I just stared at him and said, "Okay, and in my spare time I will move Pilot Mountain. You know she runs her own life and will not change or do anything that she does not want to do! For twenty years I've tried to convince her to allow me to replace the broken 1940's range in the kitchen. She still has the dead black and white console television in her living room but claims that she cannot give it up because it is a nice piece of furniture."

He knew her. He witnessed her stubborn resistance to change over the years, and heard her concrete-clad opinions about most things. But the business manager in him was uncomfortable with not tackling and solving problems and he was an expert in delegating. He sadly shook his head. "I don't know what you are going to do. You have your work cut out for you."

In my dreams that night, I was a young lieutenant whose job was to lead my soldiers into battle. I jumped out of the foxhole and yelled, "Charge," but no one followed. In the past, every time that I was adamant and insistent with Mom, she looked at me with disgust and said, "Stop it! I am not going to do that and if you cannot talk about something else, just go home!"

What can I do from Ohio? If I were there every day, she would still be determined to continue her daily routines as always. So far, she is happy plodding along with me racing back and forth every month. She denied the diagnosis and intends to continue living alone, driving, and making decisions. Her dementia has caused minor problems, especially her short-term memory, and may have interfered with rational thinking over the years. Who knows how long the disease has been slowly affecting her brain. Many more years may pass before she becomes unable to manage on her own.

If I postpone returning to my career, I will be so far behind in my field that I may never catch up or find a position. What about working and building my own retirement income? How can I afford to pay for Mom when she can no longer live alone? Her savings are meager and assisted living and memory care will cost several thousand dollars every month.

Physical labor often helps me formulate solutions to problems. I forced myself to resume a task that I started weeks ago replacing the ceramic tiles in a guest bathroom. All of the measuring and planning was finished and I could allow my mind to drift while my body went through the motions of mixing and spreading mortar and placing the tiles.

I found myself sitting immobile in the middle of the floor, gazing at a big glob of mortar. There were too many problems flooding my brain. Years ago I learned that uncertainty, lack of hope, and loss of control were prime causes of depression, and ultimately, mental and physical illness. *Is that in my future?*

My heart raced and my confused mind was in turmoil. I threw down the trowel and cried. Emotional Ann was adamant. *You know that you are going to have to give up your plans and care for your Mom. She sacrificed for you many times over the years. She needs you more than ever.* Rational Ann offered a sensible approach. *You cannot live in chaos. You must develop a plan that includes how your mother will be cared for. You won't answer all of your questions or solve the problems overnight. It will take time. For now, call her! Hearing her voice may calm you.*

"Hi, Mom. I miss you. How are you doing today?"

"I'm OK. I miss you too, Hon. I was just getting ready to go eat. It is nice here. Is it cold up there?"

"It is a nice spring day in Ohio, but I am working inside. Are you having any problems?"

"Everything is fine. How are you and........ your husband?"

"Dale. I working at home and Dale is at his office. He sends his love. Do you have my number taped to the wall near the phone?"

"Oh, yes. Don't worry about me. When will you be back? I forgot what you said."

"Three weeks. I am traveling with Dale to The Netherlands on Wednesday. He has business there. We will be away for twelve days. The day after we return, I will drive to see you. Uncle Bobby knows about my trip. He said that he will be available to help you if you need him while I am gone. I will call you from Europe."

"OK. I didn't know that you were going. Where are you going?"

"Holland, where the tulips and windmills are beautiful. The time will pass before you know it. I will call you tomorrow."

"What time will you call?"

"Probably around noon, before you leave for lunch. I love you. Bye."

I wiped away the tears. Rational Ann insisted. *Ann, you have to be strong. No one will sweep in, save you, and work miracles. There is no way to make her well again. You cannot allow yourself to become depressed or sick. She needs you and you cannot make good decisions and help her if you are an emotional basket case. It won't be easy, but she needs an advocate and you must be that advocate. You can do it! You faced many problems and solved them by tackling them and learning, not running away. You are a student, a researcher, and you know that information and help are out there. You have to find it!*

Like any good manager, I had to do whatever was necessary. I may not like doing some things, but I love and respect Mom. I do not want to make her unhappy, but in the throes of this debilitating disease, changes in her lifestyle will be necessary. For Mom's safety and wellbeing, I must become a managerial decision maker. Emotional Ann sneered. *Ha! Good luck!*

The one indelible fact gleaned from higher education is that basically you know next to nothing, no matter the number of years of formal education. I must find advisors and allies with experience in caring for someone with dementia. It made no sense to go through this alone. Plus, I knew that my ever-present stress was more than likely clouding my thinking.

CHAPTER TWO

FINDING HELP

Learning and Seeking Advice

Many Americans have a mental block when it comes to facing old age and the end of life. We spend billions trying to retain our youthful appearances, proof that we are not aging. Wrinkles? A little injection or two will fix that. A little tuck of skin here and there will restore youth.

Our culture values beauty, strength, competence, and independence. Alzheimer's and other dementias signify decline, weakness, and loss. Our usual reactions to unpleasant feelings and conditions are often to ignore or resist them. So-and-so has dementia? Too depressing! Mark them off our social calendar. Why don't they put her in an institution? We ought to visit but seeing her upsets me.

Who really wants to learn about Alzheimer's or other horrible, debilitating diseases that gradually destroy the victims' brains? It was an upsetting, dismal quest, learning about the devastating disease that would gradually take my mother away. I approached it with the same enthusiasm that I would have for joining a leper colony.

My mission to learn about dementia began with a stack of books that I collected before we left for Holland. I took one with me on the plane but immediately became depressed and put it aside in favor of planning my week and focusing on the amazing sites that The Netherlands offered.

On the return flight and after we arrived in Ohio, I again resumed investigating the 'body of literature' on dementia. Some books described different types of dementia, Alzheimer's, Lewy Body, Frontal Lobe, and many others. Several were primers that explained what to expect, and how to care for a loved one who is

experiencing mental decline. Many increased my
anxiety. I dumped all of them into the trunk of my car,
hopped in, and drove south again.

My habit of reading at night until sleepy was
always pleasant and served me well. Not so as I delved
deeper into my collection of books. The dementia books
disturbed me, and again, I had to put them aside.

Sound sleep eluded me. In a nightmare, I roamed
the streets, lost, desperate to go home but could not
remember how to get there. There were big, black
holes everywhere. Suddenly I fell and landed in a room
full of mirrors and each reflected a haggard, old woman.
I gazed in one mirror and raised my hand and the old
woman raised hers. I screamed, she screamed. I sat up
and was back in my bed! My heart pounded and I was
wet with sweat. I ran into the bathroom, turned on the
light, and looked in the mirror. *What is happening?*

I had to get help. Most of my books advised
finding local resources and support groups. The next
morning, I called every agency that was even remotely
involved with dementia. The name of one person was
mentioned several times, the Director of the Senior
Adult Day Care Center. And the center was only a few
miles from Mom's house.

"Hello, yes, of course. Can you come this
afternoon?"

Her voice was calm and pleasing. I sank into the
chair in her office and dumped my whole story in her
lap. She listened, nodded her understanding and softly
said "yes" as I spoke. She must have heard similar
stories many times. She focused on my eyes and my
face. She was reading my stressed demeanor, my
desperation.

When I ran out of words, she sat quietly for a few
moments. Her eyes reflected my pain, her lips were

clenched tightly together, and she nodded slightly. "Dementia is a long journey. You must take it one step, one day at a time. The disease manifests differently in each person and the journey is different for each family. You cannot solve this struggle by out-thinking it and you cannot predict what you will need next month or next year. If you worry about everything that may happen, you will become sick, or worse. Unrelieved stress is an insidious killer."

You have probably been living with the unconscious stress of wondering what would happen to your mother if you were not here." I sat up straight. Yes. Since Dad's death, the thought was always in the back of my mind. I was her reason for living and accepting that placed a great deal of weight and responsibility on my shoulders. We were dependent on each other. She was my mother and I was hers.

"There are many issues that confront family members and caregivers. You will best learn about the disease by talking with others who are caring for their loved ones. While each person's situation is different, there are common pitfalls. Please come to our weekly support group meetings. You will hear first-hand accounts of the trials, problems, and solutions that caring people are using every day. Ultimately, you will be better prepared for whatever may come. I know that you will not be in town every week, but please come when you can. We have a meeting tomorrow, will you be here?"

The following morning, I walked into a meeting that would forever change my life. The emotion poured out of each person as they told their stories. I was spellbound. My turn came and, unexpectedly, my tears poured as I talked. I was thankful for the tissue box thrust in front of me and for the people who understood and identified with my frustration. The huge burden that I had been carrying lifted a little.

The hoarding story gushed out of my mouth as well Mom's history and my assessment of her personality, determination, and perseverance. I was not pressured to hurry. They empathized and asked questions about my life, my family support, and the details of my current struggles.

"Do you have legal power of attorney? You will definitely need that authority to make binding decisions for her. Is she able to live alone for a while? Does she prepare food, wash clothes, and pay bills? Is she a safe driver?" Their questions made me sit back in my chair as I realized that I did not know the answers. Of course she was still driving, taking the same route as always to her favorite cafeteria, perhaps stopping at a few local stores on the way home. Had she ever become lost or confused when behind the wheel? I did not know.

Years ago, Mom updated her will, designating me as her power of attorney and leaving everything to me. I did not know whether there were potential legal problems with her documents. Since I was living in Ohio, it was impossible to know the details of how well she was handling everyday life without me. During my visits, she depended on me and rode everywhere with me. At times I tried to persuade her to drive her car so that I could evaluate her driving but she always had an excuse. "Oh, let's just take your car. We may decide to do something later and I don't like driving after dark."

By the time the meeting was over, I was mentally formulating a list of tasks that would help me understand Mom's daily functioning. First, it was absolutely necessary to have her legal documents reviewed by an elder care attorney. New laws pertaining to elderly people were recently passed.

Second, her driving skills, judgment, and reaction time may have declined. Both Mom and I would be horrified if she accidentally killed or maimed someone. According to the support group, an automobile accident after a dementia diagnosis could open her to lawsuits even if the accident was not her fault. She did not have anything of real value except her home, but the trauma and anxiety would be unbearable. The major question that loomed in my mind was *would she be able to live alone until we can find a way to move home or until something happens that convinces her she must leave her home?*

Mom's Legal Plans

Mom's last will and testament, power of attorney, and health care directives were updated twenty years ago. An elder care attorney found a clause in the power of attorney document that limited my acting in her behalf in any single year to less than ten thousand dollars. That clause would prevent me from selling her house before her death to pay for her care.

After thinking about it, jolting thoughts flashed through my mind. Emotional Ann ranted. *She doesn't trust you! You are her only child and have for years loved and helped her. She intends to have sole control over that house and live there forever.* Past conversations with Mom popped into my mind. "I'm not going to live way up there in Ohio, it is too cold. I would freeze. I have Raynaud's disease, you know." She always held up her hands and wiggled her fingers.

"Mom, we will eventually return to the lake."

"I am not living at the lake. Aren't you afraid out there in the woods? It is too deserted for me. I could never stay there. You have windows everywhere and people may be watching you. Someone could be hiding in the dark when you drive in at night and attack you."

There was a standard excuse Mom mentioned at every time the subject arose. "I don't want to live with you and your family. You have your own lives and I certainly don't want to cause any trouble."

The attorney stressed that the ultimate solution to my dilemma was for Mom to deed her house over to me. Emotional Ann agreed. *If she loves you, she will agree.* Rational Ann knew better. *Her fear of losing control will prevent that from happening. Her mind will conjure up horrible ways that she could lose you and then her house.*

The second best solution was to redraw the power of attorney document, deleting the limiting clause. The attorney would do nothing until he met and talked with Mom. If she was of sound mind, understood the problem, and agreed to the change, he would help us.

Deep down, I knew that Mom's fears of 'things that might happen' would prevent her from making changes. But I was determined to introduce her to the attorney and allow him to try reasoning with her.

A huge sense of dread overcame me. A trusted family attorney, now retired, drew her will and the power of attorney years ago. The new attorney was young and the fact that he was up-to-date on all of the laws was no guarantee that Mom would trust him.

Mom's skepticism showed from the minute that I mentioned the problem. Her jaw was set and a strong-minded look was frozen on her face as we walked into the law office. She held her head erect, shoulders back, and was ready for business. Her eyes flashed first around the room and then at him, the whipper-snapper of a lawyer. He tried the warm, friendly approach to break the ice, but her answers and comments were very curt. The poor man didn't have all day and by then, I knew that Mom would take nothing he said seriously.

He presented the issues and problems logically and any normal adult would have been convinced. But Mom was not normal, she was thinking with a brain that had regressed to that stubborn, adolescent stage. Plus, she was paranoid. Yes, she understood that the current document would limit my future actions in her behalf. Certainly she trusted me. I was her only child. She did not want to cause me any undue problems in the future. No, she was not going to change her power of attorney. Her husband built that house for her the year that I was born and she was going to live and die there. She had things arranged just the way she wanted them and she was NOT going to make any changes to her will, power of attorney, or any other documents.

The attorney's sad, defeated look must have matched mine. I thought that I could see a slight shaking of his head as he looked straight at me. His non-verbal message was, "*You have your hands full,*" but he articulated something entirely different. "It is as she wants it."

The sting of Mom's obstinate refusal hurt for days, and spurred another inner debate. Emotional Ann screamed, *I told you that she does not trust you!* Rational Ann countered, *Of course she does. She does not trust the cold, cruel world. She is afraid of unforeseen events that will destroy her nest, her world. She is determined to remain in control. You will have to leave the issue alone for now. In the future, there may be ways to deal with it legally, if necessary.*

I used cognitive therapy on myself. I changed my thinking. *Mom loves me dearly, I am certain of that. We are very close. The situation could be very different, much worse.* I counted my blessings and tried to turn my thinking in a positive direction. My heart ached for two caregivers whose experiences were different from mine.

Rob's Guardianship

Myra asserted, "Rob takes good care of me." But it was too late. Theirs was the second marriage for both and Myra never designated him as her durable or health care power of attorney because they spent several years crossing state lines as they traveled around the country in their motor home before settling in North Carolina, close to her daughter. By the time they arrived and set up legal residency, Myra's dementia diagnosis prevented her from being judged, 'of sound mind and body.'

Rob had no choice. He filled out all of the paperwork, arranged for a hearing before the magistrate, and had two doctors examine Myra and give him written documentation of her dementia. Gathering the documents took awhile before he filed a petition with the court to become his second wife's legal guardian.

The magistrate interviewed Myra and, finally, Rob was granted the guardianship that he needed to make financial and other decisions on her behalf. He was required to produce notarized copies of that document each time he talked with her doctors, social security, banks, insurance companies, and the company who held and distributed her pension income.

That was easy. The difficult part lasted for years. He had to keep meticulous records and receipts of all expenditures and have them regularly reviewed by the court. It was very time-consuming and burdensome. The many other tasks of caring for her at home required most of his time and energy.

Diane's Disrupted Future

Diane glanced at her phone. Her son, Jeff, was calling. "Mom, can you come to grandmother's right away, she is hysterical! She is ranting that you stole her money and jewelry. I cannot reason with her or calm her."

Diane, a retired nurse, could not believe what she was hearing, but knew immediately that her mother had experienced some medical event. Perhaps she had fallen and hit her head or had a stroke! "I am on my way!"

Earlier that day, Diane's brother took their mother to a festival. What happened? She dialed his cell phone. "Jeff just called from Mom's, and she is yelling and accusing me of stealing her jewelry and her money. Did she act differently when you were with her?"

He was shocked. "What? I took her home twenty minutes ago and she was happy and in a good mood. We had a wonderful day together! I will meet you there."

Diane and her brother were very close to their kind and loving mother and enjoyed being with her and helping her. When her dad was diagnosed with dementia, Diane cut her workweek from forty to thirty-two hours so that she could take care of him one day a week as well as most Saturdays, giving her mother much needed relief from the rigors of dealing with his progressively worsening condition. Diane retired early, at age sixty-two, because of her concern for her mother's depression. She gladly sacrificed the extra income and settled for the lower pension that resulted from her early retirement.

After her dad's death, Diane devoted even more time to her mother. She took her out to lunch, to medical appointments, shopping, and anywhere that Mom wanted to go. Diane realized that her mother's memory was slipping and her hearing was a problem, but otherwise, she seemed in good health and had a lot of energy for a ninety-year old woman. Her mother enjoyed their outings and was always upbeat and happy. How many times had Diane heard Mom tell others that she did not know what she would do without her loving daughter's help?

Diane and her brother were designated co-powers of attorney for their mother's financial and health care issues. She loved and trusted her children, but neither could calm or reason with her. "Mom, there is no way I would take your money or anything else. I had a wonderful mother who taught me the importance of honesty."

Her mother's eyes flashed and her face distorted into a disgusted frown. "I saw you take it! Get out, I don't want either of you in my house!"

Diane's was crushed and her brother was shaken. Tears poured as she tried to find her voice. "Something is desperately wrong here, she must see her doctor right away. Did you notice anything at all at the festival that she was not herself?" He could think of nothing.

Diane made a few quick calls and Jeff agreed to take his grandmother to her doctor right away. Mom had a severe urinary tract infection and antibiotics were prescribed. Surely she would return to normal after the infection was eliminated.

Over the next few weeks, every time that Diane went to see her mom, she was met at the door and icily told to "get out." Diane was in living hell. Her mother remained steadfast in her disdain.

Diane was desperate for answers. She talked with her niece, a physician's assistant. "Sometimes, Aunt Diane, and especially in elderly people, a severe urinary tract infection will affect the brain and it is possible that she may never be the same person."

Jeff reported that a loaded pistol had appeared on a table beside the door in his grandmother's house. Alarmed, he immediately called Diane to warn her not to visit, and arranged for a policeman to remove the weapon. A butcher knife soon appeared in its place.

Diane collapsed and sobbed for hours. "What if our mother had killed one of us?"

What could she do? She could not sleep or think of anything else. Her misery consumed her. She tried everything to please her mother and prayed that she would soon return to normal. She bought little gifts that she knew her mother would appreciate, but her mom asked Jeff to get rid of them. She cooked special foods that her mother loved, but they were immediately dumped in the trash untouched. She wrote a long letter recounting how much her mother had meant to her all the years of her life and how much she missed and loved her. She heard nothing and guessed that it had been discarded unopened.

Then Jeff informed her that Grandmother found a new attorney and changed her will, making him her power of attorney. Diane was stunned. Her brother was livid. In his anger, he vowed never to see his mother again.

Diane tried to comfort and rationalize with him. "You and I both have good retirement. We don't need her money."

He sadly shook his head. "Diane, don't you realize that we have been disinherited? It is as though we do not exist."

A year passed but Diane could not stop thinking about the situation and remained frantic. Her mother's doctors would not give her any information about her mother's health. Jeff was busy at his job and was paying helpers to take her to appointments, shopping, and other places.

Diane still thinks about the situation daily. When she shares her story, a sad countenance surrounds her. "I cannot bear missing out on the amazing love that we once shared. I would give anything to be with Mom during these final years of her life."

Is Mom Driving Safely?

Roberta breezed through the driver's test and received her license when she was sixteen years old. Pop beamed proudly at his smart daughter. As they emerged from the office, new license in her hand, he proclaimed, "Now you can take your mother wherever she wants to go."

It was a new world for women in the 1930's. Neither of my grandmothers drove automobiles. For Mom, life offered more options, more freedom, and a wider range of challenges. She loved it all. Soon after that summer, she became a day student at the local women's college. If Pop's car was available and her brothers had not placed 'dibs' on its use, she drove her college friends around the town square on Saturday nights. It was on one of those evenings that she met my dad.

Mom and Dad bought a brand new Chevy the year after they married, several months before he was drafted. While he served in the Army, she worked for the federal government issuing rationing slips and soon paid off the loan on that sweet car.

Mom drove through the snow to Pennsylvania, taking three other wives with her to see their husbands before they were shipped overseas. One of the men was amazed at her skill and courage. "Roberta, you are the best woman driver that I have ever seen."

She was indeed a good, safe driver. She never received a citation or wrecked a car. In the 1950's, before Dad died, he bought a sharp, two-door, yellow and black Buick. It served her well on the late night trips to and from the hospital. She drove it for years, long after people pointed and exclaimed, "Look at that old car."

After I married and returned to college, I gave her a newer Buick, one with power steering. By then, I was making daily trips back and forth to grad school. It made sense for me to opt for a more economical Honda and she needed my Buick with power steering.

Yes, she was competent behind the wheel, but is she now? I had not ridden with her in years. Was I still confident about her skills and abilities? The rational Ann intruded into my reminiscence. *You do not know for certain.*

As the venom from a snake spreads through its victim, the dementia diagnosis was slowly coloring every certainty that I had about Mom's daily functioning. What if she forgets where she is going or becomes disoriented and does not know where she is? What if she is roaming around the streets as though in a maze? I will be unable to help her when I am miles away in Ohio.

Rob, a support group member, told a very unsettling story about his wife when she was in the beginning stage of Alzheimer's disease.

Rob's Surprise

Friends leaving the campground passed by and tooted their horn to say a final goodbye. Rob smiled and waved. He and Myra made many friends there. It was a good week. He resumed checking the motorhome, preparing to move on to their next stop.

They loved that particular campground. The one-way, narrow, winding road through it was scenic and each campsite was special with wooded privacy and serene beauty. The idyllic setting was worth the added difficulty of negotiating the hairpin turns in their large motorhome. Once he attached the Jeep behind the motorhome with the tow bar, it was almost impossible to maneuver both around the tight curves.

"Myra, everything is ready. You drive the Jeep, follow me, and as soon as we get to an open area, I will stop. Pull the Jeep close behind the motorhome so I can attach the tow bar."

She agreed, everything was ready, and they started their engines. Just then, a Buick came around the curve and Rob waited for it to pass by, but Myra did not wait. She accelerated and fell in behind the Buick without glancing around. Rob's mouth dropped open in amazement.

"Oh No! I do not believe this. She did not even look at me or realize that she was following the wrong vehicle!"

He clenched his jaw and wasted no time as he frantically tried to catch up with her. The motorhome was just too big and slow around the curves. Myra drove out of sight and there was nothing that he could do!

"Stop! Please stop. Please wait. Please! You are following a car, not the motorhome!"

His heart sank as he approached the exit gate, there was no sign of her! She must have followed the Buick out of the gate, and then, who knows where? She may have gone straight toward the city or she could have turned north or south onto the toll road. Which way?

He rubbed his hair and then his eyes. He frowned and bit the inside of his lip. His mind was racing. What is the logical thing to do? He had to stay there. If he tried to follow her, he may choose the wrong direction.

Hands shaking, he dialed 911, and shouted into the phone. "My wife is lost and she has Alzheimer's!"

It seemed to take forever for the police to record all of the information that they needed. He knew that with each minute she was traveling farther and farther away from him.

All police and highway patrol personnel would be alerted immediately. Reluctantly, he hung up. Now what? The adrenalin was still flowing in his body. He wanted to move and move fast. He stuffed his cell phone in his pocket, stepped outside, and ran laps around the motorhome until he thought of something else. Did she have any money? Did she have her identification? Where was her cell phone?

He climbed back inside and found her purse, wallet, ID, and phone, all there in her seat where she should be sitting, beside him in the motorhome. He knew that the Jeep was one-quarter full of gas, she could go about 100 miles, but which way? The registration was in the glove box. Of course, what was he thinking? The license plate number would inform the highway patrol of her identity. His mind was scrambled. He needed to calm down and think.

He plopped onto the diver's seat, took slow, deep breaths, and watched traffic. Perhaps she would realize her mistake and turn around. Could she find her way back to him? What else could he do? I have to do something! "I have to talk with someone." He called friends who lived nearby.

"Rob, what's going on?" His friends were flabbergasted. "Oh no! What can we do? We will be there right away. Perhaps we will see the Jeep on the way. We'll call you!" They hurriedly hung up.

Rob shook his head and stared in the direction of the busy roads. He mentally berated himself. *I am so stupid! All of my careful organizing and planning is not worth much now. I should have driven the car to the gate and then walked back to the campsite. Why didn't I think about asking for a friend's help?*

"Dear Lord, please keep her safe. Please let some good person find her soon, please."

He winced at the awful outcomes that his frantic mind concocted. *No, I refuse to think about horrible things, I know that the good Lord will take care of her.*

The disease was obviously progressing. She had never done anything like this, nor had she ever been lost. After she was diagnosed with mild cognitive impairment, they decided to spend a few years traveling and enjoying places they had never seen. They sold their home, put all of their furniture in storage, and began their new, nomadic lifestyle, agreeing that eventually they would settle in a home near Myra's daughter. Their nice motorhome was comfortable, and with their little dog, they had three wonderful years traveling together. In winters, they stayed in a campground on a lake in Florida, close to Myra's son.

It had been good and Rob was grateful for that time together. Although he tried not to dwell on it, he knew that the day would come when the enjoyable plateau would end. He had noticed a recent decline in her short-term memory and increased confusion. Although she looked out over the passing landscape as they traveled across the country, he knew that she had trouble focusing on the interesting sites, and the constant barrage of rest stops and restaurants overwhelmed her.

Big decisions had to be made soon, and changes were imminent. *That is, if this nightmare safely ends and I gets her back in my arms.* He shook his head as guilt overcame him again and he began ruminating about her whereabouts. He wondered if she was afraid and upset. Again, he prayed for good people to find her and help her.

Their friends arrived, but they saw no sign of her on the way. They stayed with him all afternoon, trying to be positive. It was late in the day and the atmosphere changed to gloom. There was no word from the police or highway patrol. Rob checked with them, and was again disappointed. In spite of the bulletin, no one had found the Jeep. Their friends needed to return home.

"We will do our best to find her on our way, Rob. We hate to leave you." Rob warmly thanked them and promised to call as soon as he heard something.

As the sun was setting, he was still sitting in the motorhome and his mind was still jumping around everywhere. With darkness approaching, potential problems were again bouncing around in his head.

Then, ring, ring, it was their friends. "We found her! She is OK! We spotted the Jeep in the fringe parking of the mall as we were passing. It was visible from the road. There are only a few cars at the mall this late in the day. She is in the back seat snoozing. We will stay with her and let her sleep until you get here."

"She's OK? Oh, thank you, thank you! I'll be right there!" *Whew. Thank you, Lord.* Tears of relief welled up in his eyes.

Can Mom Continue Driving?

Soon, I must return to Ohio but not with peace of mind after hearing Rob's story. Mom would again drive to her usual destinations, grocery store, her sisters' houses, and the cafeteria for her favorite cooked vegetables and apple pie.

I cannot remember the last time she prepared a meal at home. For years, customers would find a sign on the door of her hardware store that read: *Be back in 25 minutes.* She locked the door, traveled the same route day after day, and enjoyed a hot lunch at her favorite cafeteria. Surely that firmly ingrained pattern would prevent her from becoming confused and lost. Wouldn't it?

I knew that I could not leave without observing her driving. "Mom, I want to see how your car is running before I leave for Ohio. Why don't you back it out of the garage and drive me to lunch today?"

"You do that while I get ready."

As I approached the garage, there was an obvious problem. In my best calm, conversational voice, I told her about it. "Your car license expired two months ago. It is amazing that you have not received a citation."

She seemed puzzled, and thought for a minute. "Oh, yes. A policeman stopped me a couple of weeks ago and said that I should get a new license plate. I forgot to tell you."

She wrinkled her brow, obviously concentrating, trying to remember something. "He also said that I have to renew my driver's license. Will you look at it?"

Oh dear. This is a new can of worms. I wondered if she could pass the driver's exam.

Briefly, it occurred to me that this was the perfect solution to stop her driving. Then my own panic set in. I am still living in Ohio and cannot run back and forth every other day. I have already worn out one car, accumulating over 200,000 miles. My inner, calming voice took over and reassured, surely she could safely do something that she had been doing for sixty years.

The car had to be inspected before the license plate could be renewed. A quick call confirmed that the service station was free at the moment. "Mom, I will follow you to the service station. You know, the one across from Linda's salon. We will leave it there and have lunch while they inspect it." This was a good opportunity for me to observe her driving skills and her memory.

"OK, but I need to take some things out of the trunk first. I don't want to worry about someone stealing something out of it."

My intuition was correct. The trunk was full of *stuff*. I have no idea where she found the assortment of old, burned, cooking pots, broken stools, cracked plastic tubs, and much more.

"Mom, what is all this?" I stopped myself before I uttered the word 'trash.'

"Oh, the neighbors down the street had a yard sale and these are good things that did not sell. I can make some money at my own yard sale." Shaking my head in disbelief, but realizing that we did not have time for a 'discussion' that I would never win, I helped her unload them into the already overflowing garage. Off we went.

She always took a convoluted path through local neighborhoods instead of opting for the faster, but busier highway. She gave the appropriate turn signals, obeyed the speed limit, and all stop signs. I was pleased.

My smile faded when she made a wrong turn, headed east not west, and then another, south, not north. Two blocks later, she paused for what seemed like an eternity at a stop sign. No one was behind me so I placed my car in park and reached for my door handle, intending to casually stroll to her car and offer directions when she took off abruptly! She remembered how to correct her mistake. I sighed with relief as we drove into the station. Test passed, kind of.

Can Mom Pass the Drivers' Test?

One hurdle remained, the driver's license that expired in two weeks. The middle of the afternoon would likely mean fewer people waiting in line. It is difficult to say which one of us had more anxiety. She dreaded any and all tests and I worried about her survival if she could not drive to get food and have social contact. Also, if she failed, how would she emotionally handle the defeat?

Her squeaky-clean driving record saved the day. All that was required was a vision test and identification of blank road signs. Her name was called, she hopped up, her steps were quick and sure, and she happily chatted with the female examiner.

As I sat there, I was as apprehensive as the day that I turned 16 years old and Mom brought me to this very building. I passed the written exam and went outside to take the driving portion in Mom's Buick. An examiner rode with me and we glided around block with no problems. As we turned into the parking lot, he said, "Now pull up to those barrels and back into the space between them."

Mom was watching with her fingers crossed. I failed each time I tried to parallel park that big tank. I shifted into reverse and slid backward into that space as if I had done it one hundred times. I will never forget the surprised look on Mom's face. I was pleased with myself, clutched my license, and bounced out the door.

My happy flashback was shattered by the glum, defeated look on Mom's face as she walked toward me. She handed me a card printed with road signs. "Here, you help me. She told me to study these and try again."

We reviewed each signs many times while the examiner was testing someone else. The examiner called, "Roberta," and I buried my face in a magazine but was hiding, not reading. It seemed to take forever.

This time, her step was lively as she approached me with a big smile spread across her face. Bingo! We were leaving with the prize! She was ecstatic.

"Four more years! I can drive for four more years before I have to come back!" Mom was pleased, clutched her license, and bounced out the door.

CHAPTER THREE

HONORING EMOTIONS

Mom's Denial

The week after Dr. Stone diagnosed Mom's dementia, she did not remember the diagnosis or anything about that day and was determined to continue living her life as usual. She took Aricept, the medication he prescribed, but it soon disappeared from her group of daily pill bottles. "It makes my head hurt and gives me horrible dreams. I can't take it." She also complained about diarrhea and pain in her stomach, common side effects of Aricept.

She embraced the new anti-depressant and happily added it to the group of prescription pill bottles that sat on the clothes hamper in the bathroom. The hamper was located in the perfect place, facing the toilet, and was never opened because it was filled with old clothes and rags from 1960's. I hoped that the prominent location jogged her memory and made her ask, "Did I take my pills today?"

Over the years that followed Dad's death, she took many medications for her 'nerves,' her word for recurring bouts of depression. When her doctors or anyone referred to the pills as anti-depressants, she responded, "I'm not depressed, my medicines just help my nerves and make me feel better."

The psychiatrist, Dr. Stone, chose an anti-depressant that proved helpful in patients with obsessive-compulsive behaviors, especially repetitive checking tendencies. Every time that Mom locked her front door on her way out, she returned, unlocked it, and 'checked' the stove, even though it had not functioned in years. I was doubtful that the medicine would banish that habit.

Because Mom only agreed to the MRI when I insisted, I did not tell her that it was scheduled for the next day. When we first settled in Ohio and I was busy coordinating moving vans and setting up our house, she cancelled appointments with her doctors or simply did not show up. When I asked why she gave an assortment of excuses. She forgot about the appointment, did not want to go there because it was too much trouble, or thought that she was fine and did not need to see the doctor.

The day of the MRI, we went to lunch first. "Where are we going this afternoon?"

"You have an appointment at two for the MRI that the doctor ordered."

"What? I don't want to have that. I don't feel like it today. I was hoping to do something fun."

"It won't take long, Mom. After that, we will have fun." Since we had vegetables for lunch, why don't we go to the dairy bar and have a sandwich and ice cream?"

Promising ice cream always worked. Her thoughts and actions reminded me of teenage behaviors. Her short-term memory loss helped her forget her worries and enjoy our days together. We shopped at her favorite bargain stores, laughed, made the most of our days together, and I tried not to think about the looming challenges.

I attended the support group meeting that week and was looking forward to another session before returning to Ohio. The members were warm, friendly, respectful, and eager to help each other. We listened intently as each person shared the stressful events of the previous week. We were bonded by our responsibilities and caregivers roles. Each of us knew that the others deeply cared and that their thoughts were with us during the coming weeks. After the meetings, I felt valued and understood by my new, trusted confidants. I told of Mom's MRI, her forgotten diagnosis and her denial. Some had similar experiences. Others faced situations that were worse.

Betsy's Anger

Betsy's eyes narrowed and her forehead wrinkled as she scowled at her daughter. "The answer is NO! I am NOT going to see a doctor about something that I do not have! There is nothing wrong with my memory! Do not mention this to me again!"

Pam winced, stared at the floor, and bit the inside of her lip to prevent saying something that she may regret. In truth, she did not know what to say to her mom. Betsy turned away and busied herself with rearranging do-dads on top of the dresser. Pam cleared her throat, and changed the subject. "Come on, Mom, let's see if Dad would like a piece of the pie I brought."

They found Michael reading in the family room. "Dad, would you like to try the yummy lemon pie I made this morning?"

He stared at Pam with raised eyebrows. He knew that she intended to mention to Betsy their concerns about her memory. Pam shook her head and rolled her eyes. He got the message. They headed for the kitchen.

Later, as Pam was leaving, Michael followed her outside, away from Betsy's keen hearing. The news was no surprise to him. He had experienced similar outbursts when, twice before, he tried to talk with her about his concerns. They both knew that something was wrong with Betsy.

"Dad, will see Dr. Campbell next week for an exam and was thinking that I might mention Mom's problems and our concerns. He knows all of us and perhaps he will test her memory during her next appointment."

"Good idea. Be sure and tell him about her uncharacteristic outbursts and anger, but I hope he won't tell her that we mentioned it." Michael dreaded enduring Betsy's temper and knew that she would be angry if Dr. Campbell told her they were concerned.

Betsy's forgetfulness was not evident when she stomped out of the doctor's office. She remembered exactly what the doctor said. "Your family is worried about your short-term memory. How long have you been having problems?"

Betsy promptly informed him that her family was imagining things. She remained angry and fumed for days. From that time on, Michael and Pam were careful to limit their discussions about her memory to times when she would not be able to hear them.

Jack's Turmoil

Jack was a workaholic. In college, he paid for his education by jockeying several part-time jobs. After graduation, he found a job with potential for advancement with a large corporation. From the beginning, he was dedicated to his job, arrived early, and usually stayed late. Over the years he was successful, promoted often, and became a vice president.

When Jack turned sixty, he began forgetting where he put his wallet, what day it was, and things that he needed to do. Maggie did not know how Jack's memory losses affected his job performance, but she worried that his problems must be obvious to the people he managed. When his company was sold to a larger corporation, new executives arrived and began making changes. Soon, the new managers insisted that Jack take early retirement.

That abrupt change had a tremendous impact on Jack and Maggie. He began expecting her to be at home with him all day, every day. Two years before that, they sold their large home and downsized into a condominium. There was no yard work, nothing for Jack to do. Each day he sat in front of the television but soon became bored and walked aimlessly around the house.

"Maggie, where are you? What are you doing? Why are you doing that? What's for lunch?"

Maggie was miserable. She had been active all of her life. In college, she majored in physical education and music. She played with the symphony and had many friends. She loved tennis and golf and belonged to several leagues. Before he retired, she was up early each day, exercising at the Y. The only time in her life that she stayed at home was when their children were young. But even then, she was always playing with them and driving them to ball or cheerleading practice.

All of that was fine with Jack when he was working. But after retirement, he became insistent, demanding, and argumentative. He knew that he was having memory problems and that realization made him angry. Most of the time he just sat in his recliner and drank. Maggie tried to calm him by telling him that forgetting things was a natural part of aging but he didn't believe her and became angrier. Finally, he went to his doctor and permitted Maggie to accompany him. The doctor gave him a memory test.

The diagnosis was that he was in the beginning stage of dementia, probably Alzheimer's. The disease would gradually get worse. The doctor prescribed Aricept, but cautioned that there were side effects, and if the medicine worked, it would only delay the disease for a while.

By the time Jack and Maggie returned home, he had forgotten everything that the doctor said and could not understand why he had to take the pills. He fussed every time she reminded him to take his pills. "Don't tell me what to do!".

Maggie realized that he was depressed and wished that she had been able to talk with the doctor privately about prescribing an anti-depressant. How could she live with his constant anger and misery?

She became vigilant and avoided saying anything that may anger him. Some days, he yelled at her regardless of what she said so she learned to keep her mouth shut and say as little as possible. She thought, "This disease has found two victims."

Dan's Acceptance

Dan and Adrienne were driving home after a pleasant evening with friends. Dan signaled a left turn on to the interstate highway.

"Dan, that's the wrong way."

He continued moving forward. When the last oncoming car passed, he started turning and Adrienne screamed. "Don't turn!"

He stopped just in time to avoid going the wrong way on a busy four-lane highway!

It was not Dan's first driving incident. He was having problems judging his distance from objects, even when walking. Adrienne was certain that something was wrong with his eyes. An ophthalmologist found absolutely nothing, but Adrienne insisted on a second opinion. Again, nothing was abnormal. He tried a third specialist and this doctor recommended Lasik surgery. Dan agreed.

Dan was sixty, a brilliant engineer with a master's degree, and in excellent health. He exercised, ate healthy foods, and was just beginning to think about retiring or at least cutting back from a busy work schedule that included teaching a course at the university. Adrienne was ecstatic! They would soon have time to travel and enjoy life together while still young.

To her, Dan was a very different, special man. Her first husband was erratic and volatile. In contrast, Dan was logical, calm, stable, agreeable, and several years older than Adrienne.

Adrienne was bubbly, extroverted, and funny. Her witty comments kept her friends in stitches. She loved to laugh. When they met, there was an immediate attraction and basic respect between them. Their personalities complemented each other. Together, they raised Dan's two children from his first, tumultuous marriage, and their own daughter.

Unfortunately, vision was not Dan's only problem. Adrienne noticed personality changes. At times he became withdrawn, disorganized, argumentative, and depressed. He was sleeping more, often nodding off during the evening news.

They were both skilled at and loved the game of Bridge, but Dan often chose the wrong suit and then became angry when challenged by other players. He always enjoyed his woodworking hobby, but was frustrated and upset when Adrienne asked him to assemble a simple shelving unit. He could not do it.

Adrienne knew that something was wrong. She

asked their doctor if it could be Alzheimer's and he immediately said that he did not think so, especially since Dan was young, had excellent verbal skills, and was much too bright. How about Sleep Apnea? Tests for that were negative. More tests indicated that perhaps there were heart problems and a pacemaker was the solution. Nothing changed after that surgery. His visual problems remained, his reasoning skills declined, and his forgetfulness increased. Still, his doctors did not suspect dementia.

Adrienne was on a mission to discover the cause of the changes in Dan. She was frustrated but determined. They spent several years searching and sought second opinions from many doctors. Finally, a brain scan was done.

No tumors were found, but there was above average atrophy of his brain for a man his age. Doctors concluded that it was dementia, possibly vascular, but probably Alzheimer's disease. After all of her suspicions, the doctors were finally convinced and prescribed an anti-depressant and Aricept.

Adrienne was not prepared. She was devastated. She had been so hopeful for a diagnosis that could be cured. That is what doctors do, diagnose and cure!

After the initial shock, Dan calmly learned about dementia and began making plans for how they would handle things. He made certain that all of the important legal documents were in place and even visited several memory care communities. He was concerned about Adrienne and wanted to help her by participating in the decision that may be several years in the future, but he was realistic that there would be a time when Adrienne could no longer care for him at home. Well aware of his visual problems and the potential for lawsuits, he voluntarily gave up driving and was content to ride with

Adrienne.

At first, Adrienne mounted an extensive search for cures and encouraged Dan to participate in an experimental study of a new medicine. Unfortunately, there was no change. She always tackled problems head on, determined to solve them. After reading many depressing medical articles, she finally accepted that unless some new medicine miraculously appeared soon, there was no hope of a cure.

It was not in Adrienne's nature to accept defeat. After fighting and finally losing hope, she turned to an old friend that she had left behind years ago. Every afternoon, she had a couple glasses of wine and convinced herself that it helped her cope. She was grieving. After many sleepless nights and additional glasses of her coping mechanism, she decided that the only thing she could do was focus on making the most of the time they had left together. She added many activities to their social calendar. They took short trips, continued seeing friends, and prepared for their daughter's upcoming wedding.

The Doctor's Self-Diagnosis

Adrienne's father was a physician, a specialist. When he was in his sixties, he experienced a heart attack and knew immediately what was happening. He wasted no time getting to the hospital.

That serious threat changed the way he looked at life. He decided to retire, reduce stress, and focus on playing golf and other activities. But in his mind, he would always be "the doctor."

After Adrienne's husband, Dan, was diagnosed with dementia, her dad became keenly focused on Dan's decline. Even though they lived fifty miles away, Adrienne's mom and dad visited weekly and enjoyed stimulating bridge games and outings to their favorite restaurants with Dan and Adrienne. Dad examined Dan's medicines and paid special attention to Dan's responses to his many questions.

On one visit, Adrienne and her mother were alone in the kitchen. "Your father is having problems remembering things. When we leave here, I have to give him detailed turn by turn directions to get us home. When he is out by himself, he is often confused and calls me for help."

Adrienne's Mom no longer wanted to drive. She enjoyed being driven to hair appointments and shopping by her husband. She began asking him to wait in the car for her so that he would not be out driving around alone.

Adrienne did not tell her mother that she suspected that Dad was having memory problems. After hearing the news, she felt guilty that her mother had suffered in silence.

"Mom, why didn't you tell me about this before now?"

"I know how tumultuous your life has been dealing with Dan's decline and the last thing that I wanted to do was to add to your problems. I am telling you now because your dad's decline will soon be obvious. He was all right for a while but is getting worse. Have you noticed how irrational his thinking has become?"

Adrienne knew her dad well and had indeed noticed strange new behaviors that exceeded his usual eccentricities. Her Mom's verification made her feel as though a thick, black smog had enveloped her. Her awful experience with Dan was playing out again.

"He has prescribed Aricept for himself, Adrienne."

"That is why he has been so interested in Dan's medicines."

Adrienne frowned, clenched her teeth, and desperately fought the tears that filled her eyes. In her family, emotional displays were downplayed and controlled. She was always 'Daddy's happy girl.' Even worse, her seventy-five year old mother faced the turmoil and stress of caring for her dad. It would be a rocky ride and a full time job given his 'feisty' personality and behavior.

"Mom, please call me when you need help. We have to stick together. You must allow me to help you. You will need me!"

"Adrienne, I am more worried about you than me. I have lived with that man for fifty years. You have many years left and I don't want you to become sick because of the stress. Many caregivers die before the person with dementia."

The Gun Collector's Despair

Over the years, Bob amassed a fine collection of many different makes and models of handguns, rifles, and shotguns, plus a huge supply of ammunition. Always safety minded, he carefully stored them in his gun safe, all except the handgun that he kept beside the bed. A law-abiding citizen, each was registered and he kept an up-to-date carry permit.

All of this was fine with Beth until that day, the day Bob was diagnosed with Alzheimer's. Beth's many years of experience as a counselor taught her much about life and mental diseases. She knew that his disease would become moderate and then progress to severe dementia. There was no way to predict the areas of the brain that would be affected, and there was no way to know how Bob's behavior would change.

When first diagnosed, Bob suggested they update their wills and legal documents and happily continued his life as before. He loved Beth and adored his three children. Once, Beth overheard him tell someone that his wife was beautiful and smart. Bob, a kind and pleasant man, loved life and his life's work. Although he was retired, he kept in touch with old colleagues and friends. Everyone respected and admired Bob.

When his doctor insisted that Bob give up driving, he balked and declared that he was still very capable. But after that, he was often sad. Bob's life was changing as he realized that he must give up the things he loved most.

Beth recognized that he was clinically depressed. On one occasion when he was particularly low, he mentioned that it would be best for everyone if he just took his gun and went to the creek.

"Bob, I know that you feel you have nothing to live for, but please think about your children and grandchildren and how they would be affected by your ending your life with a gun. They would live with that sadness forever. You have a great legacy for them and do not want to ruin that!"

It was then that Beth knew she had to do something. It was unlikely that he could be convinced to give up the weapons. Dementia meant eventual loss of his mental abilities and rationality. He would not be able to stop and think of the consequences of his behavior.

Their son suggested that she leave the gun safe

unlocked and take him out for dinner the next day. He would use his key and remove the ammunition while they were away. Beth hoped that he would not notice that the ammunition had disappeared.

All went well until Bob discovered the theft. She did not want him to call the police but he insisted. She was mortified to admit that at her request, their son removed the ammunition.

"Bob, I am so afraid that you will shoot yourself and I cannot allow that."

He was never physically violent with her or anyone else but she understood the unpredictability of people with dementia, especially when they were depressed or angry. Bob fussed and fumed. She ignored him and left the room as soon as he started complaining.

He did not remember what he did that morning, but he remembered losing his ammunition. "All of it, you got rid of all of my ammunition? How are we going to protect ourselves if someone breaks in and harms us?"

It stayed on his mind for days. He fussed and argued and when she did not respond, in desperation, he tried to strike a bargain to get ammunition for one handgun.

Beth wanted to spare Bob the constant worry and frustration of feeling that he could no longer protect his family. Eventually, he would probably forget it, but that may take a long time. He always trusted her to do what was best. Surely she could think of a solution.

Finally she said, "All right, Bob, make a list of the ammunition that you need."

She took the list to a friend who sold ammunition and asked how he could help her. Of course, there was a perfect solution. He would have the powder taken out of the bullets and Bob would never know the difference, unless he tried to fire the weapon.

It worked. Bob felt secure and soon forgot the incident. Beth was relieved but lived with guilt. She hoped that he never, for any reason, pulled the trigger.

Tim's Embarrassment

Doug left his Dad on the porch and joined his mom in the kitchen. "That is not my daddy sitting there."

"What do you mean, Doug?"

"Haven't you noticed that he talks and acts differently?"

Marjorie thought for a minute. "Well, he is more forgetful, but I attributed that to age."

Doug knew his father well. Every Sunday they sat together, read the paper, and discussed it. "Mom, something is happening that I don't understand."

Several weeks later, Marjorie was stunned when Tim thrust the checkbook at her and said, "See if you can figure our balance. I cannot get it to make sense." She accepted then that something was wrong. Tim worked in finance until he retired and always took care of the accounts and financial matters.

Doug insisted that they go to a special program conducted by the medical center. Tim was tested for four hours. Then, they performed an MRI of his head and kept him all afternoon completing physical tests. After all of that, and before meeting with the doctor, Marjorie was given a list of behaviors and asked to check those that were typical of Tim.

"As I sat there, I burst into tears and knew for certain that everything on that list described Tim. I predicted then what the doctor would tell us."

"The doctor was very plain and specific. He told us that Tim was in the beginning stage of dementia and that he should not be driving. Tim did not want to hear it. He became angry and refused to go back there ever again."

"Marjorie, do not tell anyone about this. I do not want my sisters, the neighbors, people at church, or anyone to know."

"Tim, we have to tell Doug."

"No one else except Doug is to know. Promise me you will not tell."

Marjorie looked around the room at the other support members sitting around the conference table "I went home and cried and was miserable for months. Plus, I had to keep it to myself. He even refused to tell his primary care doctor. When the doctor later found out, he told Tim that he had been unkind to me, making me carry that burden alone, without any release or support. People needed to know so that they could help us."

CHAPTER FOUR

PROCEEDING SLOWLY AND RESPECTING DIGNITY

Changes for Me, Changes for Mom

I raced back and forth and gave up traveling with Dale. Mom continued driving, taking food home, and caring for herself. Because I loved her, I wanted her to be herself and enjoy her life as long as possible. Because I loved me, I needed time to make major life changes that included, hopefully, moving south.

As the months flew by, I knew that she was no longer able to think clearly and do everything as usual. The *big* problem was that she did not *realize* that the disease was altering her abilities. She continued her habits, convinced that she was as capable as ever.

As always, she tenaciously controlled her possessions, resources, and decision-making rights. In our culture, teaching our children to be independent is a major goal of parenthood and education. Once an adult has attained those rights and privileges, taking them away, however gradual, may involve war, subterfuge, or cause depression. Who was I to tell her what to do? In her mind, I was still her little girl, except for when she introduced me as her mother.

Deep in the midst of tricky business is where I found myself. I was determined to treat her with respect and honor her dignity. I refused to handle things in ways that demeaned her. Dementia had not taken away her capacity to feel sadness, uncertainty, worry, and anguish. How was I going to do what I had to do without hurting her?

Analyzing that dilemma exhausted me. One day, an old memory of my management professor popped into my mind. *Students, once you know what has to be done, you have to summon the courage and exhibit the appropriate behaviors to achieve your goal, even though you may not relish or like what you have to do.* In other words, you have to do what you have to do, and a care manager's or mother's job is to choose and use the actions that are best for everyone concerned.

I did not want to, but found myself keeping things from her and telling little fibs when the truth upset her. Thinking back, I also used fibbing strategies when I was a teenager. How else could I deal with my determined and stubborn Mom? If she did not agree with me or approve of what I wanted to do, her response was, "I refuse to do that (or let you do that) and I am not going to discuss it." Period!

JOBS AND IDENTITIES – "I Have To Be Me"

The Hardware Lady

Every time that Mom walked out of her front door and glanced to the left, up the street, her identity, who she was and what she did everyday, was reinforced. The old store building and its contents were her life. She kept it just as it always was, packed full of stock that was useful in the 1950's and 1960, galvanized tubs, buckets, and plumbing, enamel pans, stove pipe, hand tools, children's metal wagons, and loose bolts sold from open bins.

She did it all by herself, employees were expensive. When she was in her seventies, she walked up the street, placed the open sign in the window, but seldom moved wheelbarrows or stock outside as in the past. Instead, she kept the door locked and sat in the rear behind a counter, in the midst of empty, dusty, cardboard shipping boxes. She stayed low and cautiously peeped over the vintage cash register so that strangers passing by would not stop. The old door rattled as potential customers grasped the handle. If she recognized the person, she unlocked the door and explained that she had been in the stock room. Otherwise, she continued hiding.

Sometimes, an old customer would stop by, rattle the old door, and peer in long enough to be recognized. Unfortunately, old customers grow older and while some were stopping by for a 'chat' with a friend, she rarely made a sale, just a few dollars here and there. With no stock out front, a faded 'open' sign stuck inside the door, and no one is sight, logic told people that she was not there. Even then, if someone asked if she was still in business, she said, "Oh, yes, but I am not there everyday." She was living out her familiar habits and patterns of the past, wearing the role that was as comfortable as old shoes.

Because she was determined to go there, I did not make serious attempts to intervene but was concerned. I wondered how she felt sitting there alone, no new stock, no customers, and in my mind, no hope. The world had left her behind. I worried, rationalized, looked for positives and somehow managed to keep my mouth shut except for sometimes asking questions.

"Do you feel safe there by yourself?" She reminded me that she kept the door locked unless she knew the person. "What would you do if someone pulled a weapon and wanted money?" She worried that they may hurt her because she did not keep much money and the thieves may not believe her. That is why she kept the door locked. "What if someone attacked you?" She would kick them in the . . . .(censored).

Over the years, she spent fewer days hiding in the store until finally, she seldom went there at all. While we were in Singapore, I transferred money to her account and hoped that the store would sit, unopened and untouched, until we moved back to the States.

The wood-frame building was old and except for the gas space heaters that replaced the old potbelly stoves, no changes were made. The neighborhood was zoned residential, limiting a potential buyer's use of the property. It was small, compared to the modern, mega-hardware stores and her meager stock was outdated. Mom understood the limitations but was unable to muster the wherewithal to liquidate and sell the place. It was too painful for her to think about.

"Mom, it does not make sense to pay for a business license, upkeep, and taxes."

Defeated, she finally agreed and said, "You handle it."

The day of the auction, she abruptly left in her car and did not return until late in the day, after the sale was over.

"Who bought the cash register? How much did it bring?" She was curious, but spared herself the agony of seeing it carried away. That part of her life was gone but her house remained full of 'new,' old hardware stock. For years, she continued telling people that she was 'the hardware lady.'

Claudia, the Public Relations Expert

Stuart whispered to his daughter, Kim, "I am glad that you came with us! It is difficult for me to wait outside the ladies' room for Claudia to finally come out. I feel as though the ladies look at me like I am a pervert or something."

They loved family dinners at the nice restaurant. The meal was excellent, and while Claudia and Kim went to the restroom, Stuart remained at the table sipping his coffee.

Kim led the way back to the table. Quickly, before Kim could turn and stop her, Claudia slid into an adjacent booth next to a well-dressed elderly gentleman who was talking with his attractive companion. Stuart's eyes widened with disbelief. He could not conceal his amusement when he saw the man's expression, a mixture of surprise and suspicion.

"So, how are you doing?" asked Claudia. "Are you two married? How's that going?"

Stuart was immediately on his feet. The man's unease and reddening face prompted quick action. He apologized many times, took Claudia's arm, and insisted that she return to their table.

Claudia loved everyone and talked with everyone. Those qualities served her well over the years in her public relations jobs, before the onset of dementia. She was warm, personable, charismatic, and had strong verbal skills. Several business managers offered her jobs after only short conversations. It was easy to see how people were drawn to her. She never knew a stranger and she loved going places, anywhere, with Stuart. She smiled and waved at strangers, and greeted everyone.

"Hi, it's good to see you again. How are you today?"

Some were perplexed and wondered if they knew her. Others assumed that they did and cheerfully responded to Claudia's unending questions, many so personal that Stuart wished that he could disappear.

"She has no filters! There is no way to predict what will come out of her mouth! It was amusing at first, but now it's embarrassing and time consuming. It is impossible to get our groceries and complete necessary tasks. At home, she talks all of the time. Sometimes I get so frustrated that I want to yell, but I would never do that. It would devastate her."

Jack Wants A Job

Jack's dementia and forced early retirement turned him into an angry, depressed man. He constantly railed at Maggie. She sacrificed most of her activities except playing with the symphony and was living in a frustrating web of uncertainty. When Jack drank, usually every day, he became belligerent and difficult.

Their two grown children were disturbed by their dad's decline and their mom's frustration. Ted, their son, took Jack out to lunch, pleaded and rationalized, but could not convince him that Maggie needed to hire someone to help around the house and time away from home to run errands and socialize with her friends.

Jack did not want anyone in the house except family. Maggie was a prisoner in her own home. She was afraid to leave him alone and worried that he would scour the neighborhood or drive around searching for her. The whole family was bothered about the potential liability of his continued driving, but even a casual comment that he should not be driving threw him into a raging fit.

One day, as Ted was leaving, he called Maggie outside. "Mom, we have to find something for him to do during the day. He needs an activity that will wear him out and make him want to sleep instead of drink. Was he drinking last night?"

"He always has his cocktails."

Ted searched and found the Senior Day Care Center. The director suggested that one way to convince Jack to come there was to pretend that he was an employee, assisting with activities. Maggie had her doubts, especially when Ted told him that he was not allowed to drive his car to the center. But he wanted to work again, so he agreed. Maggie was thrilled.

Jack was happy. He lived to work. Every Friday the director gave him an envelope with a thank you note and a twenty-dollar bill in it. On Mondays, Maggie quietly reimbursed her, relieved to get her life back, at least on weekdays.

She joined the center's weekly support group. Not everyone in the group had her same problems, but they understood and empathized with her. Listening to others helped her develop tricks and techniques to better deal with Jack. He was changing every day and she had to be vigilant and diplomatic, especially when she responded to his angry outbursts.

CONTROLLING FINANCES – "Respect What Is Mine"

Mom Needs A Little Cash

I raced to North Carolina at least every third week, making my trips coincide with Dale's business travels when possible. I was rapidly wearing out another vehicle and missing the excitement of accompanying him to Europe.

When in North Carolina I attended support meetings and Mom and I continued our routines, trips to the mountains, visiting relatives and shopping for supplies. Soon after I arrived, she always insisted that she needed a little cash. One of our first stops was her bank. "Wait in the car, I don't need your help. I will only be a minute."

Once inside, she waited in line for her favorite cashier, even if that line was longer. The lady smiled and called Mom by name. Mom presented her checkbook and withdrew one hundred dollars. That amount usually lasted until I returned two weeks later. She seldom spent any of it when we were together.

Mom did not keep cash around the house. If I had to wait in the living room for her to finish dressing, I sometimes found a few dollars hidden under stacks of junk mail or newspapers, unexpected places chosen to foil intruders. If she was in another room, I quickly searched for unpaid bills or other important documents.

The city water department cut off her service twice and on my second trip to their office, I used my power of attorney to change the billing address to me in Ohio. She could still write a check, if prompted what to write on each line, but often forgot about bills that were due. If she remembered to keep them separate from everything else, I usually wrote the checks and placed stamps on the envelopes while standing in her living room. Usually, they became lost in the rubble. It took time and effort but I eventually had all of her bills sent to me. After they stopped arriving, she forgot about that responsibility.

As I waited outside the bank, I called Dale. Voice mail. He must be in a meeting. I wanted to ask how he was doing without me. *Are you lonely, bored, or painting the undercarriage of our new SUV orange?* My monkey mind still jumped frantically from thought to illogical thought, seldom resting or allowing myself to think about how much I was missing our discussions, dinners together, interesting trips, and projects.

Although I was driving more miles than ever, my world was shrinking. I sacrificed lunches and outings with friends, ignored my restoration jobs on our old house, allowed my garden to become overgrown with weeds, and put aside my preferred books in favor of learning more about dementia and brain diseases.

Mom's world was also becoming smaller. When I was not in town, she was still driving, but seldom farther than two miles from her home and she always took the same route. Luckily, her pharmacy, grocery, clothing store, hairdresser, and favorite cafeteria were close by. A young neighbor that I befriended seldom saw Mom in her yard except for when she was walking to or from the garage.

Her typical day began with long established habits, sleeping late, eating dry cereal, retrieving the morning newspaper from the front porch, listening to her favorite local radio station, and dressing so that she could drive to the cafeteria and enjoy a midafternoon lunch, usually vegetables and apple pie.

"I never really liked meat. I remember crawling under the bed when I was young and stuffing my fingers in my ears so that I would not hear our pigs squeal on the day that Pop and my brothers butchered them. I never ate much pork."

After lunch at the cafeteria, she often stopped by her favorite bargain-priced clothing store and greeted the ladies employed there. They always smiled and called her by name. Again and again she told her story of being a widow and running the hardware store for forty years.

During our daily phone calls, I asked what she had been doing, and listened carefully to her responses. It was impossible to be very effective in my mothering role from miles away. However, it was obvious that the disease was progressing since she seldom remembered recent events unless she checked her notes.

"What did you have for lunch today, Mom?"

The answer was always vegetables. My guess was that her answers were the first thing that popped in her mind rather than factual. Mostly we talked about things that were happening at that moment. Her short-term memory was fast disappearing except for an occasional upsetting event.

She seemed content and always insisted that she was fine. I constantly tried to convince myself that indeed she was. Students of Mindfulness argue that staying focused on the present moment produces happiness by releasing worry about what will happen in the future or mistakes that you made in the past. Perhaps loss of one's memory is not so bad after all. In any case, I did enough worrying for both of us.

Before she left her house each day, she tucked the cash to pay for her meal and a list of things she needed to buy into her pocket. She believed that carrying a purse was an invitation for thieves to knock her to the ground. The lists were her short-term memory, reminders that after lunch, there was an errand.

For some unknown reason, she remembered that she needed an umbrella and a white, summer purse. Were those needs stored in long-term memory or did she find an old list? Whatever the motivation, she did not remember that she recently purchased those items. Years later, I found sixty new umbrellas, still in the package, and almost thirty unused white purses, still the original bag with receipt, in various places throughout her house.

The clutter in her home was growing. She was

spending more time rifling through old boxes of pictures, notes, and mementos, leaving them scattered about everywhere. They were her treasures, saved for years. Touching and reading them renewed her long-term memory of special events, highlights of her life, and rooted her in her past.

She would tell me wonderful stories of growing up on the farm, friendships made in college, challenges of her first job, and many hilarious adventures with my Dad. I latched on to each word as if it were a jewel, recording it in my memory banks. Most of her stories were told over and over, but I never discouraged her or hurt her feelings. Her repeated stories reinforced her memory as well as mine.

She went to the same cafeteria every day, but when I was in town I would, for my sake, try to vary the routine.

"Where would you like to go for lunch, Mom?"

The answer was always the same. There was no other alternative. She quickly pushed her tray down the line, usually without waiting, knew exactly what she wanted because everything was displayed in the same place, day after day. She enjoyed delicious pie that made her think of her mother's cooking, and drank unlimited fresh decaf coffee from a cup that was instantly refilled by employees whose major responsibility was to clean the tables after patrons finished. But they watched for Mom.

Mom was always, by necessity, frugal. Food at the cafeteria was affordable and it was unnecessary to tip anyone, but Mom began tipping the employees who refilled her cup one dollar each time they performed that service.

"Mom, we cannot afford to give her one dollar each time."

She looked sadly at me over her glasses and whispered, "She needs the money."

The disease had not changed Mom's soft heart. In truth, I enjoyed watching the race among employees to see who would could arrive first and fill our cups. When I was in town, I was also the person who produced the dollar bills.

Mom would look at me with her sad expression and quietly ask, "Do you have another dollar?" For the first time in her life, she believed that she had enough money to do as she pleased.

She would sometimes say, "I may buy a new car."

Ken Frets and Checks

Mom's casual attitudes about money were typical for some but not everyone with dementia. Ken worked for many years in a financial job and always paid the household bills, made wise investments, and managed every aspect of his family's finances. Those attitudes and habits were second nature to him and he was determined to continue as always. No dementia diagnosis was going to change him.

"What is the password? I need to make certain that our money is still there." He could no longer remember passwords and constantly worried that their savings would disappear.

"Don't worry about the balances, you just checked them an hour ago. The economy is good now, and the banks are honest, we will be OK." Corinne's voice was calm even though she was seething inside. How many times had she reassured him? She was aggravated with his increasing irrationality and anxiety about money. How could she get him to realize that he needed to trust her and allow her to handle those tasks? He obsessed about having enough and that escalated his anxiety.

Corinne worked from home and his constant barrage of questions affected her time and attention to her job. Not long ago, he moved some of their accounts to another institution, sacrificing a good return for an inferior one and was not able to remember the numbers that allowed him access to the balances of the new accounts. Luckily, he had written the numbers on a pad by the phone and Corinne was able to rectify his actions.

When she spoke up and challenged his judgment, he became angry and often stayed upset for days. The sting of those days lingered in her mind. This time, she hoped to avoid his strong negative reaction to her undermining his actions and did not mention that she moved the money back into the original accounts.

"Whew!" She sighed. "He did not notice that the account numbers were the same as before and I changed the password." She smiled. "I hate deceiving him but he is driving me crazy. I spend more time dealing with his anxiety and frustrations and less time on my job and the things that I need to do to keep the house running. I am becoming just as frustrated, but for different reasons."

Bill's Great Deal

Every time Bill steps out of his house, he fumes. "That darned bamboo is taking over my beautiful yard!" For years he complained to the owner of the lot next door, but the man ignored his appeals and protests. Bill spent hours digging roots and hacking away at the stalks but the menacing plants soon reappeared.

One day, Bill found a solution! Elated, he rushed into the house.

"We are selling this house! It is just too much work for us. That awful bamboo is spreading everywhere like wildfire! It will soon be blocking the front door! No matter what we do, we cannot get rid of it! The neighbor, Jim, offered me $20,000 cash for the house and I said OK!"

Jane stopped making lunch and stared at him, her lips pursed. She shook her head, an obvious non-verbal NO. They worked for years to pay for their beautiful three-bedroom, two-bath home on the acre lot. Jane remained quiet until he finished.

Then she said, "Well, that is not going to happen. My name is also on the deed to this house, we own it together, and I am not signing that deal." She thought for a moment. "I'll tell you what. I will give you $10,000 for your half."

Bill was shocked. His brow wrinkled and his eyes squinted. "Where will I live?"

"I'll rent you a room."

He turned, and stomped out the door. She heard nothing else from him about selling the house. Later that afternoon, she hired a man to take care of the lawn at times when Bill was not at home and turned his chair on the front porch so that he could enjoy the other side of the lawn and not constantly stare at the bamboo.

DRIVING WITH DEMENTIA – "I Can Still Do It"

Mom Drives On

Although I convinced myself that Mom was still capable of driving, I believed that in her mind, the rewards associated with driving were totally different from when she was young. In those days, not everyone owned cars and men were usually the designated family drivers. After her older sister married, Mom was the only female at home with a drivers' license. When the family car was available, she had the freedom to use it. Her friends were impressed.

Those days were long gone. She did not need to prove to herself or others that she was an in-charge, capable, safe driver. She enjoyed riding in my car and relinquishing the responsibility of thinking about signals, turns, or where she was going. However, as in the past, she usually told me where to turn, which route to take, and where to park.

"Yes Mom, you are right."

Why disagree about something inconsequential? She had firmly established habits and if I could give her pleasure and avoid conflict, why protest?

The family squabbles and struggles about driving that I heard in support group meetings fascinated and dismayed me. Many husbands and some wives waged major battles that sometimes affected their relationships for months. Driving was a badge of adulthood, control, freedom, status, and self-esteem. Perhaps Mom's attitude would have been different if I sold her car or took her keys.

Bob's New Toy

Bob rushed into the kitchen, excited. "Beth, come outside! I have something to show you! You are going to love it!"

He rushed her down the hall to the door and as she passed the window, she glimpsed something red and shiny outside. He opened the door and there it was in the driveway.

"Oh, Bob! You bought a convertible!"

Bob was still driving even though he had been diagnosed with Alzheimer's dementia. He remembered that he was developing dementia but believed that he could continue his activities as usual. He always loved anything that moved, cars, trains, and planes. Beth tried many times to convince him to give up driving. Their son pleaded and their daughter appealed to his lifelong devotion to safety. Nothing worked.

"I have been driving since before I was sixteen and I am more cautious now. I am not going to stop driving. It's not going to happen!"

Beth rode with him often and verified that his vision, reaction time, and skills were still intact. He was always a wonderful husband and very good to her and the children. She knew that he would never knowingly endanger anyone, but dementia interferes with logical thinking.

As a counselor, she realized how important it was to choose her words carefully. She did not want to hurt or insult him. What should she say? What should she do? He was so proud of his new toy that rationally trying to persuade him to return the car would be futile.

"Did you pay for the car already? We really do not need another car."

He was sitting behind the wheel, lowering the top. "Of course, got a great deal. Beth, you will look so good driving this car. I was thinking of you when I saw it. It reminds me of the one we had when we were first married. Hop in, let's go for a ride."

Beth sadly shook her head. "Bob, we were young and crazy then. We are older, supposedly wiser, now."

He thought it would make her happy. He bought it for her. She did not want to distress him by being negative about the car or his behavior. Since he had developed dementia, he had given up his gun collection and many things. He was proud of the car.

"Bob, I am in the middle of making a cake and cannot go with you. She turned and disappeared into the house, but watched Bob, top down, drive out of the driveway. She immediately went to the phone.

"May I speak with the dealership manager?" Her suppressed frustration surfaced. "I am so angry! My husband has Alzheimer's and you sold him that red convertible! What were you thinking? Don't ever take an old man's money and sell him a car unless you talk with his wife first!"

The manager apologized and explained that they had no way of knowing. Bob acted the same as any customer who was in love with a special car.

Beth knew that trying to do anything was a lost cause. Bob would have to get over his excitement with his new toy. He was emotionally sold on the car and was reliving his memories of life when they were young. The obsession hijacked his mind. Hopefully, he would lose his enthusiasm soon and forget that it was sitting in the garage before he killed himself or some innocent family.

Jack Is Late For Work

Jack shook Maggie. "Wake up! Get up! It's late! I have to get there before they open!" Maggie was sound asleep. Jack jumped around on the bed, shook her, and pulled her toward the edge. He never forgave himself if he was late for work.

"Jack, it is Saturday and four o'clock in the morning. The center is not open on Saturdays or Sundays."

"I don't understand why the center won't let me drive my car to work. My car just sits at home when I could be there already."

Her words were not registering in his brain. Even if they were, he would not listen to reason and no longer believed anything that she said. What else could she do? She threw on the same clothes that she wore the day before, ran her fingers through her hair, and grabbed her purse and keys.

"Hurry up! You are too slow."

"Jack, the center is not open on weekends and during the week they do not open until seven. Look at the clock. It is 4:15 and Saturday."

She turned into the vacant parking lot. There were no lights in the senior daycare center. Maggie stopped the car close to the front door and shined the headlights on the letters on the door. "Get out and read the hours of operation on the door. You will see that I am telling you the truth."

Jack slammed the car door and stood staring at the words for several minutes. Twice, he cupped his hands, put his eyes to the glass door, and peered into the dark interior. Then he stared at the words and numbers on the door again. He reluctantly returned to the car and slammed the door again. "Well, let's just sit here and wait."

Maggie sighed. The parking lot was dark. The streets were deserted. How could she convince him that he would not be 'working' at the center today?

"I have a good idea, I'm hungry. Let's ride over to the diner and eat breakfast. It's just around the corner."

He agreed. She was surprised since he usually ate breakfast at the center. With luck, he would eat a big breakfast, become sleepy, and be willing to go home.

After they ate, he was energized and could not wait to get to work. The center was still dark and deserted. He repeated his previous actions, slammed the door, and stared at the numbers and words on the door for a long time.

"Jack, they are not going to open. They have to give their employees the weekend to rest and be with their families."

"No. I know they will open soon. Let's just sit here and wait."

Maggie reclined her seat and waited. She dreaded another Saturday at home. She announced, "Seven o' clock," and pointed to the clock on the dash. He sat and fumed. She became the town crier, announcing the time every five minutes. Finally, after two more trips to the door, he agreed to go home.

He stomped into the house, dropped into his recliner, and was soon fast asleep. Maggie crawled back in bed but she could not go to sleep. Her mind was running wild. What was she going to do? He drove her crazy every weekend. He no longer read anything or focused on television programs, although he never turned it off. She hated the constant background noise. He was bored and angry all of the time. Soon, he would wake up and start drinking.

She finally dozed off. The door slammed. She

jumped up but it was too late. Jack was driving out of the driveway! Drat! She thought she had hidden all of the keys.

Several hours passed. She paced and peered out the window. No sign of him. Everything was eerily quiet. The phone rang. She glanced at the caller ID. Oh, No! Police! Her voice cracked, fear flooded her thoughts.

"This is Officer Wilson. I am sorry, ma'am, but your husband had an accident. He is not hurt but he sure is angry. There were no other people or cars involved, he ran off the road and into a vacant building. His car is demolished. Can you come right away and give us the information we need?"

She jotted down the location, found her purse, and ran to her car. It was a building at an intersection near the day care center. As she approached, Jack was wildly waving his arms and talking to a policeman who was writing on a clipboard. Another policeman was inspecting the building. She introduced herself to the second policeman.

"We think that he was stopping at the traffic light but instead of braking, he hit the accelerator. We are going to take his driver's license. He probably should not be driving."

Jack was yelling and among all of his horrible words she heard 'license.'

"We don't have any choice, sir, it is the law. You can get them back after you pass the licensing exam."

Oh, no! She was hoping that since his car was demolished, this would be a quick resolution to the problem of his refusal to give up driving. Jack would be determined to take the driving test.

"It was horrible to drive him around. He would reach over and grab the steering wheel, making me almost lose control of the car. He continuously bugged me, trying to persuade me to take him to be tested." She finally relented but he did not pass. That did not stop him from insisting that he take the test again, but at another location.

"When we went to take the test a second time, I pressed the parking brake before leaving the car. Jack came out with the examiner for the driving part of the test and did not know how to disengage the brake. They refused to return his license."

Maggie shook her head, her lips quivered, and tears filled her eyes. "Of course he blamed me and was furious! He continued grabbing the steering wheel when I was driving."

Because of his erratic actions and jerking the steering wheel, Maggie was stopped for reckless driving by a policewoman. After her explanation, Jack was issued a warning that he must always ride in the back seat.

"He rides back there but stews the whole time. He is angry with me all of the time now. He refuses to cooperate with me in any way. He fusses about everything. The only time that he does anything without an argument is when I tell him it is time to go to work at the center."

The Doctor Drives Everywhere

"Hi, Dad. Dan and I are on our way to see you. Bella is with us."

"Well, it is about time. Where have you been? We haven't seen you lately."

Adrienne knew that it was useless trying to convince him that she was there a few days ago. Her dad was a strong, determined, 'in charge' man. His memory and rationality were slipping and Adrienne worried about her mother's ability to handle him. Adrienne and her brother repeatedly tried to convince them that assisted living would make their lives much easier, but Dad was reluctant and Mom absolutely refused. She was determined to stay in her home.

Dad was in the yard swinging his golf club when they arrived. Dan joined him there while Adrienne went in to find her mother. As she opened the door, the smell of dog urine overwhelmed her. Their small dog, Tiger, was glad to see her but began scratching on the door, signaling that he needed to go outside. She hoped to have some time alone with her Mom but scooped him up and rejoined Dan and Dad.

"It is a beautiful day, Dad. Why don't you and Dan take the golf cart out on the golf course and let Bella get exercise by running behind the cart?"

"Great idea. Come on, Dan. You hold Tiger and I'll drive."

Off they went as Adrienne called out, "Watch Bella, you know she likes to hunt and may decide to chase a squirrel."

She hoped they heard her and remembered that Bella was running behind the cart. Adrienne found her mother in the kitchen preparing lunch. She was curious to learn if there were any new problems with Dad.

"I do not believe that the Aricept he prescribed for himself is helping his memory," her mom confided.

Dan was also taking Aricept and they were discussing the side effects when the door flew open and Dad rushed in, upset and out-of-breath.

"That crazy dog of yours ran off! We searched everywhere for her." Frantic, Adrienne ran outside, screaming Bella again and again. "Dan, what happened?"

"She veered off between the houses and refused to come when I called her. Dad drove the golf cart around the houses but she was gone."

Adrienne panicked. Bella was her baby. "Come on, Dan. Let's take the cart and find her." They called, yelled, whistled, and rode everywhere on the golf course. "Oh no, Dan, what are we going to do?"

Deb stopped two golfers and asked if they had seen a brown dog.

"No, but we saw the doctor in his big black car driving down the cart path." Adrienne shook her head. That was Dad.

As they neared the golf clubhouse, Dad, in his black Caddy, was driving toward them frantically waving his arm out the window. He was grinning like a Cheshire cat, very pleased with himself. Bella was sitting on the seat beside him.

Adrienne's heart was still pounding but she tried to control her voice and her frustration. "Dad, I am so glad you found her but you are not supposed to be out on the golf course in your car."

Dad shrugged. "I was on the cart path, not the course. Besides, I have lived here a long time. What are they going to do, evict me?"

ROLES AND TRADITIONS – "I Still Care"

Mom told me many times over the years, "Take care of your family and do what you have to do. I will be fine, don't worry about me." The roles of wife and mother were sacred to her above all others. Her role model, my grandmother, was devoted to her husband, seven children, and took care of my great grandmother when she became senile. Devotion to family and assuring their wellbeing was foremost in my grandmother's life.

When I informed Mom years ago that I was returning to college, the question that she immediately asked was, "Will your husband let you do that?"

I froze, turned, and stared at her. "LET me?"

At that time, I was not accepting of generational differences or as tolerant of traditional attitudes and was easily annoyed by similar statements. Years of researching attitudes mellowed my own. The inner drive to nurture and help others bestows emotional rewards on everyone. I have changed and better understand Mom and how her early years formed her attitudes.

Mom wants me to be happy and have a good life. She always placed her own needs at the bottom of my 'to do' list. She constantly worried that Dale did not approve of my trips to North Carolina. Rather than launch into a long, philosophical treatise about the differences in values, standards, and attitudes of women from different generations, I made one simple statement that I knew she understood.

"Don't worry, Mom, he is always working and traveling on business."

Holiday Excursion

Our tradition since we moved to the lake was for me to arrive at Mom's house Christmas morning and drive her to our lake house for the day. Alex was in grad school in Washington and wanted our family to celebrate the holidays at our larger, Ohio house. After a great deal of discussion and persuasion, Mom agreed to make the trip.

On a cold December day as a few snowflakes flurried to the ground, Mom and I climbed the mountains and headed for the curvy West Virginia Turnpike. The farther north we went, the faster snow fell. Mom was nervous; her hands gripped the sides of the seat. My decision to drive our four-wheel SUV paid off. We never could have made it in my rear-wheel drive car.

I was determined to forge on in spite of my worry that we may spin off the road at any moment. Stopping for the night was not something that I wanted to endure. Mental images of unloading suitcases, helping Mom walk in the snow, obtaining meals, and staying in a strange, cold, motel room filled my head and kept me moving. Alex was already in Ohio. I knew that the snow would be deeper in the morning. My unease kept me driving forward.

Mom was quiet, her teeth were clenched, and her eyes were big and round. When the landscape flattened and I saw the Ohio snowplows, I was never as overjoyed to be in a State north of the Mason-Dixon line.

Once we arrived, comfort and peace of mind eluded me. The unfamiliar surroundings were too much for Mom. She was more confused than I had ever seen her. She stayed in her room each day until almost noon, listening to music on the radio, eating her dry oat cereal from her hand while sitting on her bed.

Her anxiety level increased daily. She repeatedly asked, "When are we going back home?" She did not enjoy our trips around the neighborhood to view the decorations and lights and ignored the caroling neighbors.

I worried so much about Mom's discomfort and unease that I could not relax and have meaningful conversations with Alex. We were rarely together since she began grad school. On several occasions, I detoured through Washington after I left the lake on my way north, but we never had enough time to visit and catch up. The best that I could do was to hug her and take her to dinner. The brief diversion added more than two hundred miles to my trip.

That trip to Ohio was the first and last for Mom. On the day we traveled back to North Carolina, Mom finally smiled, but was anxious until she was safe in her home, her little nest.

Mom still remembered that she was a mother and grandmother. She wanted to be her old self and care for Alex and me, and desperately wanted to please us. But, she suffered when she was unable to sleep in her own bed and do the same things at the same time each day. She did not want to make the trip to Ohio, but because she loved us, she agreed. I learned a valuable lesson.

If I forced Mom to come to Ohio, I would have constant guilt. Her anxiety and confusion would, in all likelihood, speed up her disease. She had lived in the same city for eighty years, and in the same house for fifty-five of those years. It was then that I fully realized that somehow, we had to find a way to move back home.

The Bucket

John locked the door of his woodworking shop and headed home for lunch as usual. Sara always had a tasty, hot lunch waiting for him. The minute he stepped in the door he knew something was wrong.

"Sara? SARA!"

The shrill fire alarm sounded. Smoke poured from the kitchen. As he ran to the kitchen he met Sara running toward him from the laundry room. John grabbed potholders and dashed through the back door with the smoking pan. He threw it on the concrete walkway and sighed. A charred mess was all that was left.

"Oh NO! It's ruined!"

"What were you cooking?"

"Food!" The word was the only answer that she could think of.

John's panic subsided, but anger rose in his voice. "Beef, chicken?"

Sara shook her head back and forth. Tears streamed down her face. His heart softened. "Sara, we are lucky that I came in the door when I did. The house could have burned down with you in it! This is serious!"

She was trembling and staring at the ground. He put his arms around her, realizing that she was helpless and overcome by sadness. He struggled to banish his anger.

"Come on, let's air out the kitchen and notify the fire department that everything is under control. What number should we call when we have an accident like this?" It was a test to see if she would remember 911.

Sara hesitated and then blurted the answer. "Johnny."

"Sara, Johnny is at work and you may not be able

to reach him. It will take him at least 30 minutes to get here. You have to remember that if you have an emergency, you dial 911."

Her confusion and memory were becoming worse day by day. John was exasperated and realized that he could no longer leave her at home alone. He tried taking her to the shop with him but having her there drove him crazy. She had to be busy doing something all of the time and constantly cleaned and rearranged his tools. They were impossible to find when he needed them. He hired a lady to stay at home with her, but Sara fired her the second day. "That woman was lazy."

Throughout their long marriage, John and Sara worked hard. Their skin was weathered and tough from all the years spent tilling, planting, nurturing, harvesting, and preserving fruits and vegetables. When the children were young, Sara raised chickens, sold eggs, and made butter from the milk provided by Nellie, their pet cow. She cooked three wonderful meals each day and taught their girls excellent homemaking skills. Her pound cakes and pies brought top dollar at community fundraisers.

John stayed at home that afternoon, called Johnny, and confided the whole story to his son. Johnny was a determined problem solver. He learned a few things from his parents. After work, he stopped by on his way home with helpful information. He had a long conversation with the director of the Senior Services Daycare Center.

John met with her and toured the center the very next day. "Don't worry, we can help you and keep her busy."

Sara began her days at the center under the impression that she had a job. She helped with simple tasks, passed out breakfast and lunch plates, cleaned the tables, straightened chairs, dusted, and folded linens. She loved working there. As soon as one task was completed she asked what else she could do. Her mission in life, working and helping others, occupied her time. The staff thanked Sara and made her feel competent and valued.

John began taking buckets of vegetables, whatever was in season in their garden, to the center for the appreciative staff. He knew that if vegetables started accumulating Sara would be determined to preserve them. He wanted to keep her away from the stove.

The bucket full of vegetables from the garden became a pattern. "OK, Sara, I am putting the bucket in the truck, lets go to the center." Sara was always ready and happy to go.

One day, there was nothing from the garden to put into the bucket. Sara was upset. She had to take the bucket! She refused to go without the bucket! John was irritated but put the empty bucket in the back of the truck and off they went.

The director smiled, welcomed them, and noticed John with the empty bucket.

"What's this about?" she inquired.

John was still frustrated. "We didn't have anything to put in the bucket but she wouldn't come without the bucket! So, here she is and here's the dammed bucket!"

Where's Beanie?

Mom stood at the open door. "Beanie! Where's Beanie? I can't find Beanie!"

Tears filled Brenda's eyes. "Beanie died, Mama." She gave the bad news over and over. Every few minutes her mother called Bennie.

Ida cried, and then ten minutes later was at the door calling again. "Beanie, Beanie!"

Ida adopted Beanie when he was a puppy. He was her constant companion and a great comfort after her husband passed away. From then on the two of them were inseparable. She held and cuddled him as they watched TV and slept. She was happiest when Beanie was sitting beside her.

When Ida began forgetting what day it was, where she put things, and recent activities, the small Beagle began gaining weight. The veterinarian warned that he was too heavy and recommended reducing his food intake. That advice was soon forgotten and Ida worried, certain that he was hungry. She fed him again and again.

Brenda was devoted to her mother. Ida lived twenty miles from Brenda but she always found time to drop in and check on Mama after work. She helped Ida with household chores, took her shopping, to appointments, and to visit relatives. She made certain that Ida's pantry was full and that she had everything that she needed.

Although Beanie was gaining weight, Ida was becoming very thin. When Brenda's husband had an accident at work and became bed-ridden for a few weeks, she used that as an excuse to move Mama and Beanie into her home, supposedly temporarily, although she had other plans.

Brenda worried about Ida's mental decline and living with her relieved some of the stress. She arranged with her employer to work second shift so that she could be at home in the mornings to cook and care for Mama. In the evenings, her husband attended to Ida's needs.

Soon, Ida began regaining weight and Beanie was on a reduced calorie diet, or so Brenda thought. He still gained. Although everyone loved him, no one could save him. Poor sixty-pound Beanie died of congestive heart failure early one morning as Mom held him and cried.

Dementia did not save her from days of grief and sadness. Then, one morning, the memory of his death was gone and old memories of his comforting companionship reappeared. She called him again, and when he did not appear, she fretted that he was lost, stolen, or hit by a car.

Brenda could not stand to see her mother cry and grieve. She held back tears every time that she had to say, "He died, Mama."

What should she do? Should she continue telling her that Beanie died? Should she invent a lie that would explain his disappearance? Would Mama remember that reason? Should she get another dog? She remembered that simply petting Beanie had a calming effect that was better than any anti-anxiety drug.

One morning while Ida stayed home, Brenda left to buy groceries. Her route took her past the local animal shelter. Something told her to make a U-turn. She sat in the car debating with herself. "Do I really want to do this?"

She was still uncertain as she walked into the shelter. Her love of animals overwhelmed her and made her wish that she could adopt all of them. Then she saw him! To her amazement, there was a young Beagle very similar to Beanie.

Decision made! She could not leave without

him. How will Mama react to the new baby? Will she think that he is Beanie? Will she turn away, thinking only of her loss of the original, beloved Beanie?

When she walked through the door, the look on Mama's face resolved everything. Ida cradled him and kissed him. "Beanie came back, didn't he?"

Reclusive Betty

Betty and her husband, Carl, led a happy life at the retirement village. They loved the outings, activities, special events, and wonderful meals in the dining room. Then, everything changed. Carl had a massive heart attack and died. Betty closed her door and refused to see anyone. She became a recluse in her own suite. Everyone tried in vain to coax her out. No one was allowed inside and she was not coming out, not for ice cream, a special outing, a walk with an old friend, nothing.

Her meals were delivered to her door. She answered the knock and took the food inside and ate alone. The staff speculated. What happened to the trash? Mail and newspapers were delivered to her door, disappeared inside, and never seen again. Standing outside Betty's door, the director of the facility tried many times to see her just long enough to know that she was all right. Betty refused.

One day, the retirement village was sold to new owner and Betty's building was changed to an assisted living center with a new managing director. Betty's suite was large and in a prime location. The new director had no choice but to implement the new owners' policies. Betty would be moved and her room cleaned out and renovated. The amount that she had been paying would cover a semi-private room.

Most of the staff stayed in their jobs and continued their duties as usual. They worried about Betty. "Oh, this will be awful for Miss Betty! She will have to move AND have a roommate." When they learned that her roommate would be of another race they were doubly concerned.

"This will kill her!."

The new director was a seasoned manager and immediately disagreed. "No, she will be fine. Just wait. Isolation and loneliness can foster anxiety and delusions. This will be a good change."

The new director talked with her. "The staff needs your help, Betty. There is so much to do around here. Are you willing to help out by checking on the other residents? Your job will be to inform the staff if you see any problems or think that a resident needs extra assistance."

Miss Betty willingly moved! She had been a wife and mother and loved being needed and useful again. For the first time in years, she was busy and she loved it. The staff was amazed. Plus, Betty loved her new roommate and they became lifelong friends.

Role Reversal

Michael was uncomfortable in his new role as the family cook. "Betsy, are you hungry? What would like for dinner? He knew better, why did he ask?

She shook her head, as if to say, "I don't know." She was sitting on the sofa, blankly staring at the TV, showing no emotion.

Hum. What to have for dinner? He checked the

refrigerator and gasped. Ice cream that belonged in the freezer was melting, dripping, coating everything in its path, and settling in a big puddle on the vegetable drawer. In the freezer, the milk that replaced the ice cream was frozen. He dumped the disintegrating cartons into the sink.

"Oh no, again?"

Broken leaves and sticks from the houseplants were crammed into and sticking out of the garbage disposal. As he cleaned up the messes, he thought about her new behaviors.

She often moved things around the house, sending him on searching expeditions. Over their fifty-year marriage, decorating and finding just the right place for things, special touches that made their home attractive, gave her pleasure and earned compliments from visitors. Her talent for choosing colors and arranging furniture in convenient and attractive ways prompted friends and church members to ask for her advice with their household décor.

Michael wondered if she was moving things around because it bolstered her self-esteem, was a long-established habit, or because she was bored. He would probably never know, meaningful conversations with Betsy were no longer possible.

As a minister, Michael comforted people through crises, shared their sorrows when their loved ones were sick or dying, and every Sunday, delivered inspiring sermons filled with love and hope. For many years, Betsy, his helpmate, wife, and the mother of his children, enabled him to pursue his life's work by taking care of everything else, the details of daily living. Now, after retirement, he was slowly losing her, the love of his life, to the ravages of dementia.

Michael was overwhelmed, out of his comfort

zone. Oh, it was not the cooking and housekeeping, he was learning how to do those tasks. Watching her fade away, become more confused and anxious, was tearing apart his heart.

When her memory first began failing, she denied the problem and fought valiantly. She tried to function normally and became angry if anyone mentioned that she was having problems. It was a losing battle and the loving, secure, competent woman that he married was no longer inside her body. Her personality was changing daily. The last time that she accompanied him to a conference in another city, she became agitated in the unfamiliar environment and was anxious until they returned home.. It was then that Michael realized that they would never again be able to enjoy trips and vacations together.

After cleaning up the ice cream and pulling debris out of the disposal, he again turned his attention to dinner. She no longer expressed any opinions or preferences. He did the best that he could to put together a meal and hoped that she would eat it. Lately, she picked at her food and ate no more than one or two bites, not enough to sustain her. He tried to persuade her to eat but she simply shook her head. Was his cooking that bad?

"I am going to prepare one of your favorite milk shakes."

She was not interested in solid foods but drank Boost and liked it when he added ice cream. Betsy smiled at him as he replaced her plate with the shake. She drank it all.

CHAPTER FIVE

GRASP THE WHEEL AND HANG ON!

MID-STAGE DEMENTIA

The Road Warrior Struggles

My 'road warrior' madness accelerated. I drove to North Carolina every other week. Mom declined again but then seemed to be on another holding pattern with the disease. I constantly worried when I was in Ohio and did not know and could only guess her condition. Our phone conversations were short and sweet and I held my breath each time we talked.

"I am fine. Everything is OK. Don't worry about me." When I hung up the phone I thought, *If something were wrong, would she even know it?*

Unnerving events triggered my skepticism. I learned from Aunt Edith that Mom told her that the manager of the cafeteria drove her home in her car, followed by an employee who returned him to his job. Mom did not mention that incident to me. *Did she remember it, or was she trying to avoid upsetting me?*

I worried that she forgot the route home but convinced myself that most likely, her car was the culprit. Soon after that, there was a car problem.

Mom called, outraged. Her car engine stopped when she was two blocks from home. A neighbor helped her by calling a nearby mechanic. He checked and replaced the battery. Mom was angry and thought that he was dishonest.

"There was nothing wrong with my car battery but he said that it was bad and charged me ninety dollars for a new one! That is highway robbery."

Shortly thereafter, I made another trip to North Carolina to assure myself that all was well. Soon after I returned to Ohio, a terrible event happened and I immediately repacked my bag and headed south again. I called and told her that I was on the way but withheld the awful news. She did not remember that I left her three days earlier.

As usual, we went to the cafeteria for an early dinner and were drinking a last cup of decaf before I divulged the reason for my speedy return.

"Mom, I have bad news. Aunt Mary passed away last night."

"Oh, no! Her surprised expression was tinged with horror. "What happened? Was she sick?"

We visited Mary a few weeks earlier, but Mom remembered nothing. She adjusted to the news well, but as we talked, her anxiety steadily rose. I hated to leave her that evening but there was no place for me to sleep. Even the sofa was piled high. I knew that the dust would assault me and the stress of cleaning off a place for me to sleep would throw her into a tizzy.

The following morning, we began searching through piles of her clothes for suitable funeral attire. She soon forgot why we were examining her clothes. When I reminded her that we needed to find something for her to wear to the family visitation and the funeral, she remembered that her best items were hanging on over-the-door hangers in my old bedroom. She nixed all of the new clothes that we found and was determined to wear old black slacks. I did not argue and left everything hanging on the door with the price tags dangling.

She struggled to remember names and faces that evening as we greeted throngs of people, old friends and family. Many did not realize that she was under great duress. Somehow, she managed to pull herself together and convince others that she was sad but fine. I never left her side.

The funeral was cold and windy. I was glad that she insisted on wearing her well-worn shoes, pants, and many layers under her coat. As we walked from the church to the graveyard, my cousin, Donna, put her arm around Mom and the three of us somehow made it through the graveside ceremony. Mom did not cry. Her life of sadness and loss infused her with strong inner control that was evident that day.

Christmas Homecoming

Joy filled my heart. My daughter, Alex, and her new husband were coming to the lake for the holidays. After graduate school, Alex completed post-doctoral work in California and Boston before again settling in Washington, D.C. The Christmas before, in Ohio, I was unable to have long talks with Alex because of Mom's anxiety.

Perhaps a holiday at the lake would return us to the happy days of the past. That thought prompted pesky emotional Ann to interject, *fat chance!* Rational Ann was on guard. *Give us a break! It could happen. We are going to try. We used to love our family time at the lake.*

After we built the lake house, Mom drove herself there, shared Alex's room, and returned to her home several days later. After Alex entered high school and was well past the age of sharing her bedroom, I picked Mom up at her house on Christmas morning and I drove her home again in the evening after dinner.

Dementia changes everything and I was apprehensive the minute I left our driveway. "Mom, I am on the way to your house. Are you awake and having coffee?"

"Oh. It is early. The K doesn't open until eleven."

"Today is Christmas day, Mom. We are having dinner at the lake. Alex can't wait to see you."

By the time I arrived at her house, I was determined to persevere no matter how much she protested. I wanted to persuade her to wear a new, colorful print blouse and black pants instead of her worn, soiled favorites. She opened the door and was already dressed. In my mind I could see the look on Alex's face when she saw Mom's stained, faded clothes. "Mom, I brought you this new outfit to wear today. It is Christmas and Alex is waiting at the lake to see you."

"Oh, is Alex is here? Do I have anything to give her?"

"Yes, Mom. I picked up holiday envelopes at the bank and put some money in one of them for Alex from you. Slip on these new clothes and we will go."

"No. I like this blouse and I am comfortable. There won't be anyone there but family, will there?"

"No, but this is new and festive. Let me help you."

"No. I don't want to change. Take it, and I will try it when I get there."

When Mom makes a decision, battles cannot be won and are not worth the time, effort, and hurt feelings. I returned the blouse and slacks to the box and helped her with her coat and gloves. After checking twice to make certain that the oven was turned off and the door was locked, we were on our way.

As we backed out of the driveway, Mom made her usual speech. "I hate that you came all of the way to get me. You didn't have to do that. There is plenty of food in the fridge. I can always make do."

"It's Christmas, Mom, and Alex is home. I am cooking dinner and we will have a good time. It would not be Christmas without you."

I wondered if Mom would remember our new family member, Alex's husband. She had met him several times in the past and acted as though she knew him.

Mom did not ask Alex questions about grad school or her work. Ann the analyzer's brain was busy wondering 'why?' Perhaps she thought that Alex's feelings would be hurt if she did not remember the details of her life. Rational Ann chastised. *Ann, stop analyzing! She does not remember because the disease has destroyed the parts of her brain that enable her to remember.*

At the dinner table, Mom touched our red tablecloth and said, "Oh, this reminds me of Christmas." All eyes opened wide and we looked at each other, at a loss for words.

After a long silence, I said, "It is Christmas, Mom. Do you like our tree?"

She admired the tree earlier but stared at it again from across the room. "It's the prettiest one you have ever had."

Everyone talked after desert and I noticed that Mom was quiet and instead of participating in the conversation, she was staring at a magazine that she held in front of her face, upside down. The discussion was lively and everyone bantered back and forth. Everyone except Mom. The conversation was too complex and we were talking too fast for Mom. She had a far-away look in her eyes and was not turning her head toward the speaker. She was uncomfortable. When we were alone together and she did not understand something that I said, she often raised her voice and admonished, "Don't talk so fast," but not that day.

Before driving her home, Alex and Mom hugged and said goodbye. Mom looked at Alex and asked, "What grade are you in now?"

Moving Home

All of a sudden, and without discussion, Dale said, "I quit my job. Let's move home."

The old saying, 'Be careful what you want because you may get it,' perfectly describes the explosion of joy, trepidation, and looming mayhem that washed over me. Emotional Ann was in a dither and immediately made mental lists and worried about the details of all that had to be accomplished in a short time. Thankfully, Rational Ann was composed. *You have been wishing for this moment and consumed by worry since the holidays at the lake. Get yourself together and go to work. You can do it! Mom needs you more than ever.*

Dale developed a new security device months ago and had tested and revised it. He was pleased with the invention, made the decision, and wham, was no longer 'a corporate man' whose expertise turned unprofitable businesses into profitable ones. His new mission was to become a self-employed manufacturer of the invention that he had been developing since watching the crisis of nine eleven. The plan seemed brilliant, if good fortune was on his side and all of the issues, logistical, financial, timing, and a host of details, fell into place as he envisioned. No stress there.

He was consumed by planning and orchestrating all of the details involved in starting a new business. My jobs were to prepare our house for sale, find a buyer, and round up, pack up, stack up, and label the bountiful contents of our lives. Oh yes, one more necessary time consuming task, continue paving the roads to North Carolina with new coats of tire rubber.

I zoomed south, satisfied my mind that Mom was OK, then zoomed north and faced a bigger nightmare.

While in Ohio, I collected a myriad of wonderful vintage 'treasures' on my outings with friends to a fantastic place, the Hartville flea market.

During the packing ordeal, I became absolutely convinced that I had been blessed with a very special 'pack rat gene,' passed down from Mom and her ancestors. The 'treasure' label was driving my dilemma--*when in doubt, WHY throw it out*? I cornered the market on boxes and bubble wrap.

One cold, overcast day, Dale laid sheets of plywood end to end on the snow and ice and all of our wonderful stuff was rolled out and loaded on two trucks. When all of these vintage gems finally arrived in North Carolina, there was no room in our small lake house. You guessed correctly--storage spaces. A major lesson was learned from the whole experience. Our marriage would likely last until we have to move all of that good *'stuff'* again.

Problems Solved?

On the day that I handed the house keys to the new owners and drove south, I was flooded with melancholy thoughts of the past and apprehension about the future. We maintained two residences for many years. What now? In Ohio, we enjoyed large spaces, room for hobbies, and being surrounded by souvenirs collected in our world travels. The peaceful setting surrounding the lake house was amazing, fresh air, nature, and quiet solitude. But trying to live there in a small house would be unnerving. Add to that driving fifty miles every day to help Mom and Dale needing my assistance in launching a new business. "Help!"

I pondered the problems as the miles passed and convinced myself that we needed another house, one close to Mom. If she visited us every day, surely she would become accustomed to staying there. No one would be willing to take care of her in her home and she would never allow anyone in there. I could never convince Mom to allow me to clear out a space to sit, sleep, and eat. If I somehow convinced her, my allergies would soon drive me to fresh air outside.

A major issue that Dale and I agreed on long ago was that we really wanted to keep the lake house. Perhaps we could continue to use it as a weekend retreat and live close to Mom and our new business. Dale was considering a business location that was twelve miles from Mom's house.

After a few days of on-going discussion with Dale, I contacted a realtor and began the search for an affordable house that was suitable for Mom and us. Then I began to think seriously about living in the same house with my mother. Those thoughts were disconcerting. When I left her in the late afternoons, closed my car door and drove away, I often screamed at the top of my lungs in futile attempts to release pent-up frustrations from my body.

All Is Well, Or Is It?

The notion that my life would be easier when I no longer made bi-weekly excursions was an impossible dream. My long trips were replaced by daily drives. Being with Mom five days a week convinced me that she was in mid-stage dementia. Her abilities and behaviors were rapidly changing. Both of us struggled.

Every day that passed, she seemed more frightened and confused. I was constantly practicing my mother role, calming, soothing, and assuring her. She desperately held on to her old patterns and habits and was frustrated and overwhelmed. On some days, she could barely gather the strength needed to plod through.

In the late afternoons, she was even more confused. 'Sun-downing' is the term used by health care professionals to describe heightened anxiety and increased confusion in the late afternoons. She was usually ready for me to leave so that she could settle into her nest and rest.

Occasionally, there was a good day when she seemed to be her old, agreeable self, as long as I did not challenge her determination and control. Those rare days were followed by the new 'normal' days when she was driven by irrationality and obstinacy. Most new destinations or encounters confused her, and as a result, she became difficult, somewhat like a young child who pulls away and loudly declares, No! If I made the mistake of commenting that perhaps she did not remember something, she immediately corrected me. "My memory is better than yours!"

After I moved, she gave up driving altogether but never admitted it. She probably did not realize that fact since her car was parked in the garage. She told her doctor or anyone who asked that she was still driving.

"If I get a chance, I put down my dish rag and go."

Her comments sometimes agitated me and I found myself thinking unkind thoughts. *Mom, you have not washed dishes in thirty years.*

When old customers greeted her at the cafeteria and asked how she was, her answer was, "Oh, I am busy all of the time. I have a home and a daughter to care for." I smiled and nodded.

It was impossible to predict what Mom would say or how she would react. I paused and carefully choose my words before responding to her questions or statements. Being with her was mentally challenging and physically draining. I was always tired and needed weekend breaks to talk with Dale and reconnect with myself.

Every Friday, we filled take-out cartons with her favorite foods. All that she had to do was warm it in her easy-to-operate microwave oven. Years ago, I found a microwave with round dials, similar to her old stove. On Mondays I was often dismayed to discover that the cartons were untouched. I asked myself, *what did she eat?* As I waited in the living room for her to finish dressing, I noticed that bananas, Snickers, and cookies had disappeared.

Before the microwave, Mom used an old hotplate to warm food and heat water for instant coffee. To use it, she had to dig it out from under empty take-out cartons, cereal boxes, and newspapers. One day I found the hotplate perched on a rickety, wooden stool. That did it. After fretting about the chances of a fire in the midst of her hoarded rubble, I discontinued my long-standing argument to replace the broken 1940's stove, ignored her protests, cleaned off the counter beside the sink, and placed the new microwave there. Then, I demonstrated several times how to use it. I chuckled to myself as I thought about that day. Over time she became accustomed to using it. Can she still operate it?

My search for a house produced nothing suitable or affordable, but I remained determined. The search area was expanded to include the entire city and outlying communities. Again, we found nothing.

Compared to the peaceful setting at the lake, city properties seemed loud and congested. As I toured each possibility, I found myself questions. *Can we all be happy here? Will Mom be afraid to stay here? Will I be able to find people to sit with Mom so that I can run errands and stay sane? Will Mom tolerate sitters staying with her?*

For the first time in my life, I wanted and needed a sibling, someone who knew Mom well, understood, and could take over when I needed a break from it all. In the past I was never bothered by that desire. Why want something that I can never have?

My support group was my salvation. They understood, empathized, and I knew that I was not alone. They became my extended family. If only they knew Mom. There was never enough time in our meetings to fully convey an accurate description of her. She was complicated and did not fit the traditional role of 'mother.' Only someone who had been with her through the years would understand her.

As time passed, I understood that the mere existence of siblings does not guarantee that they will be helpful. Some people are just not cut out to be caregivers.

One support group member shared her frustrations. "I have a brother, but he is not helpful and his behavior causes me even more problems. He refuses to stay with Dad and claims to be uncomfortable just being around him. He worries that he doesn't know what to say or do. I make excuses for him to Dad. Dad loves him and would be happy just having him in the same room. He is so stubborn! It breaks my heart."

Mom Steps Down Again

Mom's days of performing and completing tasks were in the past. Her brain no longer allowed her to plan, sequence, and perform any activity. Even small tasks were overwhelming. She still signed her name but took a long time to write a check. She was oblivious to the annoyed people in line behind her as she slowly wrote each line and asked the clerk several times for the date, name of the store, and correct amount. My offer to write the check was usually refused, but when she agreed, she always followed with, "OK, but I'll sign it."

Newspapers were still delivered daily. Her lifelong habit of donning her robe and dashing out onto the porch to secure the newspaper before it was stolen was forgotten. I collected them when I arrived and was tempted to cancel delivery, hoping that she would not notice, but was never that brave. She tossed them, unrolled, on the growing mountains of 'stuff.' Mail was sometimes opened but never read or understood. She occasionally asked, "Is this important? Do I need to do anything?"

I longed to know what she was thinking and understand her concerns and worries. I struggled to empathize with feelings that were driving her behavior, but I could only guess. I desperately wanted to help her but I did not know what to say or do. The best that I could muster was to be kind, loving, and silently muddle through. I never argued or corrected her but found ways to diplomatically handle everything as best I could. I was frustrated and sometimes cried all of the way home in the late afternoons.

My Day With A Mission

As I left the lake each morning, I called Mom, often waking her, and urged her to be dressed when I arrived. She was sleeping later than ever.

"Mom, I am on my way and will be there in about an hour, around eleven o'clock."

The phone jogged her awake from a deep sleep and she was confused.

"What? Where are you? It's the middle of the night."

"No, Mom, it is ten o'clock in the morning. Please get up and dress so we can go get something good to eat."

The hour drive was an accepted fact of my life and gave me time to think and plan. I was determined to get Mom out of that mess, into fresh air, and provide one nutritious meal each day. Was the food we took home Friday still there? If my plan for that day was successful, I could answer that question. I lost sleep plotting how to accomplish my goal.

Her favorite cafeteria was our first destination. I often longed for a different restaurant. I gave up trying to convince her that we needed a change. New places created anxiety and she focused on everything negative that she could think of about the new experience.

"Why don't they take our order? We don't have all day! This broccoli is not good. The cooks at the K know how to prepare it."

The familiar ache in my stomach reappeared as I wound my way through Mom's neighborhood and turned into the driveway. Ding dong, I watched and waited to catch a glimpse of her cautiously peeping out of the small window high on the front door.

"It's me Mom." Click, click, multiple locks turned.

"I'm not ready yet, I just got up."

"That's OK, take your time."

She disappeared to fluff her hair and apply bright red lipstick. Slowly, I stepped from the bright sunlit porch into the dark, foreboding (living?) room. Mold and dust assaulted my sensitive nose. She retreated to the bathroom and I left the heavy, wooden door wide open so that I could see. The blinds and multiple layers of filthy curtains were tightly closed. One of the light bulbs in the overhead fixture was burned out. I made a mental note to replace it before leaving later in the day.

The living room was rarely washed by daylight. The sunshine helped as I carefully stepped over a stack of old books beside the door. Why are these here? She had been shuffling things around again, perhaps fortifying the door at night with an extra layer of protection.

There was no place for me to sit. The once beautiful, damask covered Duncan Phyfe sofa, as well as all of the chairs and tables were piled with stacks of old mail, newspapers, scribbled notes, chocolate candy turned white with age, empty wrappers, burned out light bulbs, coins, clothespins, nails, and small items from the hardware store. Everything was coated with a thick layer of dust. Piles of neatly folded, but probably dirty, clothes served as her current closet. The faded gray-violet carpeting chosen for its Robin's egg blue color forty years ago was barely visible, obscured by more old mail, newspapers and plastic bags, some empty and some containing items purchased long ago. She was no longer bothered by the state of her house, but no one other than me was allowed inside.

"I'm ready!"

Her cheerful voice signaled that she was in a good mood but her smile disappeared when she spied the open door. "Close the door."

She was wearing her black and white uniform, and as usual, the blouse bore faint food stains. I was long past being bothered and embarrassed by her dirty clothes and seldom suggested that she change. My requests hurt her feelings and were useless.

Although Dale installed a washer and dryer in the basement years ago, she never used them. In the past, she hand-washed everything, even the sheets, and hung them outside to dry. The soil was a good indicator that she had given up on that. When I tried to take laundry home, she refused and became irritated.

"Washing fades everything."

I had also given up expecting her to bathe daily and to have her tinted, dark brown hair washed and styled at least every other week. As in dealing with any teenager, it was important to carefully pick my battles. The dirty blouse was not worth upsetting her since I had other, more important issues on my agenda.

Finally, we were out the door and almost in the car before she turned around to check the stove. I patiently waited as she unlocked the door and reassured herself that a stove that had not functioned in years would not burn down her house.

We always took her preferred route to the cafeteria and she made the usual comments along the way. "It's thirty-five miles per hour along here. A policeman usually sits right there and will give you a ticket if you go one mile over the speed limit. Park right there, it is the best place. Are you warm enough in that thin jacket? It's awfully cold today. Why aren't you wearing any socks? My feet would freeze."

I wanted to scream but refrained and gritted my teeth. Rational Ann intervened. *Calm down, you know that she can only comment on the events that are happening now.* Emotional Ann countered. *She has always been critical of you.* Rational Ann prevailed. *Get out of that mood. Your mother is sick and cannot help herself.*

Even though we arrived before noon and waited in a short line, Mom was impatient. "Why can't that lady make up her mind? I know what I want before I get here."

She certainly did, she chose the same vegetables every day. To my surprise, a spicy, grilled chicken dish was on the menu and I was delighted to try something new. My enjoyment of hot and spicy foods developed years ago in Singapore. Experience told me that Mom's disapproval was coming.

"You're getting that? How can you eat that? It would kill me!" She led the way to an acceptable table. "I don't know why you insisted that I get all of this food, I can never eat everything." I usually reminded her that we took extra food home for the evenings but as usual, resisted commenting.

My stomach churned and it was not because of the mildly spicy food. I nervously waited and as we ate and mentally prepared for the worst. A second cup of coffee was promptly poured by one of the observant employees. My dollar bills were ready.

After desert, I realized that an unconscious sigh escaped from my mouth. It was time for my strategy. I began by acknowledging the problem as my fault. "Mom, I forgot to mention that you have an appointment with Linda this afternoon. It has been weeks since you had your hair washed and styled."

She was surprised and her protest quickly

followed. "Oh no, not today, it is too cold outside. Why didn't you tell me before now? I don't want to go today. It's not dirty."

I took a deep breath and began my rational plea. "It is too late to cancel now, Mom. Linda is expecting you and will lose business if you don't show up. I will park right by the door so that you won't get cold when you leave the salon. Think how much better you will feel with clean hair."

Her hesitation and disgusted look made my pulse quicken. Sometimes at unexpected moments, the kind and loving mother who taught me to empathize with others' feelings reappeared. "She does need the money. She isn't married and has to take care of everything by herself, you know. I can't go like this though. I want to go home first and put on an old blouse."

"Of course, Mom."

Diversion Accomplished

Linda smiled as we entered and Mom greeted her warmly. When I asked what time should I return, Mom's smile was replaced by panic. "You won't forget me and leave me here will you?"

"Of course not. I have to run a quick errand but will be back before Linda is finished."

As Mom placed her coat on the hook and found a safe place for her purse, I grabbed Linda's arm, pulled her toward the door so that Mom could not hear us. "Please take your time. I know that she will try to persuade you to use a black rinse but that is so harsh against her fair skin. Will you invent an excuse for using a softer brown? Perhaps you can be out of black."

I rushed out, quickly started my car and as I drove away I gazed into my rearview mirror expecting to see Mom trying to stop me. As I drove, my proud elation was soon replaced by dread. Deep feelings of sadness and loss overcame me as I passed the old hardware store building and houses that were at one time filled with friendly neighbors and my playmates.

As I turned into the driveway, the overgrown bushes and badly peeling paint that I usually ignored slapped me in the face. Several thousand dollars and a good painter would solve that problem but Mom barely had enough for basic necessities. Dale and I paid the last time that it was painted.

I grabbed several large industrial-sized garbage bags from my trunk, determined to gather as much trash as possible in the short time available. As I turned the key and stepped inside, I again sighed. My amazement never went away. The living room resembled the shaken contents of a snow globe that had settled into a huge pile.

No time, Ann! I shook off my apprehension and went to work. First, I tackled the kitchen, holding my breath as I slowly opened the fridge. The stench of spoiled food made me step back. Why didn't I bring a mask and gloves? Stacks of Styrofoam take-out boxes, full of unrecognizable, mold-fuzzed globs flew into the bag. Spoiled milk gurgled down the drain and I pried a sweet drink loose from a glass shelf. The refrigerator needed a thorough cleaning but I had no time for that. There was room at the top of my bag for a few stacks of dirty, empty takeout cartons. After I pressed everything down, there was just enough space left for several handfuls of plastic wrappers that protected newspapers from the rain.

Nearly tripping on bags full of unpacked canned

food, I stopped just long enough to look around. I could easily spend several days just in the kitchen. The small table, chairs, countertops, old stove, and the floor were still piled high. How could she know that I had touched anything? I knew better than to peep into the cabinets. Dishes, books, and yellowed but neatly trimmed newspaper articles would topple out.

I ran out and stashed the first bag in the trunk of my car. Once before, I made the mistake of leaving several securely tied trash bags in the garbage cans beside the garage and trusted the city sanitation workers to make them disappear. Much to my chagrin, I later discovered that she hauled them back into the house and unpacked the contents.

The short hallway from Mom's bedroom to the bath was my next target. I was determined to clear enough from the narrow passageway to prevent her from falling at night. I insisted that she turn on a nightlight in the bathroom, and thankfully, that had become a habit. She usually took the portable phone I had given her to bed, if she could find it and remember to charge it. I had very little faith that she would be able to find and use it. We had a major argument about getting an alarm necklace that would immediately call for help. "I don't need that and I won't wear it." After ignoring her protest, I learned that the devise must be tied to a whole-house alarm system. Issues of installation, cost, and remembering to use it made me abandon that idea.

Surveying my work, I made certain that there were no obvious bare spots. I winced at the thought of her angry disapproval. "You leave MY things alone! I don't want you or anyone messing with them! If you can't do what I say, you can just go home!" It was an eternal struggle. I didn't want to disobey her wishes and raise her anxiety, but she was living in a health hazard.

Glancing at my watch, I knew that if I kept her waiting after Linda finished, her angst could remain for days. Her trust in me was essential. My support group members cautioned that upsetting events often influenced their loved ones for days.

Handfuls of dated ads and junk mail were flying into my bag. Suddenly I stopped. Rational Ann halted my progress. *Remember last time! You MUST examine each piece of paper that you discard!* The day Mom and I were searching for a utility cut-off notice in a pile of old mail and I found an old photograph of Dad standing in front of his roadster flashed through my mind.

"Achoo, achoo." Itching eyes, running nose, and constant sneezing mandated a mission to find a clean water glass so I could take my antihistamine. Dust!!! I went outside for fresh air and paused to think about this monumental problem.

Hoarding is an obsessive-compulsive disorder that sometimes affects people with dementia. Some of the caregivers in my support group were dealing with 'savers.' They were exasperated, especially if they had to live in the midst of everything. At least I went home at the end of each day, well aware that I could not stay here. Hiring someone to stay with her? Impossible. Mom would rebel even if I could find the right person willing to tackle all of this. We were headed for a crisis.

As I stuffed another trash bag into my trunk, I looked up the street, squinted, and stared at the vacant hardware building. I wished to once again see the familiar sight of porch swings, wheelbarrows, and kids' metal wagons sitting out front.

Dad rolled my first big girl's bicycle down the street under the cover of darkness and carefully placed it by our Christmas tree. It had blue metallic paint, a luggage rack, and whitewall tires. In a gallant effort to disguise it from the one displayed in the hardware store window, Dad added white leather fringe around the seat and the ends of the handgrips. Of course I knew, but loved him even more.

I could still see my Dad, wearing his Johnny Bull solid leather shoes, tan, suede jacket, and wide-brimmed hat as he took long strides down the street to eat a hearty lunch. Mom cooked dried beans all morning and served them with cornbread and freshly grated coleslaw. "Come on, Boots," his favorite name for me, "Let's mix all of this together and make a tasty mess." His special touches to my plate made it all seem so good.

In the evening, I watched for Papa to lock his shop door and head my way. "Hello, Doodlebug!" He always reached in his pocket and produced a dime to reward his granddaughter who skipped all the way up the sidewalk to greet him. Tears welled in my eyes, everyone was long gone--Daddy, Papa, Grandma, Aunt Ruby, the neighbors, and now, little by little, Mom slips away.

The door locked, the last bag of trash safely stored in my trunk, I backed out of the driveway. My chest tightened and my stomach ached. Emotional Ann warned, *she is going to be furious*! Rational Ann chimed in, *you somehow have get her out of this mess*! I quivered inside as my mind prepared for her return home. I hoped that she did not realize that I had been 'messing' in her private sanctuary?

IRRATIONALITY AND CONFUSION

The Doctor Wants To Marry

Adrienne and Dan were on their way to visit her parents. Her father's dementia was worse and she worried about her mother, he was more irrational than ever. To remind him of their visit, she called his cell phone.

"I am glad you are coming, I have great news, I'm getting married."

Adrienne's eyes flew open in surprise. She expected anything from her dad but this shocked her.

"You are? What does Mom say about that?"

"Oh, she thinks it's great, she likes Judy."

Judy was a young woman who helped her mom several hours each day with light housework, preparing food, and had taken over the tough job of bathing her father. Her mother did not particularly like the bathing part but he was ornery, and when she insisted that he bathe, the request often escalated into a major battle. Ignoring hygiene is one of the first signs of dementia but because her father was a physician, Adrienne was surprised that he refused to bathe. When Judy told him that she was drawing his bath water and would help him, he happily agreed.

Adrienne stepped inside. "Hello? Where is everyone?"

Her dad was nowhere in sight, but Judy was marching down the hall toward her, obviously on a mission.

"Your father asked me to marry him and, of course I passed it off as a joke, but he keeps pestering me."

Adrienne thought for a minute before she calmly

responded. She did not want to be searching for Judy's replacement. She was already overwhelmed dealing with Dan's dementia.

"Judy, don't be upset. You know how ridiculous Dad can be. Try to accept this as just another of his wild, funny ideas. This may sound crazy, but why don't you tell him that you will marry him but have to wait until your divorce is final? He gets these ridiculous ideas, thinks about them for a while, and then forgets them."

Judy considered the suggestion.

"But that is not true and may make the situation worse."

"He does not know that you are happily married, and if he did, he has forgotten. If you refuse or make a big deal out of it, he may become fixated on it for a long time. If you agree but put him off for a while, he will probably forget about it and stop dwelling on it."

Judy frowned. "Do you think that your mother is upset? I do not want her to have the wrong idea."

"I doubt it, she understands him. They have been married for fifty years. Where is she?"

"She is in her room, enjoying some time by herself."

"Don't worry about Dad, he will forget soon. I will talk with her."

Adrienne found her mother in her room with the door closed. "Hi, Mom, how are you?"

Mom sighed, frowned, and seemed frustrated. "Did your Dad mention that he wants to get married? He tells me that I am too old. He wants a young wife who will move with him to Hong Kong of all places."

Adrienne was sad for her Mom but knew this was just one of Dad's passing fantasies. "I think he looks in the mirror and sees himself as a young man, Mom.

Dementia does strange things to his brain. The other day when I was checking his computer, I was amazed to see that he frequently looks at porn sites. He seems to be going through a stage of hyper-sexuality, but we both know that he would never actually do anything with other women. I am so sorry that you are enduring this. I know he hurts your feelings."

Her mom sighed. "Yes, he has occasionally said hurtful things over the years, but his crazy ideas are popping into his head daily now.

"Adrienne pleaded, "Won't you reconsider and let me call that nice assisted living community?"

Her mother flashed an annoyed smirk. "Absolutely not. I don't care what I have to tolerate, I am not leaving my home!"

You Moved Us

"Beth, you moved us overnight. I don't know how you did that. All of this stuff and you moved it."

Beth knew that it was futile to rationalize with Bob. His dementia triggered his irrationality and confusion and the best response was one that would simply verify his statement. "I had good movers, Bob."

He was satisfied. Over the years, Beth organized twenty moves to cities in the southeast every time that Bob changed jobs. He was smart, enjoyed his work, and accepted many promotions. Sometimes, Bob went to his new job without his family and lived in temporary quarters while Beth waited until school was out for the summer and then singlehandedly managed the relocation.

Those were the good old days when they both had unlimited energy and enthusiasm. Dementia gradually changed him. His steps were short and it took five minutes for him to walk from the bedroom to the den. Beth helped him dress, walked beside him, and waited until he was seated in his favorite chair to tell him about the day's events.

"Jerry is taking you out to lunch today, Bob, while I have my hair cut and get groceries." Jerry was one of their neighbors and a good friend. Bob did not realize that Beth paid Jerry to care of him two days each week. Beth suggested the arrangement to Jerry and at first he did not want to take the money. She insisted. The money guaranteed his availability. She needed time to run errands and unwind from the stresses of constantly caring for Bob.

"Why is he over here all of the time? I don't want to go. It's too much trouble. I need to get out in the yard and work. The grass is too high."

Beth knew what to say. "Bob, you need to get out of the house for a while. The yard does not need mowing and Jerry is really looking forward to lunch at your favorite café." He reluctantly agreed. While they were at lunch, the yardman mowed and Beth pampered herself with a new hairstyle.

Bob was no longer able to care for their large yard but in his mind, he still mowed. Before she hired a man to take over the lawn, Bob traded in two perfectly good lawn tractors because he thought that they were 'no good' because he could not remember how to start and run them. Plus, it was too dangerous for him to try and operate them.

The last time he tried to mow, Beth found him he lying on the ground under the jacked-up tractor, supposedly making an adjustment. She gasped when she realized that the jack was old and unstable. After she calmed down, she agreed that the mower was indeed no good, and offered a solution.

"Let's just give this no good contraption to our son, he needs a lawn mower. He can probably figure out what is wrong with it and get it fixed." Before Bob could change his mind, she called her son and told him to come get the mower as soon as possible. As soon as it was out of sight, Bob forgot about it.

Although Bob shuffled along, he refused to use his cane or walker. One day when Jerry was with him, Bob insisted on walking outside to check the yard. They walked to the bottom of the driveway because Bob wanted to look out over the lawn. It was difficult for him to walk back up the incline to the house. Thankfully, Beth drove in at that moment, stopped, helped Jerry get Bob into the car, and then drove into the garage.

Bob's confusion gradually worsened. He repeatedly asked Jerry, "Where is she?" He wanted Beth right beside of him and tried to find her if she was out of his sight for more than a few minutes. Beth was his memory and his security.

Many days, he did not realize where he was. "Beth, when are we going to the house up there where we belong? I know we moved but I don't like it down here."

"Bob, this is your dream house that you always wanted. We built it and have lived here for twenty years." The minute she said that, she became irritated with herself. Truth and rationality never worked. She should have assured him that they would move tomorrow.

"No, I want to move up there." She thought that he was probably referring to his parents' farmhouse. Growing up, he and his siblings had wonderful lives there and talked about the good old days every time were together. At times, Bob's long-term memory was still sharp. He loved those conversations.

Their children tried to persuade her that it was time for him to be in a memory care facility. Ten years ago, Beth had a stroke and they worried that stress would trigger another. She refused and insisted that she would hire caregivers around the clock when necessary.

"Mom, he is getting worse everyday. You and two other people will not able to take care of a person with late stage Alzheimer's. It will kill you!"

Tommy Needs to Go

Julie wanted to scream but somehow, she held it in again. Tommy paced nervously back and forth. "Let's go, let's go. When are we going? Hurry up, I'll be in the truck."

She plopped the pot on the counter. There was so much to do! Tommy could not settle down, sit, or rest. He had to be moving all of the time, jumping from one place to another. He kept her hustling.

He flipped through TV channels, tossed the remote into a chair, and scattered newspapers around the room. He roamed around the house, opened drawers, rummaged through closets, and shifted things around. Several times each day, she heard the water running and found him in the shower. He always changed clothes afterward and tossed the 'dirty' ones he put on after the previous shower on the floor.

Tommy wanted to work. He often ran across the lawn to his workshop and rummaged until he located something that he could fix. He removed the bolts, screws, and turned it into an unrecognizable mass of parts. Then, he tossed it aside and frantically searched for something else.

Tommy had frontal lobe dementia. The part of his brain that controls impulses and enables understanding the consequences of actions was impaired. Sadly, he no longer prioritized, organized, or completed tasks. Before dementia, he was the man who managed a large maintenance department at a huge manufacturing complex; a man who could repair anything.

He was angry that Julie would not allow him to drive. Even though she always locked the truck and hid the key, he managed to unlock it, sit behind the wheel, and blow the horn. At times, she ignored the insistent beeps. They lived in the middle of twenty acres and she doubted that anyone was bothered by the noise. One day when she left him sitting in the truck, a neighbor frantically knocked on the door. Tommy disengaged the parking brake and the truck rolled backward down the driveway and stopped in the middle of the road with Tommy inside, grinning at her as she ran down the driveway. Thankfully, they lived on a sparsely traveled rural road and he did not crash, cause an accident, or end up in the ditch.

The horn blasted again and again. How did he get the door unlocked? Julie closed her eyes, crossed her arms, and squeezed herself in frustration. Raising her voice or telling him, "No, we are not going," just made him even more determined. She weighed her options. She could endure his frustrating temper tantrum or suffer through another trip to a store or restaurant.

She was defeated, grabbed her purse, gathered her strength, and knew that she was in for another taxing adventure. "OK, Tommy, let's go to your favorite super store and buy the things we need."

As soon as they stopped and before she turned off the engine, Tommy jumped out, grabbed a stray shopping cart, and zoomed into the store. She chased him but could not keep up. She pulled another cart from the rack and scanned the store hoping to head in his direction. Catching up with him was impossible. The best she could hope for was that an innocent shopper wouldn't be run over as he dashed by.

She hurried down the aisles grabbing grocery items as she went. No time to check her list or consider brands. Occasionally, she saw him rush by the intersecting aisle and loudly called his name. He moved so fast that before she could run there, he was gone.

She no longer cared whether she had everything she needed. Where was Tommy? She positioned her cart in a central location and waited. He buzzed by with a cart filled with items she had no intention of purchasing. "Tommy, leave your cart there and come with me. I want to show you something that I am thinking about buying."

It worked. He forgot about the cart and she followed as he pushed her cart toward a checkout line. "OK, Tommy, what do you have in your pockets?" He flashed a sheepish smile and reluctantly pulled several items from his pockets. She put two of them in the cart, but held one behind her back while he placed the groceries on the conveyor. When he was not looking, she quickly deposited it on a shelf. Whew!

As they pushed the cart toward the truck, her spirits rose as she thought about her luck, this was not as bad as previous trips. Tommy set the bags in the truck and pushed the cart to a rack. She started the engine and waited, what was taking so long? Where was Tommy? She turned, Oh No! Tommy was urinating on the pavement beside the cart rack!

You Are Not My Boss!

Jen sat at the conference table with other support group members and shared the events of her past week. Her lips were drawn together and she shook her head back and forth. Her expression was a mixture of sadness, exhaustion, and exasperation. "No matter what I do, I cannot please Curt. When I try to help him put toothpaste on his toothbrush and urge him to brush, he snaps at me."

"Have you brushed YOUR teeth? Don't tell me what to do, you are not my boss!"

"I carefully choose every word so that I convey a kind, positive attitude. But everything that I say, however I say it, angers him."

Before dementia struck, Curt was an attorney and advised others what to do and how to legally accomplish their plans and goals. Since he worked alone, no one noticed his worsening dementia until a judge realized that papers Curt submitted were not correct. After that, Curt's world rapidly changed. All of a sudden, his second wife ruled his life and told him what to do.

"I moved Curt from upstairs to the bedroom on the main floor because of his unsteadiness and difficulty negotiating the steps. When he slept upstairs, he was afraid to walk around at night. But now, he often roams around the house. The noise he makes plus my concern for his safety make it impossible for me to sleep, even upstairs. About the time I fall asleep, he opens and closes cabinets and eats raw rice with milk, thinking that it is cereal. When I get out of bed and try to help him, he angrily fusses. One night he had wet pajamas and when I tried to help him change, he pushed me away and wanted to know if I had changed mine."

The bright spot in Jen's life is occasionally caring for her two-year old grandson, Teddy, and giving her daughter a chance to run errands. Teddy's world is full of joy and wonder and he plays with his toys in the floor at Curt's feet in the great room. "Lately, every move that Teddy makes prompts Curt to yell, NO, STOP THAT. I have to turn my head because Teddy's terrified look makes me cry along with him."

Sad sighs penetrated the momentary silence in the support meeting as Jen paused. "You know, even though Curt is stern, Teddy loves him. We were having dinner at a restaurant and it took Curt forever to eat. Everyone finished but Curt still had a plate of food. Teddy was tired and cranky since it was past his usual bedtime. My daughter and I left to put Teddy to bed and my son-in-law stayed behind with Curt. Teddy is just beginning to talk and adds an 'r' to Curt's name, "Crurt." When we put Teddy into his car seat and started the engine, Teddy wailed, "Where's Crurt? Where's Crurt?"

"I think that Teddy is beginning to understand that Curt is more like him, a two-year old, and not a legitimate adult like his mommy and daddy." At times, Teddy gathers his nerve, toddles over to Curt, presses his index finger into Curt's knee and says, "Crurt, you No!"

LIVING IN THE PAST

Bill's Daily Drive

Jane and I settled into facing chairs located in front of her wide window in the living room. As Bill backed out of the driveway, she said, "Bill is a seventy-year-old teenager. He calls me by my full maiden name, Mary Jane Deal, and says it over and over. He used to do that when we were in high school."

While watching a ball game on TV, Bill's thoughts were of the days when he was a star athlete in high school and excelled in every sport. "Thirty points! Did I ever score that many points in any one game? Yes! I was pretty good, wasn't I? If it weren't for you I could have played ball in college."

Jane marveled that a disappointment he experienced years ago was on his mind. "Yes, you came home to date me that weekend instead of staying and trying out for the team, and not because I asked you to come home."

"Oh, yes, I remember. I was so in love that I didn't even realize that they were having tryouts." He smiled.

There were other signs that Bill's long-term memory guided his daily behaviors. He loved wearing his old penny loafers and recently began turning up the collar of his jacket as the 'cool' guys did in the early 1960's. He refused haircuts, allowed his gray hair to grow, and combed it just as he did back then.

Every morning, Bill and his friends, mostly former associates at work, met at the mall, drank coffee at the food court, and talked. Before he left home, he always asked Jane if she had seen his cell phone. It was in his pocket, charged overnight, and placed there by Jane each morning. Their home phone number as well as Jane's cell number with ICOE, for in case of emergency, were programmed into its memory. He climbed into his shiny truck, took the same route, and parked in the same place each day.

Jane knew that he was still a safe driver and he hated riding with her. Bill taught driver's training before he retired and when forced to ride in her car, he constantly gave her instructions. "You know, I have convinced myself that he can still handle driving but how can I keep from worrying?"

Later, as our discussion ended, her phone rang. "Hey! I don't know where the heck I am." Jane glanced at the clock. He had been gone for two hours.

"Are you driving? Well, look around and tell me what you see. Is there a sign with a street name?" He must have turned off of his usual route. "Stay on the phone, Bill, and tell me what you are passing."

"Okay. There's the barbershop. I know where I am now. I will be home soon."

Jane took a deep breath. Confusion while driving was not a good sign. "Several days ago, he arrived at the mall and found that someone had taken his favorite place to park. When he left the mall, he was stunned. His truck was not there! All of the entrances at the mall looked the same. He did not call me but returned to his friends and they drove him around until they found it."

Bill's pattern was the same every day. As soon as he came home from the mall, he poured himself a glass of bourbon and settled into his favorite chair in front of the TV. He drank and snoozed, and then drank more. She hid all bottles except for his daily allotment. While he was gone, Jane checked the bottle and added enough to bring it up to the amount that seemed to be just enough to satisfy him and keep him from complaining. He was not happy if he suspected that she was rationing his drinks. "Don't touch my bourbon!"

She wondered how much longer he could continue his daily solo trips to the mall. Driving and being with his friends made him feel vital, a regular guy, and in control. He told her that he did not want to lose his freedom. "Don't take that away from me, it is all that I have left."

It was his lifeline to who he always was and to his inner feelings that everything was still OK. It was also her lifeline. If he didn't go the mall, he would start drinking as soon as he finished breakfast. He used to mow and work in the yard, but as the disease progressed, yard work raised his anxiety. He fixated on fighting weeds, pulled up all of Jane's flowers because in his mind they were weeds, and hacked the bamboo growing next door.

Long-term alcohol consumption can eventually affect blood flow to the brain and trigger the onset of dementia. Sometimes, the problem can be stopped or at least reduced by eliminating consumption. I knew from her sad expression that she understood that Bill's lifelong habits established in college were unlikely to change.

Jenny Begs To Go Home

Jim opened the door, stepped onto the porch, took a deep breath, and savored the cool fall air as he gazed out over the valley. The morning sun was slowly burning away the fog. Sunlit hilltops rose above the fog and reminded him of his mom's colorful patchwork quilt that adorned his bed when he was a child.

As a kid, he used to hate the early morning dashes to the woodshed to gather logs and kindling for the fireplaces and stoves. Now, he took his time as he walked to the outbuilding and listened to every leaf-cracking step down the path.

Rebuilding this place was his life-long dream. After his mom and dad died, the old house was reduced to a pile of charcoal by lightening. Soon after he retired, he built an insulated, compact version of their house in the same location as his old home place. He and Jenny were finally home. Well, actually, he was the only one who called it home.

Jenny grew up two miles down the country road and they went to the same rural school. After they married, farming his dad's land was not what Jim wanted, so they left the foothills in search of good-paying jobs. Their energy and enthusiasm paid off in a growing town in the adjacent county. There, they raised three daughters and operated a successful furniture store, but looked forward to the day when they could return to their home community and reconnect with extended family and friends.

Jim loved eating lunch with his friends, stopping by his sisters' houses to talk, and enjoying pieces of their tasty homemade pies. After they first moved, he begged Jenny to go with him but she always refused. She seldom talked, even to him, and became confused when surrounded by people.

Just three weeks after he sold their house, her doctor said that Jenny had Alzheimer's dementia. For several years, she had been forgetting where she put things and Jim assumed that her forgetfulness was normal with advancing age. He was alarmed when the movers began loading their furniture on to a truck and she screamed and refused to move.

It was too late and they had to move. In the new house, she was confused, agitated, and worried. She begged to return to their old house. She couldn't find anything, even the location of the bathroom. In the middle of the night he found her in the closet, crying, and standing in a puddle.

He worried about leaving her alone, and limited his time away to short trips and quick visits with friends and family. His girls saved him. His three daughters brought food, cleaned the house, and sat with their mother. Thanks to them, he was able to get out occasionally, talk with people, and see his doctor.

He dumped the logs on the porch and sat down on the step to catch his breath. It was ironic. Jenny was physically healthy but her mind was going away. His mind was as sharp as ever but his heart was wearing out.

Later that afternoon, Jenny began pleading again. "I want to go home. When are you going to take me home?"

"We are home, Jenny. This is our home now."

"No, this is not my home. I must go home. Mom will be worried about me."

"OK, Jenny. Get in the car and we will go home."

He drove her around, and sometimes, a short trip satisfied her. Often, when they returned, she refused to get out of the car because they were not home. He asked her to describe her home and it occurred to him that she was describing her childhood home that had been torn down years ago. He tried driving past the site of her old home place but she recognized nothing.

Sometimes he was lucky. He turned in their driveway and announced, "We're home. Let's go in and see what we can round up for dinner."

"Oh, yes, this is my home."

After dinner she usually begged again and again to go home. He became adept at making excuses as to why he could not take her home until tomorrow. As they were lying in bed that night she said, "My mother would die if she knew that I was in bed with a man I am not married to."

He chuckled as she explained, "I don't want any children!"

He tried to stifle his laugh but could not help himself. "You already have three daughters."

Dan Dances

Dan's smile improved Adrienne's spirits. He and Adrienne dined at a nice restaurant with live music and he appeared happier than he had been in months. He laughed as they whirled and danced to the lively band music. Several couples were Shag dancing and Dan remembered the steps that he learned years ago. After that night, he lived to dance.

Background music played as they shopped for groceries and Dan danced as he pushed the cart around the store. They took ballroom dancing years ago, but Adrienne found that she just could not keep up with him as he pursued his newfound activity. His energy, stamina, and enthusiasm were amazing.

Adrienne's family, including her mom, dad, brother and his wife, met at an upscale restaurant for Thanksgiving dinner. A string quartet played in the background, and as they filled their plates at the buffet table, Dan began tapping his foot and humming. After they rejoined the family and before Adrienne could sit, Dan grabbed her hand and insisted she dance with him beside the table. Adrienne was mortified. No one else was dancing and the food was getting cold.

"It is impossible for me to go out dancing, laughing, and acting as though everything is normal. I just don't have it in me. He is so happy and enthusiastic when he dances, and I want him to do things that keep his brain active and make him happy."

Adrienne searched until she found a caregiver assistance service with trained employees that had nursing experience. They provided companions, drivers, whatever assistance was needed. A female nursing assistant who loved to dance, picked Dan up at home every Tuesday evening and took him dancing. Adrienne was relieved. "They solved my problem. The service was well worth the money and he needs the social and mental stimulation."

Before long, it was obvious that Dan was experiencing further decline. For years, Dan rolled the trash container to the street on pick-up day. When she asked to him to take out the trash, he responded, "Where do you want me to take it?"

He always walked the dog on a leash but neighbors called and reported that they saw him walking back and forth several times and thought that he was lost. Adrienne knew that she could no longer leave him at home alone and was determined to find a solution. She had many commitments and, for her own sanity, she needed time by herself.

She soon found the Senior Services Daycare Center. It was ten miles from their home but worth the drive. The programs provided mental stimulation, social interaction, and many activities, including his favorites, music and dancing. Volunteer musicians played every Friday afternoon. Dementia was not obvious as many danced with each other and the staff, and remembered music and dance steps from long ago. Others watched and tapped their feet to the music.

Adrienne joined the weekly support group. The caring members listened, understood, and offered tips and strategies that worked for them. For many months Dan seemed stable, on a plateau with little further decline.

Myra Needs People

Myra was bored and unhappy. She aimlessly walked around the house but there was nothing to do, no fun, no laughter. The ladies Rob hired to stay with her while he ran errands were nice, but all they did was sit and watch TV.

Rob had never seen Myra so unhappy. Since they married twenty years ago, after his first wife and Myra's husband died, Myra always smiled and enjoyed each day, even after developing Alzheimer's. She loved traveling around the country in their motorhome and her dementia didn't seem to be getting worse. She was on a plateau for a long time before Rob realized that she did not remember the details of their travels and was becoming apprehensive when they visited new places. The day in the campground when she became lost after following a Buick onto the highway convinced Rob that it was time to settle in North Carolina near Myra's daughter, Jan.

Jan was helpful and Myra loved being with daughter while Rob searched for a suitable house. She was unconcerned about the future and trusted Rob to make good decisions and handle the details. Rob always made Myra's life easy. He was her memory, planner, doer, and fixer.

But as soon as they settled into their new home in North Carolina, life became monotonous for Myra. Jan was employed part-time and had a husband and children. Rob knew that he had to find something for Myra to do. She was always active, loved being around people, and needed activities.

The search did not take long. The award-winning Senior Services Daycare Center was well known. At first Myra went there three days each week but Ron soon increased it to five days. Myra was happy again! There were so many fun games, activities, and music performances. She danced to music every afternoon with a man named Dan. The two of them were so lively that they entertained everyone.

Rob was delighted. He had a daughter and granddaughters close by and a good support group at the center. Their lives and Myra's dementia were manageable again.

The Guys' Table

Tim's eyes popped open at three, long before dawn. He got up, made the bed, dressed, put on his shoes and jacket, stretched out across the bed, and nervously waited. At four, his patience gave out.

"Marjorie, are you awake?"

"I am now. Tim, it is the middle of the night, why are you dressed?"

"I wanted to ask you something."

"Can't you wait until morning?"

"But I need to tell you something."

"What is it, Tim?"

"I need to know what we are going to do."

"Tim, we need to sleep now."

Ever since Tim started going to the daycare center, his mind focused on getting there early. It was all he could think about. The time on the clock in the bedroom was meaningless to him, as was the dark sky outside.

"I need to get there in time to get a seat at the guys' table."

"We are not leaving home until ten o'clock. It is now four in the morning. We have six more hours before we leave and I need to sleep. You will be there in time to sit with the guys and have lunch."

Somehow Marjorie drifted off to sleep again but kept waking to check on him. She knew that both of them would be exhausted long before the day was over.

He paced around the kitchen while she prepared breakfast, still wearing his jacket and ready to go. He shuffled through the newspaper, neatly folded it, placed it on an empty chair, and slapped the table. "It is twelve o'clock and I am going to miss lunch. What is taking you so long?"

"Tim, it is nine o'clock, not twelve, and I have to eat and get ready. I promise that you will be there in plenty of time to have lunch with the guys."

The guys' table was a mystery. Why was this one group so important? What did they do? What did they talk about?

"Tim, what do you talk about at the guy's table?"

"Oh, guy stuff."

"What do you do together?"

"Guy stuff."

After his positive reaction to the day care center, she could not believe that she had been hesitant to take him there. She hesitated and agonized before making the decision, worried that he would not fit in there because he never joined men's groups or focused on anything except his job, caring for their son, and the lawn.

Later that morning, she asked her support group, "What goes on at that table that makes it so enjoyable?"

The director smiled. "They laugh, tell jokes and stories, and talk. They love to play the beanbag toss game, corn hole. We don't stand and listen, we respect their privacy, but every so often I catch a little bit of their conversations."

Marjorie smiled and shook her head. "Whatever it is, Tim loves it and I never predicted that he would be willing to come here or that it would make him happy. I just wish that he would sleep all night."

The support group suggested that she try melatonin, the natural sleep hormone produced by our bodies to make us sleepy when the sun sets and we are surrounded by darkness. If that did not make him sleep through the night, she may want to contact his doctor and obtain a mild nighttime sedative.

Marjorie took the advice and melatonin worked. She gave it to him an hour before bedtime and he usually slept all night. He continued going to the center Mondays through Fridays and seemed to be on a plateau with the disease.

FEAR AND ANXIETY

Wilma Panics

Roy wiped his brow and pushed the lawnmower into the garage. He needed a cool drink of water and hoped Wilma had unlocked the door. He tried to go in for a glass earlier but the door was locked and he waited rather than awaken her from her nap. He climbed the steps and tried the knob again, but the door was still locked.

"Wilma! Wilma! It's me, open the door."

Just then, two police cars turned into his driveway and stopped. He whipped around. What is happening? A policeman yelled for him to step away from the door and put his hands in the air! Alarmed, he quickly obeyed.

A policeman stepped on the porch and Wilma opened the door two inches and peeped out. "Ma'am, is this the man who was trying to break into your house?"

Frightened, she slowly opened the door and bobbed her head up and down in silent agreement.

"I'm her husband, Officer. I live here, and have been mowing for the past two hours. Wilma has Alzheimer's disease. She called you?"

"Do you have identification?"

This was not the first time that Wilma did not know Roy but she never called the police.

"Lately, Wilma's dementia is worse, Officer. She is often confused and afraid."

Roy produced his driver's license and the police were satisfied. They would file a report so that other officers could have that information if she called again.

Roy sweetly calmed her. She recognized him, and allowed him to drink water in the kitchen. Roy was at his wit's end. He had cooked, bathed, dressed, and cared for her for several years. Her confusion mostly occurred in the late afternoons. 'Sun-downing' was the term used by his support group.

Two nights ago, Wilma screamed, "Who are you? Get out!" He had nowhere to go and finally convinced her to allow him to sleep on the sofa.

She was no longer the woman he married years ago. These incidents were awful. She was terrified and afraid of him. He sighed as he thought about the future.

He guessed that he would endure in the same way he persisted through the other changes that turned her into a stranger. They could not afford memory care and none of their children were living nearby.

Thankfully, ladies from their church regularly stayed with Wilma so that Roy could buy groceries and have a few minutes to unwind. Although Wilma sometimes did not recognize them, she was usually tolerant of the women and happy to see one or two of them who came often.

What could he do? Her doctor suggested anxiety medicine but he refused, concerned that she would sleep all day and be awake all night. He watched her as she sat on the sofa. Her facial expressions changed many times. He thought she was on the verge of crying and then, he wondered if she was in pain. After he observed her and thought for a while, he called her doctor. Perhaps the medicines would banish her terrors and give her peace of mind.

Stuart's Shadow

Stuart is Claudia's memory, cook, chauffeur, caregiver, provider, and security. When he is out of her sight, even for a minute, she is desperate. She needs assurance that he is always there and follows him around the house, even to the bathroom.

"Sometimes, I get so frustrated that I want to yell at her. So far, I avoided doing that and try to keep my frustration inside. If I fussed at her, I know that she would be crushed. She wants my attention all the time and is happiest when we just sit and hold hands. I can't do that all of the time! I have things to do around the house. When I take her out to the grocery store, I have to hustle, almost run, to keep up with her. She wants to talk to everyone and touch everything. It is impossible to shop for the things we need. I constantly apologize to strangers and pull her away."

Stuart worries that he will have another heart attack and his instinct sometimes tells him that his blood pressure is elevated. "The stress is probably going to kill me."

He devised ways to keep her occupied at home so that he can get meals on the table. She no longer follows the plots of stories on TV, but still laughs at the classic comedy programs that he recorded. She loves music, especially the songs that were popular when she was young. She is content to listen through earphones and sings along. Stuart is thrilled when he finds something that occupies her for a while.

"Music is as good as anti-anxiety pills. She is calmed by it. When she is singing, she is not constantly asking me questions, usually the same ones over and over."

Unfortunately, things are getting worse, not better. A very annoying and disruptive pattern developed when she began snoozing in the early evenings and then walking around the house all night, turning on all the lights, and calling his name.

He worries that she will open the exterior doors and disappear. He turns the handles of the double locked doors a certain way so he will know if she has tried to open them. At other times, she crawls into bed with him, asks questions, begs to hold his hand or at least hold on to him.

Their daughter, Kim, worries about her dad. Although she has a job and young children, she schedules time to stay with Claudia so Stuart can rest, run errands, or meet with the few friends who have stuck by him. Kim and Claudia were always very close. Kim's eyes fill with tears when Claudia tells her that she is not welcome there. Stuart's heart breaks when as he witnesses Claudia's rejection of their child. Although Kim knows that it is the disease and not her mother talking, it still hurts.

At his wits end, he found the adult day care center. In the beginning, he took Claudia two days a week. After realizing that she loved it there, he changed to five days a week. She chats endlessly with or at others, plays games, dances, and enjoys the music performances. He and his daughter have lunch, he has time to run errands, pay bills, keep in touch with friends, and does many things that were previously impossible. He has precious time alone, a huge blessing.

"I would be dead now if I didn't have the daily relief."

Incoming

Della's eyes popped open. It was almost daylight. She listened. Oh no! In the distance, she heard the faint sound of a helicopter. Before she could move, Vic jumped out of bed, grabbed her, pulled her to the floor, and tried to shove her under a high chest of drawers. He exploded with energy, as if a bomb went off in the bedroom.

"Incoming!" He yelled and yanked open the closet door, sending things flying! "Where is my rifle? Ammo? Get down! Don't move!"

"Vic, Vic! Wake up!" Then, she gathered her wits and used a calm, gentle voice. "It's OK. It's not the Viet Cong. It's the helicopter from the hospital. They are

taking someone to the emergency room. Look around,
Vic. We are in our home. This is our bedroom. There is
no need to panic."

This time, her soothing, rational words worked.
Vic slowly recognized her and their room. Soon after
they married, she realized that he occasionally had
nightmares about Viet Nam, but he always awoke and
knew that they were safe in their bed.

In the last few years, since he had been
diagnosed with Alzheimer's, his dreams were frequent
and in his sleep he frantically jumped around, convinced
that the horrors were real and that the war was
happening around them. Sometimes she laid on the
floor for hours, trying in vain to bring him back to
reality. Those episodes were awful. She worried about
him. His heart raced as the adrenalin coursed through
his body.

Theirs was the second marriage for both. They
met when she was a nurse in a veterans' hospital and
Vic was recovering from wounds. The man she married
was loving, caring, and appreciative of everything that
she or anyone else did for him. They had many good
years together and moved from one army base to
another. He was never fearful or physically violent
before the awful disease.

In the past, she never worried about her safety.
But as the intensity and duration of his nightmares
increased, so did her concerns that before she could
awaken him, he may unknowingly explode into
violence. So far, he had been trying to protect her from
the Viet Cong. But what if he thought that she was the
enemy?

His guns were her major concern but he would
not allow her to remove them. She tried locking them in
a chest but he often cleaned them and demanded easy

access to all of them. He was especially attached to his M-16 assault rifle and checked it each day, reassuring himself that it was ready in case he needed it. Surely he would never shoot it in the house! But he was big and strong and the butt of that rifle could be lethal.

When he was awake, he was totally dependent on her to remember things and guide him through the day. He did not like being apart from her but reluctantly agreed to go to the Senior Services Daycare Center two days each week. His veteran's benefits paid for the care and Della needed time to buy household supplies, keep in touch with friends, and have breaks from the constant caregiving.

She knew that soon, when he became incontinent or was unable to walk, she could no longer care for him at home. After the dementia diagnosis, they toured the memory care unit at the veteran's hospital. She was satisfied that, eventually, it would be the best place for Vic.

Della loved him dearly, but she was logical and practical. As a nurse, she was well aware that caregivers are at high risk of developing stress-related health problems. They had been close and happy for years. When the time came, she would be strong and resolute. The look in her eyes revealed her soft heart. "I know myself. I will make the change, but probably visit him each day at the hospital, even though it is thirty miles away."

CHAPTER SIX

HAZARDS AHEAD

MOVING FROM MID TO LATE STAGE DEMENTIA

Mom Meets Her Great Granddaughter

My spirits soared when Alex and her husband returned to North Carolina and my 350-mile drive to see my daughter was reduced to fifty miles. The following fall, my granddaughter was born. I looked forward to introducing Mom to her new great granddaughter.

"Mom, we will have a wonderful day, today. We are going to see Alex and the baby, Alana, your new great granddaughter. We will eat lunch on the way."

As we drove, Mom repeatedly asked, "Where are we going?" I calmly gave the same answer. A few minutes later, "Are we going to the mountains?"

When we arrived, Mom hugged Alex and beamed as she uttered baby talk to Alana. Mom's big smile radiated her joy. Alex held Alana and we sat in the living room and talked. After a few minutes Mom became quiet and solemnly stared at Alex as she happily updated us on the details of her new life and daily baby routine.

Mom soon turned to me and asked, "Who is that woman with that little baby?"

"That is Alex, your granddaughter. She is holding Alana, your great granddaughter."

"Who gave her that baby?"

Alex's eyes filled with tears. She laid Alana in my lap and dashed out of the room. Mom's decline was too much, her tender heart was broken. Mom's expression was blank and there was a distant look in her eyes. The love that she radiated a few minutes earlier, that same warmth that sustained Alex all of those years that they played together, was quickly extinguished as if someone had blown out a candle.

Alex's elation over new motherhood turned to grief in an instant. The fun-loving grandmother who sat beside her in the kiddie cars at the fair was gone forever.

On the way home, Mom was still confused and asked the same question over and over, "Who was that woman we visited?"

Our long day exhausted her. The next morning she slept until noon and did not remember our trip or seeing Alex and Alana. Being away from her familiar, daily routines drained her.

House Hunting Problems

It was obvious to me that mentally Mom had taken another big step down. I worried that soon she would be unable to stay alone in her home. Our house search proved dismal because nothing was suitable or affordable. One house met our needs but was expensive and in order to buy it, we would have to sell the lake house. Dale and I discussed the situation, analyzed, and debated everything again. For one time in Dale's life, he hesitated and did not want to make an immediate decision.

"The business is consuming our resources, my time, and all of my energy. I do not want to exchange the house that we love for one that we will not want to keep after your mom is gone. Do you really think that you can hold up under the constant, daily stress of taking care of her? She is declining faster now. I can tell by the strained looked on your face that you are under a tremendous burden. I cannot imagine your being able to stay with her day and night, every day. Doing that may affect your health. How will your Mom react to moving with us into a strange place? I don't think that she will be happy, regardless of what you do."

His sober words surprised me. Through all of our years together, he never challenged my decisions if they were important to me. Our unspoken bargain from the beginning was that I supported everything that he deemed important and he did the same for me.

I sat there quietly thinking. Emotional Ann revved her engine. *You have to take care of your mom, you are her rock and she will fall apart if you don't comply with her wishes. After she is gone, you don't want to regret your decisions for the rest of your life.* She made a valid point and I knew that I could do it if I committed and was determined.

Rational Ann was on the sideline but made a valid point. *This is too important to be driven by guilt. You have others to consider, Dale, Alex, Alana, and don't forget about YOU. This decision will affect the rest of your life and there is a whole lot more at stake than feeling guilty about your mother.*

"Dale, I am so caught up in my daily struggles that I have lost sight of the future. You are right. We need to take a step back and consider the big picture. I cringe to think about what I will go through living with her, the enormous stress on us, and the constant drain on me."

"Dale thought for a minute. "I know that years ago you planned an addition to the lake house. We cannot do it now, but perhaps next year will be different."

My mind soared as I considered that possibility. "My ultimate dream is living at the lake and enlarging the house to meet our needs. Alana could grow up swimming in the lake and hiking in the woods. Alex loved that lifestyle."

We sat until the silence became deadening. Finally I

said, "You have stimulated my thoughts and stoked my rationality. If we sell the lake house and buy that place, we may be forever sorry. I need more analyzing time."

I Don't Know How Much Longer I Can Handle It All

Mom was almost to my car when she said, "Wait, I have to check the stove." She seemed tired as she walked across the yard on her mission to again check a broken stove. I wondered if that firmly established habit served any other purpose. Oh well. Ann the analyzer never rests.

Mom was still in good shape physically, except for aching, arthritic joints. For the second time, she closed the door, turned the key, and crossed the yard. She quickly opened the car door, and lowered her body onto the passenger seat. As we backed out of the driveway, she took a deep breath and on the outbreath said, "I just don't know how much longer I can handle it all."

I paused but she said nothing else. "What do you mean, Mom? What can't you handle?"

"Oh, everything. Sometimes I think that I should go someplace and live in one, little room."

What? Did I hear her say that she thought about leaving her home? Hooray! My jubilation soon disappeared. The alarm went off in my head and I knew that I must carefully choose my words. She is exhausted from going through the motions of her morning routine. Although the sequence of her morning actions was repeated day after day, coordinating the mental and physical effort was becoming harder, and as a result, tiring. I drove slowly down the street on our way to the cafeteria, and carefully composed my response.

"Mom, you know you can come live with me."

"No. I am not going to live way down there."

"Well, we can get you a nice room in assisted living where you will have good meals and helpers whenever you need them. We will lock your house and keep it safe, just as it is, while you are there."

"Oh no. I am going to stay in my house as long as I can."

Mom's fears flared every time assisted living was mentioned. Her negative beliefs were planted in her brain long ago by my grandmother after she visited a friend whose family placed her in an old age home. Her mother was Mom's role model. Even though my Grandmother had seven children, cooked three meals each day, raised chickens, sold eggs, and tended a huge vegetable garden, she was determined to care for her senile mother and never considered any other option. Mom was young, but remembered her jolly, good-natured grandmother who stayed in the guest bedroom.

Mom's father died the year before my dad. Grandmother was determined to live by herself in her old farmhouse. She hobbled everywhere using a broom as a cane, even while she tended her vegetable garden. She saved everything, including small pieces of string, and packed away birthday gifts, unused. My cousin, Don, remembered earning a nickel by gathering rotten apples from under the apple tree. Grandmother never allowed him to pick the ripe apples from the tree. She cut out the worms and brown spots from the overripe ones that fell to the ground. She did not waste anything. In her later years, she developed 'hardening of the arteries," the old-time name for the disease now called Alzheimer's or dementia.

Mom and her brothers and sisters planned,

cooperated, and devised ways to care for her in her home. They hired a succession of live-in helpers. Grandmother fussed and fumed about having strangers in her home and almost fired two of them because in her mind, they were lazy. Finally, she approved one person but the nice, timid, lady was afraid to stay alone with Grandmother at night. Uncle Bill called a family meeting and everyone agreed to take turns staying there one night each week with her and the helper. Mom's fears flared and she did not want to be there alone with the two elderly ladies. My Aunt Mary Francis relieved Mom's anxiety by staying there with Mom and the elderly ladies.

Throughout all of that, I heard most of my aunts say, "I don't ever want to go to an old age home and we cannot put our mother in one of those horrible places." Those mental images were born in the 1930's when conditions at institutions were often ghastly. Care facilities are now licensed, constantly monitored, inspected, and must hire trained staff and adhere to many laws and regulations.

Regardless of what I said, Mom's attitudes remained stuck in her mind. I was spinning my wheels in a mud pit of Mom's irrationality. I did everything possible to keep her at home where she wanted to be. By her own admission, she was struggling. The daily trip and constant 'mothering' were wearing me out. I had stomach and chest pains that were not explained by anything other than anxiety.

Finding Assisted Living

Just to be safe and become familiar with the assisted living facilities, I decided to visit several that were nearby. The top attribute on my list was to find caring, competent aides who treated residents with kindness and respect. Good country food was also a plus. The size of the rooms, furniture, and colors were not as important. Mom had never lived in a palace, but would eat the meals and depend on the staff daily.

My support group empathized with my woes. Many of them had either experienced my desperation or knew that they would soon be in similar situations. Those who already placed their loved ones in assisted living or memory care communities offered advice. They thought that it was important to find good memory care close to my home and eliminate my 100-mile daily drive.

One place that had good recommendations was ten miles from my house. I dropped in unexpectedly several times, talked with the director, nursing assistants, and residents. Many of the certified nursing assistants, CNA's, were long-time employees. I watched them as they talked with and cared for residents. The rooms were pleasant and clean and the food was delicious, thanks to a good-natured country cook. On two occasions I waited outside and interviewed a son and a daughter who arrived to visit their loved one. Neither was unhappy or disgruntled.

Rational Ann thought that once Mom became familiar with the surroundings and daily routines, she would be relieved that she no longer had to worry about all of the details and problems of living alone. Emotional Ann smirked, *You are wasting time and money.* I wanted to believe rational Ann even though I knew that Mom would need several weeks to adjust to her new environment. Was I overly optimistic and analyzing everything from my perspective, not Mom's? Emotional Ann insisted. *What are you thinking? She has lived alone for forty-five years, shunned friendships, and hated making changes.*

Perhaps lack of privacy could be overcome by requesting a private room. Having a roommate was much less expensive and according to many of the directors that I met, most residents preferred the companionship and comfort of having someone in the room at night. In my mind, her unwillingness and inability to adjust to a roommate would cause major problems.

Alex urged me to make the decision and do it. I kept telling myself that the main problem was money. Most new businesses struggle for operating capital and ours was no exception. I knew that we would have to supplement Mom's minimal social security. Dale was in favor of the move and said that we could handle it. As I look back on the situation, he and Alex were so worried about me that they were willing to support any solution.

I paid the deposit and made the arrangements but did not tell Mom about my plan. I hoped that she could be convinced to try it after she saw the nice room and met the staff and residents. There was no doubt in my mind that telling her in advance would be disastrous. Her daily routines would be disrupted. Her standard response to even a suggestion of anything new and different was an immediate "NO."

To my surprise, a room became available sooner than expected. If I passed up the room, Mom's name would be moved to the bottom of the list and months may pass before we were offered a second opportunity. The room was being painted and new carpet installed.

She could move in the following week.

Decision made. Then, panic time. How can I accomplish this change? Will Mom, the mighty force, squash my plan? After much thought, I decided to first take her to lunch at the cafeteria that was close to the new residence. The room was ready and I placed a new swivel rocker beside the bed and a portable television in front of it. To eliminate the immediate need for a suitcase full of her clothes, I purchased new clothes, toiletries, towels, linens, blankets, and a comforter for her bed. Fresh flowers adorned the dresser.

Move-In Day

My nerves were on edge as I drove from my home to hers. I completely overlooked the fact that it was a pleasant, sunny spring day, but she noticed. She was happy, dressed, and ready to go when I arrived. She loved the ride.

Each time we passed a truck, she repeated the same comment. "That is the longest truck I have ever seen." My stomach ached, my heart pounded, and my head throbbed. It was difficult to chew and swallow my food, and when I did, it caught in my throat. In my mind I kept rehearsing the words that would convince her to stay in the, clean, friendly, wonderful place.

After lunch, I told her that I wanted her to see a place that she would like. She was dubious from the moment that we drove into the parking lot.

"What is this place? I'll just sit in the car and wait."

"No, Mom, let's go in. I want you to meet some nice people."

She went inside but had absolutely no interest in meeting people. The director and staff smiled and greeted Mom as though she was a long-lost relative. Mom hesitated but smiled cautiously. They asked Mom several questions about her life and she told her hardware story. I knew that they were evaluating her mental abilities and verbal skills.

The tour began in the dining room. Several groups of ladies were lingering after eating and laughing at shared conversation. The activity room was filled with ladies absorbed in creating simple crafts and there was a chapel where a few people were sitting quietly. One resident played the piano in the music room while two ladies waltzed around the room.

Finally, we arrived at Mom's room. It was spacious, filled with light, and totally opposite from the dark, dirty, dusty house she left two hours ago. The faint smell of new carpet and paint still lingered. A large window overlooked a green area outside, the perfect place for a bird feeder. There was a walk-in closet and private bathroom where I hung a colorful shower curtain and matching towels.

"Yes, this is a nice room," she agreed.

"Mom, I have made arrangements for you to stay in this room for a few days. I know you will like it here. The food is delicious and you will always have someone to assist you when you need help. You won't have to worry about anything. You will be safe and secure here."

"WHAT? You want me to leave my home and stay here? Absolutely NOT! I am NOT going to do that! Why, I would cry all night. Take me home NOW!

"The director tried to convince her. "Your daughter wants you to be cared for and safe. She has gone to a lot of trouble to find us and set up this nice room for you. Just give it a few days and see how you feel then."

Mom's eyes gushed tears but were glued on me. "Don't leave me!"

A gut-wrenching crying session followed and ended by her streaking out of the room and down the hall, even though she had no clue where she was going. The director convinced her to sit in the lobby while she and I talked. Employees came by and tried to console and distract her. They offered cake and decaf coffee but she refused, lowered her head, and wrung her hands.

In the privacy of the director's office, my own tears poured. She handed me a tissue and her sad expression told me that she understood my angst. She said that there was no way that they could keep her if she was unwilling to stay. "You have to face it, she is psychotic and really needs to be in our memory care building next door. A doctor will have to prescribe anti-anxiety medicines before we can take her there. Without medicine to calm her, she will upset all of the other residents. I am certain she would try to leave on her own and absolutely must be in a place with controlled access."

I was devastated. I knew that convincing her would be challenging but this news was overwhelming. What was I to do?

On the way home, Mom happily read the road signs we were passing. I wondered if she had already forgotten the ordeal.

I was overwhelmed by sadness when I left her that day. As I drove home, I accepted that nothing could change until some 'event' occurred. I hoped that the event would not be a painful, bone-breaking fall or a horrible, debilitating stroke.

The dismal future flooded my brain. Something

would happen sooner or later, and be a life-changing event. Ultimately, Mom may have to be sedated and forced to live in memory care. After that, it was likely that she would never again be happy.

Mom's Hallucinations

Two weeks after Mom's negative reaction to assisted living, my phone rang as I dressed for the day.

"Ann, I have a problem. Are you coming today?"

"Yes, Mom. I was just leaving. I will be there in an hour. What is your problem?"

"There is an old woman in my garage. I am certain that she plans to steal my car and everything in there. What should I do?"

"Is the garage door open?"

"She is in there with the doors closed. I can see her through the window. She is just sitting there to one side, right behind my car."

"Which car?"

"The one I drive. But she wants to steal my old Buick. It's valuable. She has no business in my garage. I don't want her in there."

"Did you hear her open the garage door?"

"No. I didn't hear anything but I see her. She is old. I guess she is tired because she is sitting down."

Mom was hallucinating. The windows in the garage doors were high and anyone sitting there would be lower than the windows.

"Mom, I am on my way. Don't do anything until I get there."

"OK. Hurry."

As soon as I turned into Mom's drive she opened the front door. She was agitated and her face was pale.

"She is still there and may have been there all night. I saw her when I looked out the kitchen window first thing this morning. As soon as I leave here, she will take my Buick and everything else in my garage."

I pushed the café curtain aside and scrutinized the garage door. The morning sun was shining on the window and I did not see anything through the window or reflected by it.

"Mom, I just don't see her. I think you are seeing a shadow."

"No. She is there! I am going to leave her in there. Maybe she will starve!"

Challenging her and discrediting her vision was making her angry. I did not want to escalate her anxiety, but I knew that Mom would never agree to leave the house until I did something to dispel the vision.

"Where is the garage door opener?"

"Right there on the window sill, but don't let her out."

I pressed the button and the garage door opened. There was nothing behind Mom's car. No lady. No chair.

"Well, where is she? She was there. Where did she go? I bet she is hiding."

I moved the rakes, hoes, and shovels that were blocking the back door. "I will check out the garage for you, Mom."

"No! She may attack you!"

I grabbed a shovel and opened the door.

"Don't worry, I will whap her with this."

As soon as I stepped in the garage, I looked on both sides of her car and opened the other door in front of the old Buick. She stood in the kitchen and peered out for a few minutes. Soon, she joined me.

"Well, she is not here. I don't know how she got out."

As I closed the door behind the Buick, I distracted her. "I am starving, Mom. Let's lock everything and go get something to eat. We will come back after while and check it again."

Later that day, we visited Aunt Edith and Mom did not mention the old lady, nor did I. While it was happening, it was very real and upsetting. Afterwards, the memory disappeared from her mind.

HALLUCINATIONS AND DELUSIONS

Tim's Girlfriend

Marjorie looked down and half-smiled when she confessed, "Yesterday, I thought that I would finally meet Tim's girlfriend. He was excited and asked me to wear something nice. But when we arrived, she was not here."

A loud "What?" echoed in the room.

"It all started two weeks ago. One evening after dinner, Tim mentioned a lady at the day care center. He did not remember her name."

"She is nice. I think she is interested in me."
I stopped clearing the table, stared at Tim and said, "Oh?"

"Yes. She wanted me to go home with her. But I told her that I couldn't if it wasn't OK with you. A wicked thought flashed into my mind. *I wonder if her family will care for you, too.*" She paused while everyone laughed.

"Instead, I told him that it was OK if he talked with

her, and that he needed to talk with everyone at the center."

In the beginning, Marjorie fibbed to Tim that he was volunteering, helping care for people at the center. She was convinced that if he thought he had a reason to be there, a job, he would willingly go there several days each week.

"Last week, he mentioned his lady friend several times each day. This week, he talked about her constantly until we turned out the light each night. An aide told me that he often helps a lady in a wheel chair but no one thinks that she is the one.

"The director was uncertain. "He talks with many people, not just one person. There is a lady who has frontal lobe dementia and has lost her inhibitions. But she does not talk or speak to anyone.

Marjorie raised her eyebrows. "Yesterday he told me that he went home with her and they traveled to the mountains together. She told him that she wanted to marry him but he said that he could not marry her because he was already married to me."

Several support group members looked at each other and in unison said, "Hallucinations!"

"That must be it. Whatever it is, this is the first time that he has invented something and focused on it for days. The delusion may be fading away. He did not talk about her this morning as we drove here and when we came in, she was nowhere to be found."

Luke Banishes Squatters

Luke heard his mother screaming the minute that he stepped onto the front porch. "Get out! Get out! An entire family had moved into the back rooms of her house.

She did not know who they were and had not given them permission, but vividly described them, two men, three women, and five children. They made noise at all hours and blatantly came and went using her front door! Their voices terrified her.

Luke was exasperated. She constantly complained and did not believe him when he tried assuring her that no one was there. The support group advised that rationality would never work and suggested a few other tactics.

Later that evening, Mom screamed, "Go away! Listen to me! This is MY house!" Finally, Luke tried something new.

"I'll run them out, Mom." He stomped into the back room, beat the floor with the broom handle, and yelled at the intruders.

"I said get out! You are not welcome here! Leave, now or I am calling the police."

Then, he stomped around again, loudly opened and closed doors, and reported the good news to his mom. "They are gone and will not be back. I told them that I would have them arrested."

Later that evening, she settled into bed and no longer worried about the squatters. Luke chuckled and hoped that his loud commands banished them forever.

It was Luke's turn to spend the night. His bed was in the room adjacent to Mom's. It was his old room when he was growing up. Lately, he seldom slept well there. He fought deep sleep so that he could hear his mom stirring in the next room.

"Mom, please call me if you need anything or need to go to the bathroom."

He knew that she would not. Her short-term memory was gone and it did not matter how often he said it. If she awoke before wetting the bed, he helped her walk across the room to the toilet. Her next fall could do major damage to her frail body.

Luke spent most of the night ruminating, frustrated that his mother was gradually declining mentally and physically. Sadness often overcame him and he wished that he could rid her of the horrible disease.

Luke and his brother were retired and took turns staying with their mom in her home instead of placing her in memory care. They reasoned that surely the two of them could manage a small, frail woman. She had lived in her home for over fifty years. Her surroundings, daily routines, and habits were firmly established. They worried that forcing her to move to a new environment would trigger even more anxiety, confusion, and send her into a major downward spiral.

They split her care and tried various arrangements, including one week on, one week off. Nothing seemed to work better than alternating twenty-four hour shifts. Before, they were able to leave her alone for a few hours. But now, she required constant attention.

Even on off days, Luke constantly thought about her. He shopped for her medicine, adult diapers, and favorite foods. Trips to her doctor required both of them to get her in and out of the car and one stayed with her while the other parked, opened doors, and maneuvered the wheel chair. Both wanted to discuss issues and hear firsthand what her doctors recommended.

He heard a muffled sound in her room and abruptly jumped out of bed. There she was, trying to stand and walk without assistance. Luke took her arm and gently supported her. "It's OK, Mom, I'll help you, just take your time."

Halfway to the bathroom, Luke winced as a warm blob landed on top of his bare foot. He had no choice but to keep moving forward toward the toilet. He limped, gingerly balanced the blob, and hurried Mom a bit to get there before the deluge. As he turned and positioned her to sit, he lifted his foot and deftly flicked the blob into the toilet and heard the splash.

With Mom safely sitting, he smiled to himself as he washed his foot in the tub, and then he laughed and shook his head. A year ago, he would have been appalled and disgusted. Now, he was happy at his good fortune! He didn't have to clean the carpet

Maggie Flees

Maggie sped out of the driveway and quickly disappeared around the corner. She circled back to their street and as she approached the house, she slowed, rolled to a stop in front of the house next door and killed her lights. She wanted to keep an eye on their front door in case Jack tried to leave or bother the neighbors. She hoped that by morning he no longer remembered that he was angry with her.

She shivered as she sat in the dark car. Her heart raced and pounded in her head. This time, he really scared her. She pulled the blanket that she kept in the back seat around her and was thankful that she stowed it there in case something like this happened. She ran out of the house so fast that she had no time to grab anything. Her son was right when he advised her to keep her car keys and cell phone in her pocket at all times.

Jack was unpredictable. The things he came up

with were not the truth but he believed that they were real. She left him home alone while she went to symphony practice. As she stepped out of the brightly lit auditorium into the parking lot, the night sky was as dark as her thoughts about facing Jack when she got home.

Playing with the symphony consumed her mind and took her thoughts away from Jack's decline. She dreaded going home but knew she had to hurry back there. She pressed unlock, quickly loaded her instruments, and relocked the door.

Before she could start the car, a man jumped at her window! She screamed and then realized that it was Jack! He beat on the window and she lowered the glass.

"What are you doing? You scared me to death!"

"Go Home! We will handle this there!" His face was distorted with anger.

Instead of pulling into the garage, she parked her car in the drive. Jack jumped out of his car, jerked open her door, and hurried her into the kitchen, yelling and slapping her as they went. She held up her arms and hands to ward him off as best she could.

"What did I do?"

"You're having an affair."

"No, I am NOT, I was at practice!"

She ran as fast as she could upstairs to the bedroom, slammed, and locked the door. He was right behind her. He pounded the door and yelled at the top of his lungs.

"Open this door!"

She did not answer. Suddenly, everything became quiet, too quiet. Had he gone downstairs to get a crowbar or tool to beat down the door?

She was scared, but slightly opened the door and

peeped out. "Jack?" No response. He was nowhere in sight. She ran down the stairs, out the front door, and hid behind the shrubbery in the darkness. The garage light was on and as soon as it went out, she knew that he went back in the house. She dashed to her car, fished the key out of her pocket, and made her getaway.

As she watched the house her adrenalin rush was subsiding and she looked around the neighborhood to make certain no one was watching or aware of her presence. She told herself not to worry, crime was almost nonexistent in the neighborhood. Breathing deeply, she snuggled deeper into the blanket and fought back tears. Jack would never do this if he were in his right mind. They had been happy together for forty-five years but his anger was directed only at her.

Jack always tried to tell her what to do, that was his personality. He made most of their decisions.

"Maggie, sit down and lets talk about this." Then, he told her how he wanted it to be. She didn't argue too much unless it had to do with her music. She loved playing in the symphony. Unfortunately, the practice sessions, as well as performances, were held in the evenings. After the daycare center closed for the day, he came home from 'work,' turned on the TV, poured a drink, and snoozed in his comfortable chair until she returned from practice. She tried taking him with her but he would not sit quietly and roamed around disrupting everyone.

As the sky changed from black to pink, she realized how long she had been in the car. Should she go back there now? Will he still be angry? Will he slap her again? She prayed that he would not remember last night.

By now, their son should be awake. He could

usually calm his dad. He immediately answered and she did not have to go into all of the details. Her son knew when the phone rang this early that there was a problem.

"I am on my way now, Mom. Do not go home until I get there."

Jack remembered that he was angry with her, but as Maggie predicted, their son's presence calmed him. "Mom, come outside for a minute."

"I guess he was drinking heavily last night. I am going to take him to the center and I think that he will forget everything by the end of the day. Call me if he is still angry when you pick him up."

Karen Grieves

Karen's expression resembled a dear caught in car headlights. Her eyes darted around the room as other support group members talked about the challenges they faced the previous week. Soon, all eyes turned to Karen, a new member. Her face revealed distress and exhaustion marred her pretty face. It was difficult for her to begin talking about her problems. Someone slid the tissue box across the table to Karen.

Eight years ago when Karen was in her mid-forties, she quit her job and moved in with her mom and dad, they needed constant care. Her mom had congestive heart failure and not long after, her dad began having problems remembering things. Three years ago her mom passed away.

"There is no one but me and no one helps me. Dad is driving me crazy. I am so tired, I feel as though I am his age, not mine. He constantly searches for Mom and asks her whereabouts twenty times each day? I cannot lie to him and it kills me to tell him that she passed away. At times he insists, "But she was just here. I saw her."

"Going through that routine several times every day prolongs the hurt and sadness for both of us. Another problem is that he still wants to drive, even though his license expired and the doctor told him not to drive."

"Someone stole my truck. It is not in the driveway."

"Dad, your truck is down by the barn. We moved it there several months ago. I have all of the keys."

"He wanders around the farm from the barn to the shed, and then to the mailbox. Sometimes, he starts the tractor or lawnmower and rides around. He wants to plow the garden but so far I have talked him out of that notion."

A group member asked, "Can you bring him here? Just two days a week would give you a break and time for yourself."

"We live thirty-five miles north of here. After driving that far, what would I do all day? It is too far to return home for the day and I cannot afford to go out to lunch and shop."

"Have you investigated whether there are any services in your county that would help you?"

"There is nothing like you have here. I contacted Social Services to see if he could qualify for some type of assistance and they are checking, but I have not heard anything."

"I am always tired and some days have to make myself get out of bed. My doctors say that I have fibromyalgia and psoriatic arthritis. I wish that Dad could go into memory care and I could just be his daughter again, not his nursemaid. But, we cannot afford it. He gets too much social security to qualify, but not enough to pay for his care. I am not earning any money and depending on him." Tears streamed down her face. "I want to scream and pull my hair out!"

Karen's situation was dismal. We sat silently wishing that we could somehow help. Empathetic listening reduces stress but Karen needed tangible assistance. The director of the center made arrangements for Karen to meet with the person employed by Senior Services to help caregivers find resources.

Before she left, she said, "You know, I feel better after talking today. Somehow, I no longer feel alone. I will try to return soon."

SEVERE ANXIETY AND CONFUSION

I Don't Know You

Martha forced herself to get out of bed, showered, dressed, readied breakfast, and prepared for the struggle. Most mornings, Sam was impossible to wake, refused to shower, and would not accept her help getting dressed. If he had his way, he would stay in bed until late in the afternoon. She hurried to his room and froze the minute she saw him. "Oh no, Sam, not again. This is the fourth time in twenty-four hours!"

The horrible smell made Martha gag. She grabbed the edge of the dresser and fought the urge to collapse and cry. The bed was wet again and Sam was covered with feces. Four hours ago, Martha finally went back to sleep after walking Sam to the bathroom, cleaning him, stripping the bed, and replacing all of the sheets, blankets, and waterproof pads.

During that ordeal, she prayed that Sam would settle down and go back to sleep. Sometimes, he toddled aimlessly around the house in the middle of the night. Exhaustion was a heavy weight that sat on her shoulders all of the time. Thankfully, he slept.

The mess in front of her was worse than ever. She had to do it since there was no one else. She clinched her teeth, held her breath, and began the routine.

"Come on, Sam, you have to get up and wash in the shower." He pushed her away.

"Who are you? I don't know you. Get away from me!"

Her heart sank as she fought back tears. Last week when she awakened him to use the toilet at ten p.m., he did not recognize her.   Later, at two in the morning,, she awakened him again for another trip to the bathroom. "Who am I, Sam? Do you know me?

"Sure, you're my wife. How about a kiss?"

Mornings had become a battle. "Sam, look at you. You are a mess. I'm your wife and you have to help me, come with me to the shower."

"No, you're not my wife. I don't know you. Get out of here!"

Just the mention of a shower upset him. Yesterday, she tried gently pulling him toward the shower. He grabbed her and almost pushed her through the glass window. His grip was tight and it happened quickly. She knew that she was going to fly through the glass. Just in time, she bit his arm and he released her.

Sighing, she hesitated. She needed to avoid another violent, physical response. This time she slowly backed out the door. "OK, Sam, I'm leaving." She thought, *this is harder than dealing with a tired toddler.*

Calm down, Martha, and think.

She retreated to the kitchen and set the breakfast dishes on the table. After a few minutes, she slowly walked down the hall and sweetly called his name. When she reappeared, he was sitting on the bed and seemed to know her.

"Don't you think we should get washed and have breakfast?" She tried to sound pleasant, as though nothing happened. Perhaps his memory loss would be in her favor.

"Oh, sure." This time he went with her to the bathroom.

Martha was determined to take care of Sam at home, just as she had cared for her father-in-law and her mother who had dementia. That was years ago and her younger body cooperated with the physical and mental demands. Last month, she fell and hurt her back. Pain still shot up and down her spine every time that she stooped or tried to bend over.

"Well, you do what you have to do. Sometimes I look at myself in the mirror and say, Martha, you can do this. Sam was the best husband anyone could have and you are not going to put him in a rest home. He hates rest homes."

She paid several thousand dollars to have the shower altered so that he could easily step in. In the past, he loved showering every morning. It was much easier for her to bathe him in the shower, especially if she successfully convinced him to wash his own legs and feet. Since he became incontinent, daily bathing was absolutely necessary.

The waterproof pad that she placed on the floor beside the bed was no guarantee that she wouldn't be down on her knees cleaning the floor. At times, when she hurried him to the bathroom, he could not control himself and drizzled urine and feces on the floor as he walked.

His obstinate, childish attitudes and refusals to cooperate were driving her crazy. "All his life, he happily agreed with my requests, especially when I explained why and how things needed to be done. But now, he is stubborn and constantly refuses to cooperate."

She quietly counted as she tried to remember the number of times last week that he said, "No, I don't want to. Leave me alone."

Martha smirked and admitted that the only thing that he would do without resistance is eat. "He consumes everything on his plate and then gazes at me expectantly."

"When are we going to eat dinner?"

Last week she tried to get him to understand her pain. "Sam, you know that my back really hurts when I bend down. You have to help me by putting on your socks and tying your shoes." He didn't understand. He forgot how to perform the simple task every child learns early in life.

"The thing that hurts me most is that Sam doesn't want our grandchildren to visit. He hates having the kids around and insists that they go home." She hung her head and covered her face with her hand as she fought back her tears.

"I love seeing them. We used to take our daughter's children on trips and they often stayed at our house. They are older now and understand about their granddad. But our son's little ones are young. I worry that they won't feel loved and wanted."

She paused for a minute and then shook her head as though trying to banish her disturbing thoughts. Then, she tightly closed her lips. She was finished thinking and talking about the sadness.

"Oh, well, what can I do? I just take each day as it comes. At night, I try to put everything out of my mind and tell myself that tomorrow is another day. I need my sleep."

Dan Cannot Sleep

Dan thrashed, tossed and turned, and then wandered around the house in the dark. He did not want to awaken Adrienne. He was never successful. Her eyes popped open if he made the slightest noise. She did not to complain because he cannot control his anxiety, but she is frustrated and exhausted every day.

"It is a full time job caring for Dan. He needs help with simple things. He is much harder to bathe than a baby. I have to choose his clothes, lay them out, and help him step into his trousers and button his shirt. He cannot remember the location of his toiletries in the bathroom and sometimes asks what he is supposed to do with his toothbrush."

"If only we could sleep well at night." They tried medications, but nothing worked for Dan.

After debating with herself for many days, she decided that it was time to move him to a separate bedroom. She prepared a large room upstairs and, thankfully, he agreed to the move. She was able to get more rest, but often stayed awake worrying about him. What was he doing all night? Was he sleeping or wandering around? What if he stumbled and fell down the stairs?

According to Adrienne, Dan was a trouper and adjusted well to new arrangements. The move seemed to be the right decision, but her brain was always on heightened alert. She rationalized with herself that moving him to a separate bedroom would make it easier for him to transition to memory care. After he was first diagnosed with dementia, they both accepted that such a move would be necessary in the distant future. He was tall and there was a limit to how much physical assistance she could provide.

Adrienne knew that she was drinking too much wine in the evenings but believed that she needed it to control her stress. Instead of helping her sleep, the wine was keeping her awake for several hours in the middle of the night. About the time she fell back to sleep, Dan was ready to begin the day.

She was still making two trips ten miles across town to the senior daycare center. If only she had a helper. She really needed someone to care for him in the mornings and drive him to the center each day.

Adrienne was a problem solver and when she put her mind into gear, she always found solutions. She remembered the caregiver service that provided the companions who took Dan dancing. He liked those girls.

She called and one of his dancing partners came in the mornings, used her key to unlock the door, helped Dan shower and dress, prepared a light breakfast, and then drove him to the daycare center. Adrienne needed the sleep and and appreciated relaxing in the mornings, drinking coffee, checking e-mail, and taking her time starting the day. It was wonderful to only make one trip to the center in the afternoons. They settled onto another plateau.

Sun-Downing Seth

"Seth, please! Come back inside! It is late! You will wake everyone!"

Frantic, Seth dressed only in his undershorts, ran from car to car yanking door handles.

"Stay away from me! You can't stop me! This one isn't mine! This one is locked! No! Go away!"

Stacy was desperate. Seth darted out the door before she could stop him. She threw on her robe over her pajamas and tried to reach him before he disturbed everyone. Perhaps if she could hold him, he would calm down enough to get him back inside the condo. But he dodged in and out between cars, determined to evade that woman chasing him.

"Seth, please, let me help you!"

"Stacy, what is going on?"

She turned. Tom, a neighbor and friend, heard the commotion.

"I am so sorry, Tom. We were preparing for bed when all of a sudden, he ran out the door screaming that I could not stop him. Before I could get my robe on, he was out here yelling, trying to find his car. I don't know who he thinks I am but he wants to leave in the car. I have hidden the keys. He blames me for not driving, you know."

Tom understood, this wasn't the first time that he witnessed the violent effects of Seth's disease. "I'll go around behind him, Stacy. Maybe we can corral him between us. I hope he will recognize me and we can calm him back to reality."

She welcomed Tom's assistance and was thankful for all of her wonderful neighbors. Seth's dementia had progressed rapidly since they arrived in the fall. After they married seventeen years ago, they spent winters in Florida. Stacy's first husband died from cancer in his early fifties. Seth's long, unhappy marriage ended badly, with his first wife and two adult children hating him.

Their years together, especially in Florida, were happy. Until this year, they played golf and joined in all of the community activities.

Two years ago, Seth's doctor diagnosed Alzheimer's dementia and recommended that he no longer drive. Stacy begged his son to take his keys but he refused, as did his daughter. Stacy had no choice but assume the 'bad guy' role. "You must stop driving, Seth." She worried about of the risks of potential lawsuits and the emotional distress of hurting innocent people.

Seth was determined to continue their winters in Florida. So far, she managed without the support of his children, but he was rapidly sliding into severe dementia. He was confused, angry, and impossible to control, especially in the late afternoons and evenings. The doctor called it 'sun-downing.'

In his clouded mind, Stacy was the enemy and the target of his anger. He never physically attacked her, but threw everything that he could get his hands on at her. She often pulled a chair in front of the door and sat there, blocking him from leaving and holding a big tray in front of her face for protection. Everyone in the condo complex heard him yelling, sometimes until after midnight.

Seth eluded Tom and Stacy and his belligerent voice became even louder.

"Stacy, I think that we need to call an ambulance and let them deal with him." The nurses convinced Seth to go with them. The emergency doctors calmed him, gave him fluids because he was somewhat dehydrated, and called in a neurologist who prescribed an anti-anxiety medicine.

They returned to the condo but in the back of her mind, Stacy knew that their time there would soon end.

Jon Disappears

Nan sighed, "This was the worse week of my life. Jon sat in front of the television while I prepared dinner and all of a sudden, he disappeared. He left the house! He used to stay in our yard but now wanders around the neighborhood. One day he walked into a neighbor's house. Her sick mother almost fainted. Another day, a neighbor brought him home."

A support group member asked if she would consider installing dead bolt locks on the exterior doors. Another suggested inexpensive alarms to alert her when he opens the exterior doors.

"I hate to use dead bolts because I worry about being able to locate the key if we have a fire or an emergency and need to get out in a hurry. One night he got up and walked out into the cold, shoeless and wearing his lightweight pajamas. Luckily, I was soon able to get him back inside. I will check into the alarms. At least I will know the minute he opens the doors. Thanks."

"He is always angry with me. Jon is originally from the Dominican Republic and remembers his family home and having young friends there. Even though he has been here fifty years, he constantly pleads to go home. He roams around the house looking for his luggage, pulling things out of the drawers, and scattering things everywhere. He thinks that he is packing to go home. One night, he kept me up all night. Every time I calmed him enough to get him back in bed, he jumped up again and began packing. The other day, he became angry with me when we pulled into the daycare center. He thought that we were going to the airport and when he saw the center, he threatened to hit me."

"I don't know how much more of this that I can take. It makes me so sad because I thought that I could see this disease through and take care of him at home. But now, I am having second thoughts. I don't know what I am going to do because we cannot afford memory care. But If he begins beating me, I will have no other options and will have to find a way.

A support member suggested that she contact Social Services and see if he could qualify for assistance. Others urged her to immediately begin visiting memory care communities.

CHAPTER SEVEN – FINDING AN ALTERNATE ROUTE

CARE CHANGING EVENTS

Mom Cries "Help"

At 10 p.m. on a Sunday night, I was ready for bed and hoped to sleep well, the next day would be challenging. Mom had an appointment with her doctor on Monday. Her last appointment was not pleasant. She hated everything about it, parking in the huge deck, walking through the maze of offices, and waiting for the nurse to call her name. I realized that it was difficult for her to gather the mental strength required to perform her usual 'look at me, I'm fine' routine. I worried that if I told her in advance and she remembered, she would refuse to go.

My phone rang. "Ann, I need your help can you come right now?" She was frantic.

"What is it, Mom, what happened?"

"Those women across the street put dogs in my house and I can't get them out."

"What women?"

"Those mean women who live across the street. I could just shoot them!" She was angry.

"What dogs?"

Her voice was loud and revealed her impatience as she rushed through her explanation. "They came over here bothering me and put two big black dogs in my house! The poor dogs are hungry and I don't have anything to feed them. I can't make them leave."

"OK, Mom, try to calm down. Are the dogs growling or barking?"

"No, but I don't know what they will do."

She was hallucinating again. Perhaps she had a bad dream or something happened that day. A neighbor would never put dogs in her house, even if they had a key. "OK, Mom, I will get dressed but you know that it will take me about an hour to drive there."

Most of her neighbors were elderly except for Katie, a friendly young woman in her thirties. When Katie saw Mom outside, she crossed the street to talk and always offered Mom her assistance. Mom was cautious and tried to avoid her but I wanted to become her friend. If ever Mom needed assistance in a hurry, I could call Katie. I always waved to her and, if possible, talked for a few minutes. I checked with Katie.

"I just talked with Mom and she mentioned you and black dogs. She was not very clear. Have you seen her today?"

"Before today, I had not seen Roberta for several days. My mother is visiting and while we were walking her dogs, I decided to ring her doorbell and introduce my mom. She peeped out first and then came out onto the porch. We talked and she patted Mom's Labs. As always, she was very pleasant."

Mom *was* hallucinating again. I did not tell her that she confirmed my suspicion. There was no time for a long conversation.

"Well thank you. I am certain that everything will be fine and I really appreciate your taking time to check on her."

"If there is anything I can do, let me know. I will go there anytime you need help."

I called my daughter and explained everything. I needed her professional, psychological opinion.

"Do not drive there at this hour, Mom. You MUST call the police and have them investigate even though we know that there are no dogs in her house. You may need a police report of this incident, she is getting worse. Her confusion will be noted on the report and will help you if in the future you need to declare her incompetent. Also, if she continues to live there, you may want the police check on her. Tell her that you called the police and they will take care of the dogs."

My mind raced. I imagined the terror on her face when the police knocked on her door. I have to do something, but what? By the time I drive there, she may have forgotten everything and be in bed asleep. But in her mind the dogs are very real. I cannot take the chance and wait for this to pass.

Two weeks ago, Mom told me that a man came into her house and stood over her while she slept. When she opened her eyes and screamed, "Get out," and he ran away. When I asked if she knew him she said no, and she did not know how left the house. Again tonight, she was frightened and felt threatened in her home. I decided to try Alex's suggestion before I actually called the police.

"Mom, it is very late and Dale has an early meeting and cannot come with me. I do not want to drive that far by myself this late at night. You have nowhere for me to sleep. I called the police and they will be there soon to take the dogs away."

She said nothing for a minute. I waited patiently. Then she said, "Well, hold on, let me go look." She was gone for another minute. "It 's OK now. They're gone and two kitty cats are under the table. They're sleeping I can make it until morning. Call the police back and tell them not to come." She seemed much calmer, but insistent.

"I am glad to hear that. I know you like cats and they will not hurt you. I will be there in the morning about eleven o'clock. Try to get some sleep."

I called Alex again and we discussed her recent decline. "I know you don't want to place her in memory care, Mom, but she needs constant supervision. There is no way that you or anyone can stay in that filthy house. It is a health and safety hazard. What time is her appointment tomorrow? I will meet you there."

She made valid points and I understood that Mom's solitary situation was feeding her fear. Somehow I had to bolster my resolve and force a major change. She was also correct in that I needed her with me tomorrow. I would be stronger with her by my side. Plus, the doctor may better understand our desperation if we stand together. In the past, Mom prevented private conversations with her doctor, "If you have something to say about me, say it to my face!"

"Alex, it is a long way for you to drive. What about Alana?"

"Don't worry, she will sleep in the carrier. I have to be there. I want to see her, support you, and talk with the doctor."

I enjoyed a brief moment of relief, until emotional Ann interrupted. *Tomorrow will be a disaster! That young doctor will not do anything.* Thankfully, rational Ann overrode her. *This is good. It will be difficult for him to discount the two of you. Plus, you need Alex's strength and moral support. She was always more effective than you at persuading her grandmother.*

Mom's new physician saw her once six months ago and she convinced him that she was happy and functioning well by herself in her little home. The more I thought about our visit, the more hopeful I became. The two of us will impress upon him the reality of Mom's living situation and seriousness of her recent decline. Her delusions were terrifying her and disturbing me.

But we were going to need a miracle. Mom lived on the minimum amount of social security. Getting her t to agree to changes was a problem but another more practical one was paying for those changes.

Midnight Turmoil

After hanging up the phone, I drank a of cup of calming chamomile tea, swallowed a melatonin tablet, collapsed into bed, closed my eyes, took deep breaths, relaxed my muscles, and told myself, *good night, sleep well, you need to be mentally sharp for Mom's appointment with the doctor tomorrow.* A minute later, my eyes opened, my stomach hurt, my pulse raced, and I breathed as though I had been running a marathon. I fidgeted, scratched, flipped from one side to the other and sighed with disgust. My body betrayed me. I shot out of bed and flew up the stairs to the spare bedroom.

I threw back the covers. Were these blankets dusty? I didn't care and plopped down. Emotional Ann commandeered my brain. *If Mom goes to a memory care facility, she will be miserable. The loss of everything that is familiar and comforting will destroy her. She won't know who or where she is. She will crash!*

Rational Ann tried to calm me. *Stop over-analyzing! You are fantasizing about the worst-case scenario. Alex will be there to help and she is strong and determined.* Emotional Ann countered. *But she has been away through all of the turmoil of Mom's decline, and doesn't fully understand her. What if the doctor and Alex convince you to make bad decisions?"*

Achoo! Oh great! I jumped up, turned on the lights, jerked the sheets and blankets off of the bed, and threw them in a pile in the corner of the room. Now, where are those clean sheets?

THE Appointment

When the walls faded from dark to light gray the next morning, I had turned into a zombie. If I slept at all, it was fitful. I was glued to the bed and did not want to move. Rational Ann encouraged me. *Good grief, you are awake, pull yourself together. This will be a good day. You will be getting your mother the help that she desperately needs.*

Professional clothes, a cup of yogurt, and I was on my way to Mom's. My car knew every nook and cranny of the road, thanks to the zillion trips to Mom's house. Twice I slumped, but caught myself before falling asleep. Rational Ann fussed. *Sit up straight, open your eyes, take deep breaths and focus on the road!*

As always, I called to awaken Mom and remind her that I would soon be there. She seemed alert and in a good mood but I was still jittery when I rang the doorbell. She did not mention the dogs or cats. A glance at the table proved that there was no way that dogs would fit under there with all of the bags of canned foods and who knows what. This time, I insisted that she wear a clean blouse but did not divulge that she would be seeing her doctor in the afternoon.

Lunch at the same time, same place, and the same food was uneventful. I nibbled, certain that I would see everything I ate again. We left with the standard to-go box and made a quick stop by her house to stash it in the fridge.

"Where are we going today?"

"You have an appointment with your doctor."

"Why didn't you tell me? Weren't we there just last week?

"No, Mom, it has been six months."

"Well, I just don't think that I need to go. There

is nothing wrong with me." As we turned into the parking deck, she continued her customary protests.

Alex called and she was almost there. I gave her parking, building, and office information.

"Who was that?" Mom asked.

"Your granddaughter, Alex. She is meeting us. She wants to see you."

"Isn't she in school today?"

"Not today."

Mom's mind was in the past. Somehow, I steeled myself, and was outrunning the emotional flood, praying that it would not overcome me. I did not discuss details about anything with Mom. I simply said whatever was necessary to keep her calm and moving forward.

We signed in and found seats in the waiting room. Mom settled down and picked up a magazine. Quickly, I hopped up and whispered to the person who checked us in that there were problems and that I needed to privately talk with the doctor sometime during the appointment. She promised to tell his nurse. Mom held a magazine but gazed around the room at others who were waiting and said, "We'll be here all day."

Alex appeared with six-month old Alana in a portable carrier. Mom was surprised but recognized Alex, called her name and hugged her. "What's the baby's name?"

Everyone in the room rushed over to ooh and ah over the beautiful baby. Mom smiled, made little motions with her hands, and uttered goo goo sounds. Alana squirmed, kicked, waved her little arms and then smiled. We were captivated. *If she is at all like her mother, she will be thrusting herself out of that carrier very soon.* The stress was gone, momentarily.

Mom's name was called and Alex stayed in the waiting room but grabbed my arm as I followed Mom into the examining room.

"Come get me," she commanded, her face stern and determined. I nodded my agreement and flashed a fake smile. She was practicing her mothering skills on me a few decades ahead of the time that they will be needed or wanted. It's interesting what my brain thinks of at the strangest times.

The doctor was on schedule and I introduced myself again. I missed Mom's last doctor, the one that sent Mom to the psychiatrist years ago. He promptly examined her and asked several questions about how she was doing and if she was having any problems.

"Are you still living alone?"

"Oh, yes. I've been living in my house for . . . ." Finally, she interjected, "A long time."

"Are you able to take care of everything by yourself?"

"Of course. Well, Ann helps me."

"Are you getting out often?"

"If I get the opportunity to go somewhere, I put down my dishrag and go."

I was standing behind the examining table and shook my head back and forth denying her last answer and motioned to the door, silently mouthing, *outside.* I quietly confided that my daughter, a psychologist, wanted to talk with him. I began telling him about Mom's recent hallucinations as Alex joined us.

Alex shared her concerns about Mom's cognitive decline and my health and ability to continue the daily care. He asked about assisted living and we assured him that we tried and the director said that she was psychotic and needed to be evaluated and medicated before they would accept her.

Finally he said, "Well, I almost told her that all of her physical signs were good and that she should return in six months. What do you want me to do?"

"Will you send her to the psychiatric center in the hospital for a thorough assessment?" Alex asked.

"She will have to go to Emergency first and the doctors there will make that decision. Depending on how busy they are, you may be there the rest of the day."

"Let's do it!" Alex demanded and I agreed.

We waited two hours in the Emergency Room while Mom paced and fretted. At last, they found a room and began evaluating her. They repeated the physical exam, asked questions, and ran tests. Mom and Alana were equally fussy. Alex came prepared to feed Alana but everyone else was hungry.

At eight o'clock that night, Alex faced a two-hour drive home and was exhausted. Alana was again asleep in the carrier. I demanded that she go home. She hesitated and then pulled me far enough away so that Mom would not hear our conversation.

"Mom, we have come this far. Please don't cave now. Neither you nor she can continue the way you have been."

Just then the doctors interrupted to make certain that I was legally designated as her health care power of attorney. I assured them that I was and would produce the signed and notarized documents tomorrow.

They arranged a room on the psych floor in their special unit for seniors. She would be rolled over there soon. We thanked them and Alex was relieved. I was dubious. What would I tell her? She had to stay here? Her plea reverberated in my head. "Don't leave me!"

It was ten o'clock before we began the journey across the hospital. She was rolled in and out of elevators, down many long hallways and thru a passageway to the building next door. I walked beside the gurney, touching her arm and talking so that she would know that I was with her.

Finally, we arrived at a pleasant private room with a big window and caring night nurses who brought a gown, slippers, and food. I helped her undress and together, we picked at two warm dinners the staff provided. Mom ate more than I and looked around, somewhat satisfied with the room.

"Why can't I go home?"

"They want to perform tests and need you here early in the morning."

"You're going to stay with me, aren't you?"

"Of course. I just need to call Dale and am going to step out in the hall."

Alex arrived home safely and informed her dad of our ordeal. Dale was relieved that we were able to get the help Mom needed. He knew that I was exhausted, physically and mentally.

In truth, the recliner in the corner of Mom's room did not look comfortable. Even though I somehow made it through the day with little sleep the night before, I doubted that I would rest that night.

The nurse gave Mom a sedative and whispered to me that she would be asleep soon and that I should go home. I told her that I was worried that Mom would be upset in the morning. She assured me that Mom would be kept busy and that she would leave instructions for the morning nurse to give her special attention. Sold! I bought the plan, thanks to her encouragement. I was able to slip out a few minutes later.

Mom's Psychiatric Evaluation

My eyes finally closed at two a.m. and popped open at six. I immediately began making mental 'to-do' lists. By my calculation, I was already late. Hospitals begin their days in the wee hours of the morning. Mom would be awake and upset that I was not there. As I threw on my clothes and grabbed a banana, her plea was still ringing in my ears. "Don't leave me!"

For the first time in my life, I slipped out after promising to stay. I wasted no time getting there. I'm depending on you, trusty little car. Let's make it to the interstate before the school buses begin their rounds.

Thankfully, it was easy to find a space in the parking garage. To save time, I ran up three flights of stairs. I stashed my health care power of attorney in my purse last night and thrust it at one of the nurses behind the desk, promising to stop by later to answer questions.

Mom was sitting up in bed and focusing on finishing the cereal and milk that she requested. Eggs and toast were pushed to the side. She smiled.

"I had cheerios, they were pretty good, but not as good as my oat flakes. Where are my clothes?" A nurse appeared in time to hear the question, opened the closet door and pointed to them. Mom half-smiled when she saw that her clothes and shoes were close by and secure.

"Good. When can I go home?" I recognized a look in her eyes that resembled the wild stare of a caged animal.

"As soon as possible. The doctor wants to see you this morning, and he will order some tests. You will be busy all morning. Is this your daughter?"

"Oh yes. She is my only one. She's a doctor, too.

Oh, not the . . . ."

"Medical doctor," I chimed in.

I introduced myself, thanked her for taking good care of Mom, and asked if the doctor would be in soon.

"It won't be long and he will want to talk with you," she responded with eyebrows raised eyebrows, non-verbally inquiring whether I could stay.

"Of course," I responded. "We are fortunate to have this opportunity."

As she was recording Mom's vital signs, she asked if Mom needed anything.

"I need some HOT coffee. This is barely warm. It sure is cold in here."

"I will bring coffee and another blanket right away. Dr. Perry will be in soon."

Dr. Perry was young, tall, pleasant, and caring. Mom gave him the abbreviated version of her life story, but as usual, insisted that she was fine living alone in her own home, and asserted that she intended to stay there.

"You are an amazing woman and we want to evaluate you and the medicines that you are taking and make certain that you can continue to enjoy life for a long time. This is my assistant and she is going to ask you a few more questions."

Mom was obviously pleased with his response and seemed to relax a bit as the assistant took over. Dr. Perry quietly motioned for me to step outside.

We discussed the details of the dogs, as well as her other hallucinations, living conditions, hoarding, checking, and obsessive-compulsive behaviors. I stressed my concerns that it was impossible for me or anyone else to stay with her in her house and my house was very small and in a rural area. He had the records of Dr. Stone's original diagnosis and the MRI from several years earlier. He was busy making notes and then listed the tests that were important, including another MRI.

"She will be here several days, although we won't tell her at this time. We want to prescribe the appropriate medicines that will, hopefully, halt the hallucinations and reduce her depression, anxiety, and obsessive-compulsive tendencies."

The assistant was leaving and I was amazed that Mom was in a good mood. In my best soothing voice, I assured her that I could not go with her to the tests but would be there when she returned. She agreed, and I refrained from any other conversations about the day's activities or my plans.

I made a mental list of everything that I could think of that Mom may need as I walked out to the parking deck. To save money, I purchased a parking pass for the whole week. Alex called as I turned into Mom's driveway. She wanted the details of my discussion with the doctor and was pleased that he would prescribe anti-anxiety and anti-depressant medications.

"Mom, you cannot allow her to go back to that house. It is filthy and dangerous, a major health hazard. She will not remember or may refuse to take her new medicines. You cannot stay there, even if you hired someone to come in and clean it out while she is in the hospital. The carpet and walls are molded! You and she will get sick if you allow her to go back there. Take this time to find the best place and make the change! You may not get another opportunity!"

I agreed with everything that she said and promised that I would do as she insisted. As soon as those words left my lips, emotional Ann crawled on my shoulders and pounded on my head. *Yeah! Let' see you handle this one.* Rational Ann pulled me out of the car but a nagging foreboding descended on me and I shook like a leaf in an earthquake as I walked to the front door, hesitated, took a deep breath, and stepped inside.

The smell was horrible, mildew and rotten fruit were in the stale air. I knew that Alex was correct, mold! I did not want to spend any more time there than absolutely necessary.

My plan was to find a small overnight bag in the attic but the door was locked and the key was missing. Sometimes she hid keys under vases. No, there were many notes scribbled on scraps of paper and two dollars but no key. Surely there is an overnight bag in my old bedroom. I ducked under the clothes hanging on the door and pushed, but the door would not open more than three inches. I reached in up to my elbow and tried to push aside the items that were blocking the door. I gained another couple inches, enough to peer in for a suitable bag. It was futile! I will put everything in an empty grocery bag and purchase something.

Where were the gowns and slippers? The only ones that I found were falling apart and filthy. I stuffed a few toiletries in a bag and paused long enough to marvel at the number of new tubes of Cherries in the Snow lipstick that were stacked on a shelf over the toilet and the used paper towels that were hung on a makeshift clothesline stretched over the bathtub. The tub was full of crumpled clothes, plastic bags, and dusty papers that must have been there for weeks. Tears filled my eyes.

Shaking off my impending breakdown, I needed a distraction. I told myself not to pass up the opportunity to round up dirty clothes that were good enough to wash and wear again. Lately, I had to hide her dirty clothes and sneak them out while she fluffed her hair and applied lipstick. Sometimes I was able to slip the clean ones in unobserved and at other times she caught me red-handed and accused me of shrinking and fading them with my washer.

There was no time to gather trash, I had to buy the needed items and return to the hospital. Since it was spring, finding the long-sleeved, flannel nightgowns that she preferred may be difficult.

I grabbed the trash bag full of dirty clothes, items for the hospital, and my list and was opening the front door when I paused, sat everything down, and turned around. Something propelled me back to Mom's bedroom. It was difficult to make my way to the bed but I carefully followed the narrow path and stepped over plastic bags stuffed with used tissues, old newspapers, and junk mail. It was amazing that she had not fallen. Or had she? The piles and stacks of clothes may have cushioned her fall.

I was determined to throw back the quilt that her mother made. I gasped! There was a rotting apple and a black, mushy banana! *Oh, Mom! I have been so stupid to enable you to stay here! I knew that it was bad but this is horrible.* There was no stopping my tears.

Soul Searching At The Hospital

Finding and purchasing the necessary items took more time than planned. It was mid-afternoon when I returned and she was in her room napping. I took that opportunity to talk with the nurse before the end of her shift. Mom complied with every request and although she asked about me, was not upset when told that I would be there soon.

I sat quietly by her bed, thinking. This was the

inevitable, care-changing event that I expected. After seeing her bed, a good measure of guilt was added to my desperation cocktail. Emotional Ann chastised. *How could you allow her situation to become this bad? You let this go on too long!* Rational Ann intervened. *You must put all of those guilt feelings and emotions behind you and become a manager now. The past is the past. It is vital that you go forward and do the right thing. Accept it, you have no other choice. You must relinquish your impossible quest!*

Mom stirred and I smiled and squeezed her hand. "Mom, the doctor wants to run more tests in the morning, so I brought you a few things that you may need and a new gown and slippers." She was pleased that I remembered her sleep bonnet that she wore at night to keep her hair in place. She was not happy about staying another night.

"I don't understand why I have to stay here. There is nothing wrong with me. You go tell them that I refuse to stay here tonight. This must be costing a fortune. If they want to do more tomorrow, I'll come back then."

Soothing fibs were required and I was a master of inventing those. "Mom, they will start a six in the morning and there is no way I can get up at four, drive to your house, and get you here by six. Let's change out of the hospital gown and try your new, warm one."

The distraction worked and I handed her a warm washcloth for her face, helped her with her new gown, and she tried the new, soft slippers. Alex called and after my brief description of Mom's day and a promise to call her later, she talked with her 'Gang.' Gangy was the name that Mom gave herself when Alex was a few months old. I can still hear Mom prompting, "Gan-gy, Gan-gy." I guessed that she was urging Mom to be patient and comply with the doctors. Mom soon said, "I love you, too. Be careful and don't worry about me, I'm all right."

Dinner was delivered and I was pleased that I arrived early that morning and circled Mom's preferences for the evening meal and tomorrow's breakfast. She enjoyed the food but complained that I was not eating with her.

"Mom, I need to go home early and make sure that Dale has something to eat (fib). I haven't seen him for the past two days. He was asleep last night and I left this morning before he was up (another fib). I know that you are tired and will go to sleep early since you have to get up early."

She agreed and suggested that I go home and get some rest. Yahoo! As soon as I was out of the parking deck, I called Dale and we arranged to meet at a restaurant. I needed a good meal and a chance to relax and discuss everything.

You Are Sending Mom Home?

After four days in the hospital, Dr. Perry met with me in a small conference room. "Roberta has adjusted to being here, is pleasant, and is no longer fearful of being left alone in her room. In fact, the nurses report that she walks around the halls, smiles, and greets everyone. She will be able to go home very soon."

My eyes and mouth flew wide open and stayed that way as he continued. "The MRI showed a significant increase in 'white matter' in her brain and further shrinkage. I prescribed an anti-anxiety medicine and an anti-depressant and together, they seem to be working fairly well. As far as we know, she has had no additional hallucinations. We hope that the medicines will increase in effectiveness over time."

I was dumbfounded but quickly reminded him her hoarding and filthy house. I stressed that I could not stay with her in that gory situation and she would never be satisfied living with me. I traveled over one hundred miles each day and was worn out. Her psychotic episode that occurred when I tried to move her into assisted living flowed hurriedly out of my mouth, followed by my plea for him to place her in a memory care facility.

"I sympathize in every way, but legally, I cannot force her to go there against her will. If she refuses, there is nothing that I can do." He paused for a minute while I groaned, "Unless, she is a threat to herself or others."

Again, my eyes opened wide, "She threatened to shoot the neighbors who put the dogs in her house." That was the truth.

"Does she have guns in the house?"

"She operated a hardware store for years and when she decided not to renew her gun license, she took all of the unsold guns home. I am certain there are rifles and several handguns in her house somewhere." I did not mention that she knew nothing about loading or shooting a firearm.

"Well, in that case, she cannot go back there. Our social worker will help you find a suitable place. Stay here and I will see if she is available."

I was relieved. No, I was terrified. Emotional Ann railed. *How can you do this to your mother?* Rational Ann countered. *How can you NOT do this FOR your mother?* Rational Ann was making more sense. After my anguish in her house four days ago, how could

219

I allow her to live there?
Emotional Ann pleaded. *Take her to the lake.*
You can do it. Rational Ann resisted. *She would hate*
being there and beg to go home. *You will be stressed and*
there will never be any relief. You can never leave her
alone, even for a minute, and you will never find good
sitters to drive out there.

The social worker, Susan, came in and
interrupted my mental debate. She exuded an aura of
kindness, caring, and empathy and before she said
anything, I was comfortable confiding in her. She had
read Mom's chart and talked with her. She knew that
Mom was determined to return home, and was willing
to listen to my rambling story, my guilt was oozing out
of my mouth.

"Ann, if you take her home, it will be for a very
short time. Families who are successful in keeping a
loved one at home through the final stages of dementia
usually have several family members involved in the
daily care or are able to hire nurses around the clock."

She made sense. "Since I have come this far and
an 'event' has happened, delusions of dogs in her house,
it is best for both of us to go forward and find a good
place for her."

She assured me that I did not have to convince
Mom. "Doctor Perry will tell her that she must
temporarily go to a nice convalescent center where
nurses can make certain that the new medicines help
her and are effective. It will not be necessary for him or
anyone to go into all of the details and discuss the
future."

Susan inquired about Mom's finances and asked
if I had any preferences as to place. She assured me that
my ordeal with Mom about assisted living was not
unusual among dementia patients. Since I had chosen

that facility a few months ago and they have a nice memory care building, with my approval she would contact them first.

I agreed and crossed my fingers, hoping to be so lucky. She would call as soon as she had news and left me with a list of local care facilities and suggested that I visit as many as possible.

Mom was in her room preparing for lunch. I hugged her and we talked about lunch but I did not divulge one bit of information about the plan. Instead, I told her that I had an appointment and would be back later in the afternoon.

As I was driving out of the parking deck, I knew exactly where I was going. I needed the sound advice of my friend, the Director of the Senior Day Care Center. My phone rang and Susan had been in touch with my preferred memory care facility.

"I have good news!"

"I desperately need good news."

The director and her staff remembered Mom and they still had my deposit. A room was available in the memory building, but Mom would have a roommate. I agreed and said nothing about a private room. The nurse from the facility would interview Mom that afternoon. She suggested that I contact Social Services about whether Mom could qualify for financial assistance.

Everything was moving so fast. This morning I was preparing to spend the day with Mom, and this afternoon, everything was magically falling into place. Everything *except* dealing with Mom once she is told that she will not be going home.

Seeking Validation

By the time that I arrived at the Senior Center, I was again in the throes of a mental debate with myself. By the time I collapsed in a chair in the director's office, I was uncertain and ready to take my to my home.

"Well, you have accepted that she cannot go back to her house and live alone. She will continue getting worse. If you take her to your house, the three of you will be in a continual, stressful battle with yourselves and probably each other. You know yourself and your husband. Are you willing to care for her twenty-four hours a day with little or no relief? At first, she won't be satisfied anywhere other than her house. It seems that it is time to turn this over to the professionals who are trained and know what they are doing. It will take a little time but she will begin new daily patterns that will be beneficial for her and you."

I knew that she was right. But how can I possibly make it through the transition? What will I say to her? How can I bear hearing, "Don't leave me?"

"Let them handle it. They have done this many times and know what works. They will probably advise you to stay away for a week, perhaps two. You should heed that advice. You will be surprised when you see her again. Tell your husband to take you somewhere for a vacation. Spend the time with your daughter and granddaughter. They need you. They are your future."

CARE CHANGING EVENTS

Leah's Love Prevails

Leah glared angrily at her three daughters sitting across the table. "I know what you are up to and I am not having any part of it! I'm leaving!" She pushed her chair back and started toward the door.

The director of assisted living stood up and said, "I'll walk you to the door, Leah. Please, everyone, finish your lunches and I will return soon." The family was surprised at Leah's angry outburst. She was always a quiet, loving woman.

Leah's dementia was diagnosed five years ago and her decline was gradual. Three years ago, her daughters became concerned, decided that she could no longer live alone, and hired a live-in helper. The costs of around-the-clock care mounted up and Leah's savings were depleted.

Her daughters had employed husbands and children who still lived at home. What could they do? Leah flatly refused to move in with one of them. After days of discussion, they accepted that the only solution was for the three of them to rotate and care for her in her home. Every third day, one of them arrived in the morning and stayed through the night.

Their husbands were not happy with the situation. Melanie's son was still in school and she had two married daughters and grandchildren. Family outings and vacations were impossible because of her time-consuming caregiver role. Finally, Melanie's husband told her that he was considering divorce.

Melanie was shocked and desperate. She had to take her turn caring for her mother. What could she do? She called her college friend who was the director of an assisted living facility.

"Yes, we can help you. We have a nice semi-private room available and can begin the process of getting your mother qualified for financial assistance. Bring your mother and come for lunch in our dining room and invite your sisters and their families. Let me talk with her, I think she will like it here."

Melanie and her sisters doubted that their mother would willingly go there, but since the director was certain that she could convince her, everyone agreed to go for lunch. After Leah stomped out, they looked at each other, deflated and certain that the situation was dismal.

"Leah, here is my office, come in and talk for a minute." Leah was educated, cultured, and a woman of faith. Hesitating, she was polite and agreed to talk. "Leah, Melanie and I have known each other for a long time. I know that you raised your daughters to be strong, loving, married women who take care of their families and are good wives and mothers."

"Yes, I did and they all turned out to be wonderful in every way."

"Did you know that Melanie's husband has asked her for a divorce? He is very unhappy. All of your girls are running themselves crazy trying to care for you. Their families still need them at home."

"Oh, no! A divorce! Oh my, I did not realize."

"Leah, I think God has another plan for you. You are still able to help people and do his work. How would you like to work here greeting people who arrive? Many new residents are upset and nervous about being here and you could help them calm down and know that they are in a good place."

Leah was quiet as she thought about everything. She did not realize that she was causing so many problems for her daughters.

"OK, I'll do it. Let's go tell my girls."

"Would you like to see your room first? It is near my office."

Leah moved in with her new roommate and came to love the woman. They were best friends. Every day, Leah sat at the desk beside the entry and greeted people with a smile. She loved her new job. She assured anxious, new residents that it was a wonderful place and that they would be happy.

Dan Fears Falling

"No! I will fall!"

Dan stood at the top of the stairs. Adrienne's morning helper tried to steady him and encourage him to take each step one at a time, slowly, carefully. Her job was to help Dan get dressed, give him a light breakfast, and take him to adult daycare.

"I will go in front of you, Dan. Hold on to the stair rail with one hand and put the other hand on my shoulder. You can do it." But he was terrified and would not move. The commotion awakened Adrienne and, finally, the two of them coaxed him slowly down the stairs.

Dan's fear resulted from a near-fall the morning before. Mentally, he had taken another step down, a decline that was serious. His peripheral vision was worse than ever and probably fueled his fearful fixation on falling. Adrienne understood his fears and worried that if he fell, he could hit his head and never recover. She had visions of being in a panic while he laid at the bottom of the stairs, writhing in pain.

What should she do? The situation was complicated. He was incontinent and required constant clothing and bed linen changes even though he was wearing adult diapers, day and night.

The life-changing problem that Adrienne dreaded had arrived. People in her support group advised that incontinence is often the key event that signals it is time to seriously consider memory care. Keeping him at home involved more than she ever imagined. She knew that she could not do it without her helpers.

What should she do? Her stomach ached as she debated moving the love of her life out of their home. For several nights, she could not sleep and walked around the dark house wanting to vomit. Finally, she realized that she was so exhausted that she was on the verge of becoming ill. She stopped in front of a mirror and said, "You cannot deny reality. It is the best thing for him and you."

She revisited several care facilities and chose an assisted living community close to her home. Some of the residents had dementia, but did not wander and did not need to be in a memory care unit with exterior doors locked. To her amazement, Dan agreed to the move. She knew that he was still concerned about her and understood her stress, unlike many victims of the disease who become self-centered. He wanted the best solution for both of them. He was still the Dan that she fell in love with years ago.

Bob Wants To Move 'Up There'

Bob slowly toddled along, holding his cane tightly. His steps were short and unsteady but he refused to use his walker. Beth and their daughter, Linda, matched his gate and held his arms as they guided him to the car. Beth was patient and vigilant. She knew the pain and misery that resulted from a hip-breaking fall. The statistics of elderly who fall, break their hip, and never recover were dismal.

Fear of falling was not the only problem that influenced her decision. He was incontinent. His weight and size made it impossible for Beth to handle him by herself. She could not persuade him to shower or bathe. Unfortunately, his incontinence demanded regular baths.

The problem that tore her heart out was that he was no longer happy in their home. He continually begged to go to the house 'up there.' Beth guessed that he was thinking of his childhood home.

Her parents instilled in her the importance of being strong and courageous when facing tough times in life. She felt guilty that Linda cancelled her appointments to be there and help her. Beth insisted that she could handle the situation. "You can fuss all that you want, Mom, but I will be there early and go with you."

As they drove out of the long driveway, she was relieved that Linda was with her. She could feel her heart pounding in her head. Linda's words kept playing in her mind.

"Mom, he is so bad now that he won't know where he is."

"Where are we going?" Bob's words broke her inner turmoil.

"We're going to physical therapy, Bob," Beth lied.

They were expected at the assisted living memory care community. As soon as they walked in, the staff greeted Bob warmly and showered him with attention, making him feel at ease. He loved basking in the limelight. At lunch, his seat was at the head of a table full of women and a few men, all Alzheimer's and dementia patients. Bob seemed comfortable being around them.

Beth signed the admission papers and then she and Linda slipped out while he was distracted having lunch. Beth slumped in the passenger seat. She had no idea where they were and was still shaking as they drove into the garage.

The house was deathly quiet. Pepper, Bob's companion dog met them at the door wagging his tail in anticipation, but no Bob. He dashed into the garage and circled the car. Tears filled Beth's eyes.

"Pepper, he is not coming home. Come here." She patted him and he followed them into the house.

She set her purse on the counter and walked to their bedroom. Bob's things were everywhere. She stared at their wedding photo hanging on the wall. Tears rolled down her cheeks. She did not move his things, but turned and walked to the sitting room where she collapsed on Bob's chair. For the next two hours, she cried until there was no more fluid. Then she sat motionless, all of her energy drained.

Linda wrapped her arms around her mom and said nothing. They sat there together, silently being with each other. After a few hours, Beth still sat motionless. Her arms and legs were so heavy that she could not lift them. Linda brought her a cup of warm soup and stayed quietly by her side.

The next day their son, Mac, arrived to stay

overnight with his mom. He decided to go see his dad but thought it best that he go alone.

"I am so glad to see you," Bob exclaimed.

He was dressed and sitting with other residents in one of the large rooms with comfortable chairs and a television. They walked around and then went to Bob's room. As Mac prepared to leave, Bob began packing his clothes.

"I'll go with you."

"Not today, Dad. I have to go to work, but I will come back soon."

The third day, Sara, their youngest daughter, knocked on his door. Bob was trying to stuff a big magazine into the memory box that Beth placed on the table beside his bed before she left. Bob turned and flashed a big smile.

"You have saved my life." Sara worried that he would want to leave with her but he never mentioned it.

The following day Beth could wait no longer. She was nervous but determined to see Bob. Before she walked onto the patio where he was sitting, she stopped, took a deep breath, and made sure that she was smiling. Bob smiled as soon as he saw her, as did another woman resident who was sitting beside Bob, comforting him. The woman quickly stood up and gave Beth her seat.

"You see that lady over there, I couldn't make it here without her."

"Bob, it is wonderful that she is helping you."

They sat for a long while, mostly without saying anything. He was comfortable just being with her and holding her hand. She did not entertain him. When Beth finally rose to leave, Bob stood up.

"Are you ready to go home now?"

"Bob, I have to go back to work." He believed

what she said even though she had been retired for ten years.

An aide walked her out and asked how she was adjusting. She almost uttered a few choice words but stopped, thought about Bob, and said that she was satisfied that she made a good decision. It was a good place and it was time. Earlier in the disease, Bob would never have believed her explanation that she must return to work.

Marjorie Needs Time

Marjorie reluctantly opened her eyes. Daylight poured through the blinds. She closed them again and shuddered. "Oh, no! I still feel horrible. If this virus or whatever it is keeps me down much longer, I am going to shrivel away!" For three weeks she had been unable to eat or drink anything without becoming violently sick.

She heard Tim shuffling around in the bathroom. "Marjorie, I am going to be late again. Get up. I have to go."

"Tim, I feel so bad, I am sick."

"I am sick, too. I need to go. Get up."

Marjorie looked at him through half-opened eyes. He was dressed but not in the clothes that she laid out yesterday. His trousers were navy blue and his shirt, dark green. Who cared? Coordinating him today was not worth the effort.

"Val is going to drive you to the center today. You will be there in time to eat breakfast with the guys. Don't worry."

"Tim peeped through the blinds. "I don't see her. I have to go. Where is she?"

Marjorie dialed her helpful neighbor. "Good morning. Tim is ready and I'll send him out when you pull in the driveway. I appreciate your driving him again this morning. I am still weak. Doug is taking a day off from work and will be here in an hour to drive me to the doctor. I may need another IV since I still cannot eat or drink."

As Doug dressed, he worried about his mom. He had never seen her sick for so long. The stress of caring for his dad probably lowered her immune system and made her susceptible to the virus.

His phone rang. People at work were always calling. He recently received a promotion and was trying to learn a new job. He had his hands full with that situation, but his mother's health was more important than anything.

Marjorie's participation in the support group at the daycare center convinced her that Tim's decline would soon make it impossible for her to keep him at home. During the last meeting she confessed, "If it weren't for Tim coming to the center during the week, I would have pulled my hair out by now."

Several weeks ago, her support group warned that she needed to begin searching for a suitable memory care facility. The group members were experienced and she trusted their judgment. She narrowed the choices to two memory care communities that were located within a few miles of her house and placed Tim's name on their waiting lists. If she was feeling better after seeing her doctor, she wanted Doug to tour the one that she favored.

That afternoon, Marjorie was determined to take advantage of Doug's day off. "Well, Doug, this place is fairly small, they only have forty residents, but it has wide open spaces for meals and activities. You know how your dad likes to keep busy. There is ample space for him to walk around. It is nothing fancy but is clean."

Doug thought that it was wonderful. The management and staff were obviously well trained and dedicated. "I like this, Mom." He asked the director, "How long do you think that it will be before you have a room for my dad?"

"Well, this is unusual but a semi-private room is becoming available. We will have it ready by the middle of next week. If you like, it is yours. If not, I have a fairly long waiting list."

"Mom. Let's sign the paperwork today while I am here. You cannot do this much longer. By the time another room is available, you may need one too."

Marjorie found a nearby chair and sat. She took a deep breath and tried to think. The virus and all of the medicines were still clouding her thoughts and she could not concentrate.

"This is a big decision, Doug. I cannot decide without thinking it over for a while."

Doug shook his head and made certain that the director noticed his exasperated expression. He understood his kind, loving mom. She and Dad had been married for a long time and this was a major decision that will initiate a huge change in her life.

The director had seen spouses hesitate hundreds of times. "This is Friday afternoon. I will try to hold the room for a day or two but I cannot promise. We are not supposed to do that. The corporate rules specify that if there is a family emergency and we have a room available, we must immediately fill the vacancy. I cannot predict what will happen in the next two days. I understand your situation. As soon as you decide, please call immediately."

As he drove Marjorie home, Doug again urged

her to act. "Mom, what will we do if someone comes along and takes the room? I wish you would call her. I am afraid that by Monday we will be searching for another place."

"Your dad will be home in an hour. Between now and then, I will think about nothing else. Thank you, Doug, for taking today off and helping me."

"Mom, I am not married and I have no children. Watching Dad decline over the last few years has been the hardest thing that has ever happened to me. I was so lucky to have both of you. I cannot stand the thoughts of you getting sick or having a damaging illness. We have to do what is best for you and dad."

Early Saturday morning, Marjorie began giving Tim an extra dose of his anti-anxiety medicine. He was fine on days when they were going places or he was going to the center. At home, he paced, fussed, scattered things, and tried to get out of the doors. She had deadbolt locks installed soon after he slipped out one Sunday afternoon while she and Doug were talking. Doug found him walking on the side of the road a mile from home. The locked doors made him angry and sometimes, he threatened her. "I am going to smack you!" Then he would hit the wall or the side of the refrigerator.

Sundays were always special for Marjorie. Doug went with them to church and then to a restaurant for lunch. Tim was fine and sat quietly in church. As soon as they arrived home, Marjorie encouraged him to take his medicine but he knocked it out of her hand. Marjorie was patient and he finally swallowed it.

They went into the sitting room to talk and Tim began ranting. "I have to go up yonder. You promised you would take me."

"Tim, the center is closed on Sundays. No one is

there. We have to wait until tomorrow morning."

"You lied to me. You said you would take me. I will not put up with this." He rose, frantically looked around the room, and bent over Marjorie until his face was five inches from hers. "If you don't take me I am going to bust through that window and go there by myself." He looked over his shoulder at the large window, stood up, and turned toward it.

Doug jumped up, grabbed his dad and sat him in his chair. "Dad, do not talk to Mom with that tone. You will sit in that chair and do as Mom says. She cannot take you today because they are closed, the doors are locked, and the workers are home with their families."

"Mom, we are not doing this any longer. You have to do something. I cannot concentrate on my job or think about anything but this. I will not leave you here by yourself! You have to call the director first thing in the morning! This situation is going to consume us until you do! Please!"

Marjorie had no other options. Tim's disease was going to get worse, not better. She did not want Doug to suffer.

The medicine took effect and Tim snoozed in his recliner. She convinced Doug that everything was under control for the rest of the day and evening. She would give Tim another dose with dinner. Doug reluctantly left after Marjorie assured him that she would be OK and that she would make the call first thing the following morning.

Marjorie watched Tim sleep and then went to the phone and dialed the director's number. She left a message and hoped that she had not waited too long.

Tim went to the daycare center as usual, for the first three days of the week. On Thursday, she took him to his new home. The staff opened the side door so that they would not have to wait for someone to unlock the front door. They walked into a large room with a dining area on one end. Tim was served breakfast and did not notice when Marjorie left. He was accustomed to the same routine at the daycare center.

That afternoon, Marjorie saw her doctor and learned that he had cared for his mother with Alzheimer's. "Marjorie, go home and rest. Do not visit Tim until two weeks have passed. He will be settling into his new life in memory care, getting accustomed to new routines, people, and activities. If you go there, you will pull him back into your world and renew his dependency on you. People don't understand how cruel that can be. Dementia makes it impossible for him to mentally live in two worlds. He will have peace of mind after he settles into his new home."

Ida's Recurring Infections

Brenda's eyes popped open but she laid still and listened. Her mother softly moaned. She jumped up and bent over her mom. "Mom! Mom, wake up! Are you OK?" Brenda gently shook her mom's motionless body. Ida stirred and moaned again.

"Mom, we overslept. It's morning! Time to get up." Ida groaned. She lifted Ida's head and shoulders and tried to prop her on several pillows. Ida's pulse was strong, her hands were cold, and her night diapers were dry. That was unusual.

"Mom, let's get up and eat breakfast." Ida closed her eyes and slumped. "Your forehead feels warm. I am going to get the thermometer."

Brenda turned on the light to read the thermometer. She gasped, blinked her eyes, and again

checked the reading, 103. She removed one of the
pillows to keep Mom from toppling over sideways and
called the doctor.

The nurse did not hesitate. "You must
immediately take her to the emergency room." This
was the third time in two months that Brenda heard
that command.

"Mom, we have to get you into the pickup truck
and to the hospital."

Ida needed fluids and antibiotics administered
intravenously. According to the nurse, the symptoms
indicated another severe bladder infection.

"How could this happen again?"

Ida had rapidly declined over the last six months.
She no longer walked and either sat in her wheelchair
or in the truck while with Beanie while Brenda
completed short jobs at local businesses. Brenda
accepted the part-time job, confident that Mom could
ride along and pet Beanie while she waited. She was
convinced that Ida enjoyed riding around town, and
once she was safely belted into the truck seat, she was
fine. The daycare center was no longer an option for
Brenda. They did not have the one-on-one staffing and
constant care that Ida needed.

The emergency room doctors were suspicious
that something was wrong in addition to the bladder
infection. More tests revealed the problem.

"Pneumonia! Oh no! How can that be?" Brenda
did not believe it. "She never touches anything but our
house and truck. She never sees people who are sick."

"Your mom is inactive, always sitting. When she
eats or drinks liquids, she inhales some of the food or
beverage into her lungs and that causes infection. It is
aspiration pneumonia and very common in the later
stages of dementia."

Ida was admitted to the hospital for several days and Brenda stayed by her side, thinking about the future. She was unwavering in her resolve to take care of her mom at home. She knew that she had to help Mom move around and drink more. She would start pureeing all of her food. She was determined! "I will quit my job and find ways to keep this from happening again."

The Doctor Is Down

Adrienne's dad pulled out his chair at the breakfast table, hesitated, and turned white as a sheet. Her mom rushed to him but he passed out cold and fell on her.

Mom knew that she was hurt. She strained, and eventually managed to get out from under his dead weight. The excruciating pain became worse when she tried to get up. She somehow pulled herself along the floor all of the way to her bedroom where a phone was on a low table. She called her son but he did not answer, and then she tried Adrienne.

"Your father is lying on the kitchen floor and I think he is dead. I am hurt and cannot get up."

Adrienne's pulse raced and she yelled into the phone. "Mom, stay there and do not move, the paramedics will be right there!" Then she dialed 911 and her brother's receptionist. His medical office was only five minutes from Mom and Dad.

Dad was alive and rushed to the hospital. His breathing was labored and pain stabbed from inside his chest. His congestive heart failure struck again. He was lucky, a second time but this time, his heart attack was almost fatal. The doctors guessed that self-prescribed medicines had triggered the attack. He was notorious for diagnosing and prescribing medicines for himself as well as everyone else in the family. Now that his dementia affected his rationality and memory, self-medicating was not a good idea. No one could convince him of that.

Mom's hip was shattered and she was badly bruised. Her doctors rushed her into surgery and she came through without complications. Her prognosis was good, IF she followed instructions. It was not long before she became her determined self again. Both Mom and Dad were admitted to the same rehabilitation facility for six weeks, and every day Mom received physical therapy.

Dad's doctors thought that it was unlikely that he would survive heart surgery. He was still in great pain and confided to Adrienne that he did not want to live that way. They increased his medicines, doubtful that he would get better. To everyone's amazement, the medicines worked and before long Dad was feeling better and begging to go home. He was persistent and, of course, he was impatient and wanted Mom to go home with him.

Mom was horrified. "Please don't send me back there with him."

Adrienne suspected that her mom had hidden the true extent of Dad's mental deterioration for a long time. She kept him driving the car by giving him minute-by-minute verbal directions. She was very attached to her home and determined to go back there but knew that she could not function the same as before the fall. Adrienne and her brother arranged for around-the-clock nurses and soon, they were back in their familiar environment.

"Those poor nurses had triple duty with Mom, Dad, and their incontinent dog, Tiger. They had to lift him on and off Dad's bed, carry him outside, and watch to make sure that he did his business."

After a while they were able to manage without three full shifts of nurses, but neither was able to resume driving. Mom depended on her son and daughter-in-law to take her everywhere.

Several months passed before Adrienne's Dad had another attack and was again rushed to the hospital. His congestive heart failure was worse and, as before, the attack was serious. Doctors finally stabilized him, adjusted his medicines, and insisted he be placed in a facility with around-the-clock care. For the short term, Adrienne and her brother sent him to a large medical center with many heart specialists in Adrienne's home city, forty miles away. When he was strong enough to be transferred to long-term nursing care, Adrienne chose the same facility that cared for Dan, her husband.

Dad did not protest and Adrienne thought that her mom was secretly relieved. She tried to persuade her mom to move into assisted living at the same facility, hoping to have everyone in the same location. But Mom was resolute and had other ideas. No! She would stay at home and ride with her son to see Dad. Adrienne knew that it was useless and a waste of time and energy to argue with her. Plus, she had enough to take care of with Dan and Dad.

Curt Falls

Jen needed a break and thought that a pleasant lunch in town at one of their favorite restaurants would give her the relief she needed. She slowly walked beside Curt to the car, mindful that he was, at times, unsteady on his feet. "Where would you like to eat lunch, Curt?"

"I want to go to the little place near my office, the one that I love." Jen knew it well. Curt and she often met there before they were married, when he was still working.

"We can try going there, but the area is so busy at lunchtime. I will have to find a parking space on the street. Perhaps we will be lucky today." They found a space just around the corner from the restaurant. Jen dropped quarters into the meter and helped Curt out of the car.

There was a thirty-foot gradual incline to the corner. Curt's steps were small and deliberate and as they neared the corner. He slowly leaned forward and seemed to be losing his balance. Jen grabbed his arm. Her heart pounded as she stared at his face and his eyes. She had seen that look before, twice, at the beach when they were on vacation. Both times, Curt collapsed onto carpeted floors.

"Curt, Curt!" His body stiffened and began toppling like a huge, falling tree. Out of the corner of her eye, Jen saw a man on the other side of Curt and screamed for help. Jen was thin and recovering from a horrible car accident that sent her to a convalescent center for two months. If it had not been for the kind stranger who grabbed Curt and gently laid him on the sidewalk, Curt would have either fallen on her, or his head would have slammed the pavement.

As soon as he was down, he regained consciousness. Another man helped, and the three of them managed to get Curt safely in the car. When they arrived home, Curt seemed all right and did not remember the incident.

Jen immediately talked with his doctor and asked

if he thought that Curt had experienced a TIA, a transient ischemic attack. The doctor said, "The symptoms you describe, loss of balance, weakness, facial and limb paralysis, and the fact that it lasted only a minute or two, certainly indicate a TIA that is caused by a temporary blockage if blood flowing to part of the brain. There is no way to know for certain unless we order a brain scan and other tests. Be watchful and call me in a few days if you want those tests performed. The tests will be informative but they will not change anything. At this point in his disease, there is nothing else that we can do for him."

Jen began to worry and think about what would have happened if those kind men had not helped her. Given her size and injuries, she knew that it was time to begin searching for memory care.

Myra Needs Peace and Quiet

Myra retreated into the corner and drew up into a tight ball. She screamed, "No! Tell them to stop!" The voices and music at the daycare center reverberated through her head. The kind staff members recognized the anxiety attack and intervened. "Come on, Myra, let's go into the quiet room and rest." They wrapped her in a warm blanket, dimmed the lights, and one stayed by her side, assuring her that everything was OK.

Myra had thrived on the lively swaying and dancing to the music at the day care center, but no longer. The disease had progressed and she needed calm and quiet. The noise distressed her and the activities were too taxing and over-stimulating. As a result, she yelled and screamed every afternoon. Those behaviors were so unlike Myra. The experienced, caring staff recognized that her needs had permanently changed and her environment must change. They were sad to say goodbye to the once lively, vivacious Myra.

Rob was prepared for what he had to do. He anticipated that this time would come because he heard similar stories at the weekly support meeting. His new role was an around-the-clock caregiver. Rob was organized, rational, but knew that he could not do it alone.

The trials of other caregivers galvanized him to seek out and contact local resources. The Shepherd Center provided a weekly volunteer who sat for a few hours, allowing him time to get out of the house, even if he just shopped for household supplies. His family often saved his sanity by taking him to lunch and staying with Myra while he exercised at the local Y. He made arrangements for a visit from the Hospice doctor to see if she was ready for their palliative-care-at-home program. She was, and Hospice provided her medicines, a hospital bed, wheelchair, and twice weekly medical care visits at home.

Bathing was always a problem for Rob. From the very beginning of the disease, Myra resisted his assistance at bath time. At the center, he paid a small fee for baths in the special "spa" room and she loved it. But she hated showering at home and threw her 100-pound body into a rage, swinging her arms and kicking at Rob, determined not to cooperate. She was incontinent and Rob, almost twice her size, was determined to bathe her. He hated every minute of the struggle but sat her on the bench in the shower and tried to dodge her flailing arms and pounding fists.

His size and strength served him well as he easily lifted her from the bed to the wheelchair and then to other chairs in the house so that she could change positions often. He rigged a seatbelt to the middle seat of the sofa so that they could sit together in front of the TV. The clever device enabled him to make short trips to the kitchen to retrieve juice or snacks without worrying that she would topple onto the floor while he was gone. He managed to become a 'decent' cook and was patient and loving during the forty-five minutes necessary to feed her each meal.

Although she seldom uttered a word to him or anyone, he constantly told her that he loved her and gazed into her eyes as he engaged in one-way 'conversations.' He was confident that she knew and loved him because she still smiled at him when he returned home from shopping.

One evening while he was feeding her dinner, Rob began asking her questions, trying to stimulate her brain. "Myra, do you know me? Who am I? What is my name?"

Myra seldom said anything and tried to ignore his questions. He persisted and finally she looked straight at Rob and said, "Don't you know?"

Rob laughed as he told the support group his story. "You know, you have to find joy wherever you can."

Jack's Last Rant

Maggie's expression was solemn as she told her story. Her face was drawn and reflected many sleepless nights. "We planned our traditional family week at the beach. We usually travel in a caravan of several cars packed with kids and beach paraphernalia. The kids and grandkids love it."

"This year, I had a symphony performance and had to travel a day later than everyone else. The children tried to convince Jack to go with them, but he insisted on waiting and riding with me. He sat in the back seat as the law required, but was agitated. He reminded me of a child, asking over and over how much longer it would be until we got there."

"My hands were shaking on the steering wheel. When we turned into the parking area, I felt as if a thousand pounds was lifted from me. Just seeing the kid's cars made me relax and I was really looking forward to the week. Jack would have something to do and other people to help keep him occupied."

"Soon after we arrived, my daughter, Shelly, and I left to buy groceries. While we were gone, Jack paced, yelled, and constantly asked where I was. The boys told him many times that we were shopping and they tried distracting him. They begged him to go with them to the pier. He refused and would not go anywhere or do anything. The longer we were gone, the angrier he became."

"When we returned, he still refused to calm down. He was so upset that he commanded me to take him home, stormed out, and sat in the car. Everyone was worried about what he would say or do around the children. I was exhausted from the morning drive but knew that he would ruin the week for everyone. I convinced them that I was fine and could safely drive him home."

"The minute we got home, he rushed in the door and started drinking. I was so tired that I went upstairs, intending to rest, but he kept calling me and before I could run down the stairs, he was ranting, pacing, and throwing his arms around everywhere. I went to the kitchen, sometimes food calmed him, but he followed me, yelled, and slapped me. I was trying to get away when the phone rang. I answered it but Jack knocked it out of my hand. Shelly heard me screaming and called the police."

Jack was as nice as could be to the police officers. He invited them inside and offered them a drink. When they told him that he would have to go with them, he smiled and went right out the door. One officer stayed behind a few minutes to make certain that I was all right. He said that Jack would be evaluated at the hospital's psychiatric center and that I could go there later but he was uncertain if the doctors would allow me to see him."

"He was there for seven days. He did not forget that he was angry with me. The doctors did not want me to visit unless someone on the hospital staff could stay in the room with us. They tried several different medicines, but nothing seemed to control his anger toward me. The doctors thought that Jack had fixated and blamed me for all of the changes in his life. They said that it could last for months, maybe longer. The doctors would not allow him to come home since it was not safe for me."

"We had to scramble to find a place for him. Even though the doctors had him highly medicated, no facility wanted to admit a person who is violent. Finally, we found a place, but they asked me to only visit when it was convenient for a staff member to be in the room while I was there."

"All of a sudden, I am no longer caring for Jack. I don't know what to do with myself. I have been trying to think about everything that has happened and sort through it all. I was so focused on living with him and not upsetting him that I never thought about anything else. I am amazed that I did what I did. I don't know where all of my energy came from. I had to be smart and do and say things that I never thought were in me.

I could never have done it without the support of my children and the people at the daycare center."

Claudia's Obstinacy

"Claudia has changed. She no longer constantly talks and asks me questions. Sometimes she doesn't even know me. When I tell her that we are going to eat or watch TV, she just stands there. She can't remember how to sit down in a chair. The day-care staff mentioned her changes. She stays off to the side, away from the others, and no longer participates in activities. She carries the doll that I gave her everywhere."

The tension and stress radiated from Stuart's body. Support group members were concerned about his health and asked how he was holding up.

"I am physically and emotionally worn out. I have learned so much from this group. But now, I don't know what to do. My daughter is worried about me. She is afraid that I will have another heart attack. She comes every morning and helps me with Claudia. Sometimes, she can persuade Claudia to get up when I cannot. But, she is a nurse and has to work and has two kids. I look at her face and I know that she is also exhausted."

Last week, Stuart mentioned that he was thinking about visiting several memory care communities. "My daughter finally convinced me, took a day off from work, and we toured four. My daughter knows what to look for and asks the right questions. We narrowed it down to two places and put Claudia's name on the waiting lists for both." Stuart pressed his lips together, looked down, and shook his head. When he looked up, his sad face revealed his inner turmoil.

"I don't have a choice. This is killing me a little bit at a time. I look in her eyes and the vibrant Claudia that used to be there is gone. Her hollow, vacant look and expressionless face tear my heart out. I worry that she is suffering, but I know that she isn't. She is in a world of her own, holding her baby doll."

"We have been together for a long time and went through everything together. I cannot imagine my life without her. I wish there were another way, but it's too hard for me now. If I don't place her, I won't make it."

Jon Leaves

Nan looked down and was silent for a moment. "Where do I start? Monday afternoon when I arrived here to pick up Jon, and before I could step out of the car, my phone rang. The daycare aides were calling me to come as soon as possible.

"Jon was agitated and they could not control him. He came out in his bare feet. He threw his shoes in the trash, and insisted that they were too small. We put them back on him and he walked out the door toward the car. Quick as a flash, he sat down on the pavement, took off his shoes, and threw them several feet. I examined his shoes and he had stuffed his socks into the toe of each one. No wonder they would not fit his feet."

"When we arrived at home, he pushed in front of me and set off the door alarm. While I turned off the alarm, he ran out of the house and disappeared. I looked everywhere, alerted the neighbors, and finally called the police. He moved fast because they had already received several calls about a man in our neighborhood who was trying to break into houses. He pushed his way into one house and uttered words that the residents did not understand."

"The police took him to the psychiatric unit at the hospital. It did not take them long to evaluate him and calm him with anti-anxiety medicine. The doctors said that he could not come home."

"The week before, I took your advice and found a memory care facility that accepts Medicade and luckily, they still had a room available. I will have to private pay until we can get him qualified to receive assistance."

"I visited him yesterday and he knew me. He had on someone else's shoes and I searched but never found his shoes. I hope they reappear. I put nametags in all of his clothes. When I prepared to leave, he gathered his things and intended to leave with me. The aides distracted him and I slipped out."

"I am still in shock and trying to reconcile all that has happened within one week. One good thing is that for the first time in months, I am able to sleep without waking up every few minutes."

Michael's Surprise

"The reason that I was not here last week is that there has been a big change. Before I give you the details, I want to thank all of you for being here for me week after week and helping me in so many ways."

"As you all know, Betsy demanded to have things her way and I gave in rather than live in a battle zone. When it was time for bed, she refused to change into her nightgown and slept in her clothes. Many of you reminded me that it really did not matter what she wore to bed."

"Helping her bathe or shower was impossible, she steadfastly refused. Ellen, you are a nurse and when you convinced me that using baby wipes was sufficient and that elderly skin did not need a daily bath, my problems with that issue improved."

"When she stopped eating solid foods, my family and I thought that her world had come to an end. You recommended giving her Boost with ice cream and that is all that kept her alive for the last two years."

"As we discussed, I had to have breaks and tried to find ways to get out for a few hours. My family and friends did the best that they could to stay with Betsy, but they have busy lives and obligations. Occasionally, I was able to call on church members to sit with her while I visited our sick and shut-in members.. That work has all but stopped. Betsy only allowed a few people that she remembered to stay with her."

"Our children worried for a long time. They watched their mom change from a loving, welcoming grandmother into a stranger, a woman who did not remember their names and became upset when the little ones visited. Too many people and too much stimulation made her uncomfortable and our grandchildren did not understand that her changes were the result of the disease."

"We finally had a family meeting. After gradually losing their mom, our children did not want to lose me also. They were concerned that the stress from Betsy's around-the clock-care was too much for me. After talking about everything, we decided to place Betsy's name on the waiting list of a memory care community operated by our faith."

"As often happens, a room became available sooner than expected. Rather than turn down the room and have her name placed at the bottom of the list, we made the decision that it was time."

"I agonized but kept my feelings to myself. It was

impossible for me not to manufacture a worst-case scenario in my mind. I was convinced that Betsy would be angry and miserable not being at home. I wondered if I could endure her unhappiness and disappointment."

"Our marriage has been wonderful. I thought and prayed and finally accepted that our life together would never be the same, regardless of whether Betsy was at home with me or being taken care of by the good people at memory care."

"Last week, moving day arrived. I dreaded it and expected the worse. What would I say and do if Betsy begged to go home? I did not tell her where we were going."

"Once we arrived, the staff knew how to ease the transition. They welcomed her and whisked her away to the lunchroom while I was busy filling out and signing the admittance forms. I wanted to slip out and disappear without seeing her, but knew that my heart would not allow me to do that. I found her walking down the hall on an aide's arm. As she approached, she smiled, blew me a kiss, and walked on by. Whew! I was amazed and relieved."

Marie's Near Miss

Marie sat on the bed and crossed her arms and held her chest while she waited for Dave to shower. Was she sick? Strange feelings flooded her body but she had to get him dressed and ready for daycare. His clothes were in the closet and the door was open. She was weak and grabbed the open door to keep from falling. What was happening? It was morning and she slept all night. Was she still tired?

Dave was wet and needed her help drying with

the towel. Oh, dear, the horrible feelings again! Was she dehydrated? She leaned on the sink and drank a glass of water, but that made her feel worse. She realized that she could not function and may pass out and called 911.

The ambulance crew remembered them from the week before when Marie called to have someone help get Dave up when he fell. Dave rode in the ambulance with her.

As she was rolled into emergency, she worried. Am I having a heart attack? She willed herself to be positive and told herself that it was just a virus. The doctors would prescribe something and then she and Dave would be on their way home. He was agitated and did not like being there, probably because he was in this same hospital two months ago and was diagnosed with congestive heart failure. She had changed his diet and was restricting his fluids and salt intake. His dementia was fast moving into the severe stage.

Her pulse raced, her heart beat irregularly, and her blood pressure was low. "You are lucky. You made it here before having a heart attack. Has anyone in your family had heart problems?" Marie's eyes opened wide as she thought, *the odds are against me.*

"My father had by-pass surgery, my mother died of congestive heart failure, my brother's heart suddenly failed when he was sixty-four, and my sister died from sudden cardiac arrest when she was only forty-four."

The doctor immediately said, "You will be here for a few days. We need to run several tests and find out exactly what is going on."

Marie called the adult daycare center and the director sent an employee to get Dave. She took him to the center and later drove him home and stayed the night. The next day, he accompanied her to work and they repeated the procedure for the three days that Marie remained in the hospital.

All tests indicated that she was OK. The doctors said, "Stress, stress, stress."

Marie's children were horrified. Something had to change! Her daughter was employed, pregnant, and had a two-year old at home. Her son offered to take an extended leave of absence, come home, and stay with her. But with the daycare director's help, Marie lined up helpers to come in daily and that made life somewhat easier.

"Mom, Dad is getting worse every day. You cannot continue this even with part-time help. It is too stressful! We have to place Dad in memory care."

Marie wanted to take care of Dave for as long as possible, but the doctors were correct that she was under extreme stress every minute that he was home. He was on a special diet and constantly fought with her about food. He loved to eat. His fluids were restricted and he frequently experienced urinary tract infections that affected his whole body and made him even more difficult to deal with.

How could she argue with her children? The time had arrived. What if she had died that morning? Her children would be left with huge problems and her grandchildren would grow up without either of their grandparents. The search for a good, convenient memory care community began.

Jane's Ultimate Challenge

"Well, things are not going well. My doctor thinks that I have six to nine months to live. The melanoma is finally getting me."

"Thirty years ago, I took a job advising the managers of several care facilities across the State. Driving between them was part of the job, and I remember feeling the hot sun on the side of my face as I drove. I was too caught up in my busy life to even think about using sunscreen daily. Skin cancer was not widely discussed or publicized then. In college, we slathered our bodies with coconut oil and fried ourselves in the sun."

Surgery, five years ago, removed the cancerous facial tissues, but by then, it went deep into her lymph nodes. It reared its ugly head with a vengeance and was spreading throughout her body. A recent scan revealed tumors in her lungs. She inhaled oxygen as we talked.

I watched her face as we sat beside each other on her sofa. She lowered her chin and half-smiled in her mischievous, introspective way. "I always thought that congestive heart failure, my genetic gift, would get me. My Mom, Dad, and my brother died from heart problems." She frowned. "I was hoping that I could make it to eighty."

"I am slowly giving my nine and twelve year old granddaughters hints, gently transmitting the message. I'll say, 'I NEED you to go to the basement and bring a roll of paper towels upstairs. You know, climbing the stairs really wears me out and makes me weak and short of breath.' They are smart girls."

"Bill is another story. Last week, we went to see our lawyer. He knows all about Bill's dementia. I told him what is happening. Years ago, we designated each other as health care and legal power of attorney. Our lawyer revoked those documents and is redrawing them, giving our son that responsibility. That will save Mark a lot of time and trouble when he has to take care of his dad."

"On our way home, Bill was confused and didn't understand why we did that. I told him that we did it because I will probably die first."

He said, "What? You can't do that! I can't make it without you!"

"Mark will take care of you. You'll be all right."

"No! I have to die first."

"He did not remember that we had the same conversation many times recently." Jane shook her head and sighed. "Regardless of how often I tell him, he does not remember."

We sat there in silence for a few moments. Honestly, I did not know what to say to the kind, strong woman who helped so many people through many crises. Then she chuckled and her checks crinkled, her eyes twinkled, and I waited.

"I looked at him and said, "Well then, Bill, you better get on with it."

CHAPTER EIGHT

ACCEPTING AND LETTING GO

A Week of Respite

The foaming surf engulfed my ankles. I kicked it with my bare feet and stomped up and down the beach. I hated the out-of-control anger that spilled out of me. My stoic family upbringing compelled me to stifle these unwanted emotional outbursts. Showing them in public was worse than inadvertently exposing one's underwear. But, emotional Ann hijacked my brain and invited anger and her friends, frustration, regret, misery, and despair to my party.

After all of those frantic years traveling down desperation road trying to keep Mom happily and safely in her home, the fight was over. This is a fate that I did not want her to suffer.

My family avoided me. Dale was nowhere in sight and Alex rested on a lounge chair under an umbrella with Alana beside her, sleeping in her carrier and covered with a light blanket to protect her new, delicate skin. Alex made the last-minute arrangements and insisted that we drop everything and trek to the coast. "Mom, pack your bag! We are going to the beach for a week together. You need to get away and relax! We need it!"

Barbara, the manager of Mom's memory care community, recommended that I stay away for one or two weeks so that Mom would develop new daily patterns and familiarize herself with her new home. I knew what that meant, Mom needed to shift her dependence from me to them. Alex believed that I would be fighting with my car to transport me the easy ten miles to check on Mom, if I remained at home for the week. She conspired with her dad and here I am, ruminating and throwing a tantrum.

My chest and stomach ached and my skin itched

as if bugs crawled all over me. How can I do this? How can I all of a sudden disappear? Mom's plea, "Don't leave me," rang in my ears and I picked up a shell and hurled it toward the ocean. Emotional Ann screamed, *you should have moved her to the lake.* Rational Ann insisted, *do something, call Barbara!* I fished my phone out the back pocket of my jean shorts.

"Your Mom is fine. She likes her new roommate and they stay in their room or walk around together. She eats everything on her plate. The nurses and aides like her and take good care of her. She is always kind and thanks them for their help. If possible, give her more time before you see her. I know that it is difficult for you. You were caring for her every day. The uncertainty you are feeling will soon pass. I think you will be pleasantly surprised when you see her next week."

As I stuffed my phone securely in my pocket, emotional Ann whispered in my ear. *Do not believe her. She is lying. You know better. She is miserable and will beg you to take her home the minute you walk in.* Rational Ann countered with logic, but I did not pay attention to her. The angry, emotional Ann continued her rampage and commandeered my thoughts.

On our way to the coast yesterday, I cried until I had hiccups that would not go away. By the time we arrived, I was exhausted and quiet long enough to realize that I was having an anxiety attack. Acknowledging that fact did not help, I remained miserable and I watched passively as my family happily unloaded bags, food, beach paraphernalia, and a myriad of baby equipment and supplies from the van and SUV. They worried about my health and Alex wanted this week to be a transition that would chip away my desperation. Rational Ann advised, *you owe it to them to 'get a grip' and not ruin our first family vacation in many years.*

For dinner our first night, Alex searched online and found a highly recommended fish restaurant. We ate at a table beside a huge window and the view out over the marshes at sunset was spectacular. I struggled to keep dry eyes as I stared out the window and grieved that Mom would never again appreciate the coastal sunsets.

Alana awoke, squirmed in her carrier, and smiled as we waved and jiggled her. I laughed and before long her gyrations yanked me out of my funk. The distraction relaxed my mind and body and I enjoyed our meal and slept well that night.

A crashing wave threatened to cover me and I raced toward the dry beach to save my phone. Movement felt good and I headed down the beach, hoping that a brisk walk would stimulate my brain to release 'feel good' brain chemicals. Rational Ann suggested, *you need positive thoughts, not negative ones. Be thankful that many good outcomes have fallen into place.*

Mom was out of her filthy, unbearable house and well cared for. Barbara and a nurse drove forty miles to the hospital to personally move Mom into her new home. I am uncertain whether I could have done it. Taking her there after she was discharged from the hospital, fibbing that it was just temporary until the doctor was certain that her new medicines were working, and enduring her distress as I left would have given me nightmares. I cringed as I thought of her plea, "Don't leave me!"

Early yesterday before she was discharged from the hospital, I set out a few family photos in her room, filled the closet with clean clothes, and met her new roommate, Hilda. She was kind and resembled Aunt Margie. I was relieved and hopeful that they would be satisfied together.

Would it occur to Mom that she would never return to her little home? Surely, complex thoughts of the future were all in past. She lived in the current moment with the mind of a young child. She will likely be happy if the food is good and she is comfortable, cared for, and treated with respect.

Dad and she moved into their new house before the furnace was installed. My first memory was being snatched from my bed, carried into the kitchen, and dressed in clothes warmed on the only source of heat at the time, a coal-fired stove.

The back door in the kitchen opened toward my grandmother's house and all that I had to do to be entertained was crawl to the sturdy screen door and shriek at the top of my lungs. Immediately, one of my grandparents or Aunt Ruby rushed across the yard, scooped me up, hugged me, and read wonderful stories while I gazed at colorful books. I was told that my first sentence was, "Come get Ann."

As I turned and retraced my steps along the edge of the surf, I wished that I could yell for someone to come get Ann. There was no one who could save me from my grief, guilt, and anger.

The ocean water was still cool in May. Sadness washed over me like the waves nipping at my ankles. I turned to face the ocean and waded out knee deep hoping to again hide my pain and tears from Alex. Rational Ann whispered in my ear. *You cannot live your Mom's life, nor can you save her. You have to live your own life. You know that If it weren't for this disease, your mom would want you to do that.*

The squishy sand felt good. My feet were happy.

If only I could get control of my brain. Ruminating and fuming my way through the week would not help me nor make anyone happy. I mentally surveyed my favorite books for one to help me cope and live peacefully with myself. Oh yes, Eckhart Tolle's, _The Power of Now_. Perhaps I can take his advice and focus on the events that are happening moment by moment and shut out all of the miseries of the past and uncertainties of tomorrow.

I turned and gazed at my beautiful granddaughter snoozing in her carrier. Her little face looked just like mine when I was her age. Her proud parents, unlike me, waited until after they finished grad school to have a child. They lounged on the warm sand, thoroughly enjoying the ocean breeze and the time away from their daily routines.

Down the beach, Dale was walking toward me with our dog and Alex's Labrador retriever. There were only a few other people on the beach so he bent over and removed their leashes. Unhampered, the ecstatic dogs raced toward me, dipped in and out of tidal pools, and chased sea gulls as if they could actually catch them.

Rational Ann insisted, _this is your life now. Relax and enjoy today! Your Mom had the best life possible given her temperament and resources. Even if you were there with her, you can never bring back her mental clarity and make her happy._

I walked toward the umbrella and sat on the blanket beside Alex. "Why don't you walk down the beach. I will gladly stay here with my precious granddaughter."

Return to Real Life

Tomorrow, eight days after Mom was transported to her new home, I must gather my wits, march in fearlessly, and face her. At the beach, I lived each day in a different world, one with promise and a future. Watching Alana's reactions to her new world enthralled me. I had missed many wonderful moments with my daughter and granddaughter. The week together was my happiest in many years. Constant worry and physical exhaustion magically dissipated.

Memories of past vacations when Mom played with her granddaughter added to the stew of sadness that simmered permanently in my heart. I lived with that pain but wondered if I could ever get past the despair caused by the horrible disease. Mom faced the end of her life and I faced life without her.

I trusted Dale's expert driving as we led the way home to North Carolina. The flat, swampy sand country of South Carolina could not hold my attention and allow me to live in the present moment. My mind buzzed with uncertainties. Will she know me? Will she plead to return to her dusty, but comforting, little house?

There was only one past occasion when she did not know me. We were eating lunch at the cafeteria and I briefly left the table to wash a sweet desert from my hands. When I returned, Mom seemed surprised and said, "Oh, hello. When is Ann coming?"

My support group warned that the day would come when she did not know me, but I was not prepared for the disappointment. "I am Ann, Mom." I was only away from the table for a minute. Did her mind drift to another time and place and my quick reappearance bumped her back to the cafeteria before she could reorient herself? Similar situations happen when I am abruptly awakened from a dream, but I immediately recognize my family.

Dale slammed on brakes to avoid hitting a deer that sprinted across the road. I instinctively grabbed our dog and after my heart slowed, my apprehensive thoughts returned to tomorrow. How should I greet her? What will I say? Lying to my mother was never easy but I had learned the hard way that a kind fib may save her from days of mental anguish.

Two years ago, Aunt Edith, who was three years younger than Mom, fell down steps and hit her head on the concrete driveway. She was in a coma when Mom and I arrived at the hospital and she passed away a week later. I convinced Mom to go to the family visitation at the funeral home but it was difficult for her.

Mom was over-whelmed by the people who patiently waited to hug her and speak of the sadness. Some asked questions after they expressed their condolences. I stood by her side, announced names and, at times, answered their questions. She pretended to know each one. It was a taxing task and I knew that Mom barely made it through the evening. Seeing Aunt Edie lying in the casket was almost too much for her. She was relieved when we left and exhausted when she collapsed in her bed.

The next morning, I rang her doorbell, prepared to help choose appropriate clothes for the funeral. She would be determined to wear her worn out old black slacks and a stained blouse. I hoped that she bathed, even if it was with a washcloth and sink basin of water. When she opened the door, I was surprised to see that she was still in her pajamas. "I am sick and don't feel like going. Tell them I am not able."

"That's all right, Mom. You are very tired. Everyone will understand."

Last year, Mom mentioned that she had not seen Edie in a while and asked if I had talked with her. Before I thought about it, I said, "Mom, she died two years ago."

She shrieked, "Why didn't anyone tell me?" She did not remember the accident, hospital, or funeral home, and was upset and grieved again. After that, I told many fibs to avoid provoking anxiety attacks. I did it to be kind.

The Dreaded Visit

The drive to Mom's memory care community was short compared to my usual fifty-mile trek to her house. That daily trip was time consuming and costly but provided a buffer, an interval to prepare myself mentally for the day's activities. By the time I arrived, I had summoned my resolve, patience, and kindness, and stuffed my anguish, frustration, and unease into my car's glove box, and locked them away for the day. I was ready and determined to make the day a good one and was thankful that she was still with me, at least physically.

My visits were especially trying during the last year. She made hurtful, critical comments about my clothes or what I did. She acted like a self-centered young child. Rational Ann continually reminded me that the disease was in control of her behavior, but I never truly relaxed until the day was over. As I drove away from her house, I often screamed to release my pent up frustrations.

My hands trembled as I left the interstate highway. I did not know what to expect but guessed that lots of soothing, fibbing, and distracting would be required. Lack of control and uncertainty were lethal poisons that I regularly ingested during her decline. Rational Ann advised, *push away your fears, don't worry about something that may never happen*! Mom's motto was, *buck up, you can do it.*

The window in her room provided a view of the driveway and there was a parking space directly in front of her room. I opened the trunk and took out a new bird feeder. She always loved birds and this one would provide hours of entertainment. The nicely manicured area between her window and the driveway was covered with mulch and attractive shrubs. The sod was soft and I easily pushed the wrought iron holder into the ground.

Satisfied that the feeder was straight and placed in the perfect spot, I moved close to the window, cupped my hands, and peered in through the open blinds. She was sitting in a high-backed Queen Anne style upholstered chair and was staring straight at the window but did not acknowledge me when I waved. Instead, she stood up, turned, and faced an elderly lady who appeared in the doorway.

I walked across the veranda to the front door and rang the doorbell. Because it was a memory care building, all exterior doors except for the one that opened onto a privacy-fenced, secure garden were kept locked. An engraved sign beside the doorbell warned visitors: *Please be careful entering and leaving as residents have a tendency to wonder.* Hum! Surely this is a pun, a trick to insure that a smile adorned all visitors' faces. It worked for me!

I greeted everyone that I passed on my way to Barbara's office for a full report before seeing Mom. "She is settling down, becoming familiar with the routines, and participating in several activities. We had to put an alarm on her ankle because she tried to slip out two or three times when she first arrived. But that has not happened in several days and we can remove it now. She may be in her room, let's find her."

She was in her room with her roommate, standing by the desk, admiring several plastic multi-colored necklaces. Hilda put one around Mom's neck. Barbara silently backed out of the room and allowed me to greet her alone.

"Hello, Mom. How are you? What are you doing?" I hugged her.

She smiled and addressed Hilda, "This is my daughter."

Yea! She knew me. Hilda directed my attention to her jewels. "Look at my pretty necklaces."

"They are beautiful, Hilda." There was a doll on Hilda's bed and I asked its name.

"That is my baby, Jenny. She is still asleep."

"I brought a new birdfeeder, Mom, and put it outside your window. It is a miniature little red schoolhouse. The birds will soon find the seeds."

They admired the bird feeder through the open blinds. I gave Mom a new pair of black knit slacks that were soft and flexible, and held them up to her waist to verify that they fit.

"Do you like these, Mom? They will be warm and comfortable." She agreed.

Just then Hilda asked, "Who are you?"

"I'm Ann, Roberta's daughter. Do you have a daughter?"

"Yes, her name is Jenny. She should be here soon."

"I hope so, I want to meet her."

I was still nervous and tried to think of something to say.

"Why don't we walk down the hall? You can show me the dining room."

"I can't," Hilda said. "I have to stay here and take care of my baby."

"Well, Mom, let's go for a walk. I want to see everything."

"OK. First let me get my things." She went to the closet and grabbed several hangers with clean clothes.

"No, Mom. You don't need those, we are going to walk down the hall."

"You're not taking me home?"

"Not today. I have to go help Dale at work. He needs me. You will have dinner here." I learned long ago that if I mentioned a task for Dale, it was an excuse that she always understood and accepted.

"Can you give me some money? I cannot pay for my dinner."

"Mom, you don't need to pay for anything. I have already paid for everything. You must eat, enjoy the food, and don't worry about paying."

That satisfied her and we walked around. I cheerfully smiled and greeted everyone. Mom showed me the dining table where she ate meals with three other ladies. The TV room was deserted except for us, so we sat for awhile. I was certain that Mom no longer watched TV and was unable to follow and understand programs. TV's were allowed in private rooms but not in rooms shared by two residents.

We walked back to her room and she sat in her chair that faced the window. "What is that red thing outside my window?"

"It is your new bird feeder. I filled it with the seeds that the birds love. You will love watching them eat. "

I checked her clothes closet and made certain

that her toothbrush and red lipstick were in the bathroom. "I have to go help Dale now, Mom. I will see you tomorrow."

"Oh, what time will you be here?"

"I will be here about eleven and will eat lunch with you."

"OK. I'll be ready."

I bent over, hugged her, and hurried down the hall. Barbara gave me a shadow box to take home and arrange with pictures and mementos. The hallway was adorned with many memory boxes that proudly exhibited pictures from residents' past lives.

An employee walked by and I asked if she would please open the door for me to leave. A female resident rushed to me. "Are you leaving? Can you take me home? I have to take care of my children. They will be coming home from school soon."

"I am so sorry. I am late for work."

I wasted no time hopping into my car but paused to smile and wave toward the window just in case Mom was watching. As I turned on to the road, I realized that fast thinking and compassionate fibs were now an important and necessary part of my new role.

I asked myself, now what? Where am I going? What am I doing? My heart ached. I pulled into the parking area of a small store, turned off the engine, and took deep, long, breaths as tears rolled down my face.

"Help! I'm lost."

MOM HAS A NEW HOME

Daily Life in Memory Care

Habits, schedules, and routines, each day was the same as the day before. Nothing changed. Life moved in rhythmical, predictable patterns. After a few weeks, Mom knew what to expect and adjusted to her clean bed, tidy room, bath schedule, snacks, meals and the other residents, especially the three ladies who shared her table in the dining room. Three shifts of kind aides babied her and took care of her. Their jobs were not easy. Somehow, they managed to always smile and cheerfully help Mom wash, dress, and tie her shoes.

I greeted her caregivers warmly, remembered their names, and learned about their lives, boyfriends, husbands, and children. They beamed when I thanked them for taking good care of Mom.

At first, I tried to visit every day and sometimes ate lunch or dinner in the dining room. There was a five dollar charge for my meal and the food was good. The cook specialized in country-style cooking and the meal usually included meat, two vegetables, fruit and a light desert. Mom liked the convenience of walking the short distance down the hall to the dining room and always recognized her chair at the table with the three ladies. The staff alerted me ahead of time when one of the ladies was not going to be there for lunch and, if convenient, I filled in for the absentee.

Although the food was tasty, for me lunch was stressful. There was no conversation, no idle chit-chat about the day's activities and no noise except for clanking forks and spoons. The silence disturbed me and I racked my brain for things to say or ask.

No one remembered yesterday, the day before,

or recent visits from loved ones. I quickly discovered that they occasionally remembered details of their lives when they were young, where they grew up, lived, or their young families. At times, one of the ladies talked about needing to go home to care for her family and gave detailed descriptions of tasks and housework that she performed yesterday. I was always thinking, *what can I say now*? One day, I realized that I was judging the situation from my perspective. *They were not uncomfortable eating in silence, I was.*

The layout of the community made it possible for Mom and me to walk in a big circle and end back at her room. The resident's rooms were located on the outside of hallways and each had windows. The central core of the building held the laundry, chapel, hair salon, and other special-use rooms.

As we walked, I smiled and greeted residents. A few of them began to watch for me. They may have assumed that I was an employee since I always summoned a staff member when they had a problem or needed something. Mom often corrected their assumptions, proudly declaring that I was hers, "This is my daughter."

One day, a lady argued with Mom. "No, she is MY daughter."

Hilda's Daughter

One morning I met Hilda's daughter, Jenny. She was friendly but frustrated as she checked her mother's clothes and possessions. "Oh, I am so irritated with this place! Mother's clothes disappear and strange ones are hanging in her closet. Everything is clearly marked with her name. I take her laundry home and do it myself and

I still cannot find her things. I hang each outfit, slacks and matching top together and place it in her closet. Every time I come, Mom is wearing mismatched clothes. Why can't these people do better? I want them to put a lock on Mother's closet but they will not do it. They claim that it is difficult for a staff member to get the key every time that Mother messes and needs a quick change of clothes. Do your mother's good clothes disappear?"

"I have not noticed a problem, but Mom prefers black slacks and print blouses and they all coordinate. If something is missing, I just assume that it is being laundered." I did not tell her that sometimes Mom's eyeglasses are nowhere to be found and I have to walk around and look at other residents' faces. When I spot them, the aides handle the situation. Or, if I cannot find them, a bulletin is quickly issued and before long, they reappear. They have a box of eyeglasses in the nurse's office with no names on them.

Hilda and Mom were easy going about their clothes. I wondered if either would protest if she realized that she was wearing another person's blouse. Why upset the staff about clothing? They were busily changing diapers and making sure the residents were satisfied, did not fall, and drank fluids. I was more accepting of circumstances than Jenny.

"Well, Mother has matching sets of everything. I am going to have another serious talk with Barbara. These women just don't listen to my complaints. I have been thinking of moving Mother. This situation upsets me." As she hurried down the hall, I thought about Hilda's difficulty in having to learn new people and new patterns at a different place. The confusion on Hilda's face warranted a hug and reassurance.

"Don't worry, Hilda, everything will be all right."

The Boss

I stayed for dinner one evening and walked with Mom to the dining room. The aides were busy preparing beverages in a small service area adjacent to the dining room. A new resident, a distinguished looking man wearing a dress shirt and slacks, sat at a table with three other men. The minute he saw me he stood up and pointed at me. "You, come here."

I looked behind me, certain that he was addressing someone else, but no one was there. I did not say anything and focused on seating Mom in her usual place. He repeated his command, loudly, and moved his index finger in a circle as he pointed.

"You! I said come here and I mean come here RIGHT NOW!"

My eyes widened and I looked from side to side hoping to see an aide. The room became quiet and all eyes turned toward us. He then stood up and hurried toward me. Out of the corner of my eye, I saw a male CNA hurrying toward him. By then, I was moving toward the nurses office, preparing to close the door behind me. He followed.

The aide intercepted, turned him away, and quietly soothed and talked as he led him down the hall. The nurse and the night manager immediately followed me into the office and assured me that everything was under control. The new resident, admitted earlier that day, was an executive at a large company before Alzheimer's struck. They thought that he was convinced that he knew me, perhaps he mistook me for one of his former employees. Unless he could be calmed and remained civil, his daughter would be called to come and take him elsewhere.

I returned to Mom's table and tried to focus on

her and the other ladies. In truth, when I left, I cautiously checked the route to the front door. The tall executive was nowhere in sight, but an aide was admitting a woman. It was his daughter. We introduced ourselves. She was my height and our hairstyle was similar. Aha. The executive thought that I was his daughter.

She was distraught. "I am at my wit's end! This is the third place that has expelled him. I have to work. He was so angry with the nurses I hired to care for him at home that they quit. I don't know what to do!"

She trembled and I reached out and squeezed her hand. "My mother was psychotic, difficult, and finally admitted to the psychiatric unit at the hospital for evaluation. The doctors there gave her a low dose of an anti-anxiety medicine and an anti-depressant. The combination calmed her without making her sleepy. You may have to get medical assistance for your father."

She admitted that she had been refusing to allow medications, fearing the side effects. Tears streamed down her cheeks and I felt her frustration. I gathered my nerve. "I have to ask, and please tell me that it is none of my business if this upsets you. Has he ever been abusive or physically violent with you or anyone? The reason that I am asking is that he is creating his own bad reputation with memory care communities and private nurses. Few facilities will admit a person who has a record of being violent. He was very demanding when he saw me earlier, and ordered me to come to him immediately."

She paused and thought for a few moments. "No. He orders everyone around. That is his life-long, outdated management style. You and I are similar in appearance and he is upset with me for making him move here and giving him no alternatives. Perhaps that generated his anger. I guess that I will soon find out. I dread facing him."

"Well, if I can help at all, even if it is just to listen, please call me."

A booming voice interrupted. He was standing at the other end of the hallway. "Kate, is that you?" We hurriedly hugged again. I gave her my cell number and expressed my hope that her problems would soon be resolved.

Call My Lawyer

Edna was up early, dressed, and hurried down the hall to the front door where she paced back and forth. Aides tried to convince her to eat breakfast but she refused, paced faster, and watched the door. Finally, Barbara arrived. "Good morning, Edna."

"I must use your phone right away! I have to call my lawyer!"

Shortly after arriving, Edna discovered that she could not go home or get out of the door. She was trapped. She became irate and remained agitated. Each morning, she waited. Each morning, Barbara tried distracting her.

"Edna, how nice you look! Have you had breakfast? Let's go to the dining room and talk."

"I am NOT hungry!" She stomped her foot and followed Barbara to her office, protesting as she walked. "No, I have to call my lawyer, now!"

Her son and power of attorney, Steve, was overwhelmed by Edna's strong will and self-determination. He was desperate. Her doctor repeatedly warned that Edna was not safe living alone in her home. Each time Steve hired someone to stay with her, she quickly found reasons to dismiss them. They were stealing from her! He heard, "My shampoo is missing again," many times.

Since Edna's husband died several years ago, she ate most of her meals at a restaurant that was two miles from her home. One day, the owner of the restaurant called Steve. "She ate, paid, and left, as usual. We noticed that she sat in her car and did not drive away. In a few minutes, she returned, took her usual seat, seemed confused, and ordered the same breakfast a second time."

Her doctor advised Steve that her dementia was becoming worse and recommended that she stop driving. Steve was unable to convince her to relinquish her keys. Eventually, he disconnected the battery cable so that her car would not start. Edna fretted, complained, and when Steve stalled, she called her mechanic. After diagnosing the problem, he called Steve, uncertain what to do. Edna threatened to buy another car if Steve did not have hers repaired immediately. He finally relented and reconnected the cable.

A few days later, Steve was shocked into action when he received a call from a lady in Georgia. She found Edna wandering aimlessly in a mall, confused and disoriented. She located Steve's name and number in Edna's car and took care of her until Steve arrived.

After they returned, the car disappeared. He fibbed that it was towed to the mechanic's shop for major repairs and hoped to gain time to find a solution. Perhaps Edna would forget about the car. She didn't and began pestering him again.

Edna's name finally rose to the top of the waiting list for memory care. He tricked her into thinking that they were going to a restaurant for lunch and slipped out after signing the admission papers.

Barbara spoke in a soft, caring voice. "I know you are upset, Edna, come into my office." She followed but paced back and forth in front of Barbara's desk.

"Edna, please sit here beside me. It is difficult to talk when you are moving around." She dropped on a chair beside the desk.

"Now, tell me all of your concerns."

"I want to call my lawyer and I want to call the police. My son tricked me and forced me to stay here! He stole my money, my jewelry, my clothes, and my car! I am going to have him arrested and change my will!"

Barbara again tried to reason with Edna. "Your son is trying to help you Edna. Your doctor signed orders that you are not able to live alone. It is not safe for you to be at home alone. Steve is protecting you, paying all of your bills, and trying to help you. He loves you, Edna. We all want you to be happy here. Please give us a chance."

Edna gripped the chair arms, her eyes narrowed, and she pressed her lips tightly together and puckered her mouth. "NO! I DEMAND to call my lawyer. My son is a thief! I will not allow it!" Barbara sighed. "All right, Edna, I will do my best. Please give me until this afternoon to arrange everything. Edna rose and stomped down the hall toward the dining room. Barbara called Steve and explained the event.

"What can I do? I cannot quit work and stay with her. If I find another memory care facility this situation will happen all over again. You are convenient to my work and home. Do you have any suggestions?"

Barbara thought for a moment. She wanted to help him but had other residents depending on her. "She has been determined to call her attorney since the day that she arrived. We will try our best to handle this situation but if she starts disrupting other residents, we will have to ask you to make other arrangements. Even if she were to talk with her attorney, he cannot comply with her wishes, given the dementia diagnosis."

Steve groaned. "Our attorney has helped our family for years and understands our problems. As a matter of fact, I think that his mother had dementia before she passed away. I will call him now and ask if he will talk with her over the phone. It is worth a try."

Later that day, Edna received a call from her lawyer.

"Edna, how can I help you?" Edna recognized his voice and wasted no time demanding changes in her legal documents.

"Edna, I am sorry but I am not legally able to help you. Your doctor has entered into your medical records that you have dementia. Because of that, anything I do to change your power of attorney or last will and testament will be illegal. In fact, if I changed those documents now, I could be penalized. Also, Steve has no choice. He is responsible for your wellbeing and is legally responsible for you. He has to make certain that you are taken care of, or else he could be put in jail."

No one was certain whether Edna understood his blunt words. She angrily stomped out of Barbara's office. Edna fumed for the rest of the day but Barbara and the staff enticed her with food, activities, and other distractions. After a few days, Edna settled into her new routines, participated in all of the activities, and appeared to enjoy her new routines.

The Resident Romeo

After three weeks in her memory care community, I was pleased to see a big smile on Mom's face when I walked through the door.

"Guess what? I may get married again."

I was dumbfounded! What could I say? Mom had been on one date and that was fifteen years after Dad died. It did not go well and she always refused to talk about it. All of a sudden my Mom is not only seeing a man but making future plans to marry?

I sat on her bed patiently waiting for her to tell me about the new man that she was thinking of making my step-dad, but she said nothing. I checked her clothes closet, commented about the cardinals enjoying seeds on her bird feeder, and waited. She seemed to have forgotten her boyfriend. Finally, I could no longer contain my curiosity. "Mom, when I arrived, you told me that you might get married. Who is he and when will I meet him?"

"Oh, he will be by here soon."

We looked at cards and pictures together but no man appeared. My patience evaporated. After making a feeble excuse about checking something, I almost ran to Barbara's office.

Barbara saw me coming and motioned for me to come in and have a seat. I dashed in and closed the door behind me. "Yes, we have a Romeo. He is infatuated with every new female resident. His interest in Roberta will last until someone new arrives. He is married and his wife is angered when she finds him holding hands with another resident. She never confronts him about it but demands that we do something to solve the problem. We moved him to another hall and assigned him to a different dining room, but he finds his way back to this side of the building. We tried talking with him but he immediately forgets everything we say."

I was silent and worried about Mom's feelings if she were jilted. "Does Mom hold his hand?"

"Your Mom does not seem very interested in him. His attention is flattering but I doubt he will pursue her for long, she doesn't want to hug and hold hands."

I decided to say nothing else about him to Mom and wait. I assumed that time and memory loss would solve everything.

The Interior Decorator

"This room would be beautiful painted robin's egg blue. Do you like blue? The beds should be turned so that the headboards are on this wall. Don't you think that would look nice?" Most of the residents simply nodded their agreement and let her finish and move on to the next room.

Even though she was living in a memory care community, Arlene continued performing the job that she loved. In the beginning, it took a little time for her to adjust. But soon, she happily resumed her decorating career and scurried from room to room with pad and pencil in hand. Residents did not complain when she waltzed into their rooms, rambled about her plans, and scribbled on her pad.

The minute Arlene saw Larry, a new resident, she smiled and rushed to him. "I am so glad to see you. Where have you been? I need your help." She took Larry by the hand and pulled him with her on her rounds. He looked around and agreed with whatever she said.

When Larry's wife arrived with his clean clothes, she found him sitting on the sofa with Arlene in one of the television rooms. She was surprised that he was sitting close to Arlene but said nothing. He recognized her and stood as she approached. She hugged and kissed him on his cheek. "You look nice, Larry, but that shirt does not go with your slacks. Let's go to your room and change into a clean shirt."

Arlene's jaw dropped as she stared at the strange woman. She did not say a word and soon they left the room. Her surprise immediately changed into misery and she bawled as she rushed to her room and threw herself face down on the bed.

Her roommate asked, "Why are you crying?"

"Some woman came in and kissed my husband and took him to a room."

Arlene remained in her room while Larry's wife hung his clean clothes in his closet and set family photos around his room. It was a large private room. His wife chose it because she was convinced that he would not like having a stranger as his roommate.

Arlene's room faced the front of the building and after she calmed down, she patiently stood by her window and watched for the woman to leave. She was soon rewarded and flew out of her room to find Larry. "I thought she would never leave. Are you ready to help me?"

She took his hand and they continued visiting residents' rooms and talking non-stop. After work, they sat on a sofa, hugged, and held hands. At dinner, she asked one of the ladies at her table to find another table so that she and Larry could sit together. The staff intervened and found a table where they could sit together.

As the days passed, they were together

constantly. When they weren't working, they would find a sofa in one of the reception rooms, sit closely together, hug, and kiss. Residents seemed to ignore then, but if the room became too full, Arlene said, "Come on," and pulled Larry to his feet, "Let's find another room." If their display became too amorous, the staff distracted them.

Mom's First Trip Out

After six weeks, Barbara assured me that I could take Mom out for lunch without worrying. She felt certain that Mom would return without fussing. Past images of her distress the day I tried to convince her to move to assisted living still loomed in my mind. I fretted and deliberated. Finally, I summoned my courage and decided to take her to the cafeteria similar the one near her house. It was a short drive, only one mile.

The staff helped her dress and when I arrived, she was ready. "We are going to the K for lunch, Mom. It is a beautiful day and you will enjoy being outside."

My car was near the door, and as I walked beside her I noticed that her steps were smaller and more deliberate than in the past but she lowered herself onto the passenger seat with no problems. Her muscle memory was still intact.

"Where are we?" I worried that she would be upset when she realized that she was no longer in her hometown and was careful to avoid that fact. I wondered if she suspected or perhaps was informed of that by aides or visitors.

"We are getting on the interstate and the K is just down the road."

As we entered, she smiled, immediately recognized everything, and turned toward the cafeteria line. She retrieved a tray and placed two rolled napkins with cutlery inside on her tray. Her usual habit of taking two was firmly ingrained in her long-term memory. Her reason, "I may drop one." Mom's mother taught her to always be prepared for mishaps and negative events.

She chose the usual, familiar foods and ordered decaf coffee. A waiter carried our trays and she whispered, "Do you have a dollar?" I was overjoyed. Old patterns remained in her brain! Then, I began to worry. Will she refuse to go back to her new home? Will she beg me to take her house? Those thoughts occupied my mind for the rest of the afternoon. Hum. Perhaps I should consider renaming myself Roberta junior.

As in the past she requested a to-go box and arranged one half of her lunch on one side and placed a few bites of pie on the other. I did not protest but wondered if the aides would appreciate storing foods that must be refrigerated. She protested as I deposited the box in the trunk of my car, "I can hold it on my lap."

"It will be safe here and we may stop at a store. Do you need or want anything for your room, Mom?" She could not think of anything immediately but soon mentioned that she would like a small throw rug to place beside her bed. We found one that she liked at a discount variety store, and she enjoyed walking around the store holding on to a cart. She also selected a colorful throw pillow.

Time to return and my nerves were on edge. As we approached her building she asked, "Where are we? This is not my home."

"Yes, Mom, this is where you are staying. There

is your birdfeeder and don't you remember the rocking chairs?"

"Oh, OK, I do now."

Whew! "Why don't we sit on the porch in the shade for a few minutes before we go in?" She agreed and I patted myself on the back, another good distraction Ann.

One of Mom's favorite, young aides came out with another resident and we all rocked and enjoyed the pleasant weather. "If you need to go, I will see that Roberta gets back to her room in a little while."

"Actually, I do need to pick up a few things for my husband's business. I have to go now Mom. Did you enjoy our day?"

"Oh yes. I love you, hon. When will you be back?"

I always gave the same answer, "Tomorrow, Mom." If I had to skip a day or two, she never mentioned my absence. As I walked to my car, I chuckled about the box that was still in my trunk. I heard myself whispering, "Thank you, thank you, thank you."

Betsy Thrives

Michael's face radiated with love as he entered Betsy's room. The day that he left her in memory care, he was relieved to see her happily wave goodbye. During his first visit he worried that she would want to leave with him but as he said goodbye, she smiled and said, "Bye." She never asked to return home. All of his mental anguish had been unnecessary. Every day, Betsy recognized him, smiled, and gave him a hug.

They often walked around together and Betsy

cheerily greeted everyone they passed in the halls. He brought an album of family photos and they enjoyed it together. Michael asked her the names of the people in the old pictures. Some she remembered and others she did not.

Michael tried to time his visits to coincide with meals. For a small fee, he ate at the large table with her, the aides, and other residents. "I really enjoy doing that. I feel surrounded by a big family". At first the kitchen staff pureed Betsy's food. But after a few weeks, she began eating solid foods again. Every support member was amazed and we applauded and yelled, hooray when he divulged the good news.

Occasionally, he took her out to eat and to family gatherings at restaurants, but avoided driving anywhere near their home, fearing that she would want to stay. On one occasion while they driving to a favorite restaurant, she needed to use the restroom. Aware that they did not have a family toilet at that restaurant and hating the ordeal of standing outside the ladies room, he detoured by their house. She went in, used the toilet, and was immediately ready to continue their journey.

Bob Takes Care of Others

Beth's relief showed on her relaxed, well-rested face. Bob was happy and content living in his memory care community. He loved being surrounded by people and when she arrived, she usually found him sitting with other residents.

"He smiles when I arrive and, as always, he comforts people who are distressed. One day last week he was sitting beside a woman who was crying. He patted her hand and told her that everything would be all right. He may believe that he works there. On another day, he sat with me for awhile and then told me that he had to go to work, stood up, and went to his room." She smiled, "He always loved his job."

Bob became best friends with his roommate, Frank, although he couldn't remember Frank's name. They ate at the same table, sat together in the TV room or on the patio, and participated in activities side by side. One day Bob stayed in bed because he had a virus. Frank hovered over him, tucked his blankets, and did not leave his side. When Beth arrived, Frank was distraught. "Will Bob get well? I want him to get well."

Each day, Frank called his wife from the phone at the nurses' desk. Beth noticed that the frequency of his calls increased and every time that he passed the desk, he stopped and called her again. Evidently, Frank's wife asked the staff to limit his calls and, of course, they complied with her request. One day, Frank was turned down when he asked to call her and Bob became outraged. He loudly complained and lectured the nurses, and when they refused to allow Frank to call his wife, Bob ranted.

"This is not acceptable and I am not going to put up with it! I am calling the FBI and will have them come in and clean out this place. This is not right!"

When Beth walked through the door, the nurses sighed. "We are so glad to see you!"

Beth led Bob out onto the patio and distracted him. When his roommate joined them Bob asked, "Did you get that problem taken care of?"

"What problem?" Frank looked puzzled.

Later, an aide pulled Beth aside. "Does Bob have connections to the FBI?"

Beth giggled. "No!"

Kindhearted Dan

Dan immediately settled into his assisted living community and was content. He loved the food and participated in most of the activities. His demeanor was pleasant, as always, and he still liked being with people, although he often had trouble communicating. Alzheimer's had attacked the speech center in his brain.

When Adrienne arrived one day she found him sitting beside, holding, and patting the hand of a female resident. As Adrienne related this story to the support group, she called her 'Dan's girlfriend.'

When the woman first arrived, the memory of her husband's death consumed her thoughts. She never smiled and sat alone in a corner wiping tears and shaking her head. Dan could not tolerate her sorrow, sat with her, and comforted her. After a few weeks, the woman became convinced that Dan was her husband.

"How do you deal with that, Adrienne?"

"In spite of Alzheimer's, Dan is the caring guy that I always loved. I don't fret or worry about it. He is still doing good things in his world. In fact, I am relieved that he is not despondent and depressed and neither is his girlfriend."

The Doctor's Eccentricities

While Dan was easy, running interference for her father consumed most of Adrienne's time and energy. Some things never change. Adrienne was never able to predict what her Dad would say or do. She tried to adjust to his unusual behavior as best she could. He was still making waves. Lately, he used words that she never heard him utter, cursing staff and calling everyone, male or female, bitches.

One of Dad's former patients worked at the assisted living community. They had known each other for years. Dad loved to see him and enjoyed his visits. One day, Dad agreed to go with him for a ride around the grounds in a golf cart. As they set out, Dad loved it, smiled, and was content for a while. Then, for no obvious reason, he began screaming.

Adrienne laughed, "The poor guy could not return him fast enough." Dad rushed back inside and yelled at the top of his lungs, "Someone tried to kidnap me. That bitch!"

Mom's Ninetieth Birthday

Mom's first year in her memory care community passed quickly. The routines were comforting and, at times, she joined group activities and patted her feet on the floor in time with the music when musicians played. Most days, she sat in her chair, watched the bird feeder, and snoozed.

Every Friday I drove fifty miles to the town were I grew up to meet with my support group. There were many new members who were as desperate as I was in the beginning. I felt useful and appreciated and shared insights from my experiences with Mom. They were my second family, my emotional outlet, and a ready source of good advice.

After hearing updates on my interactions with Mom and others in memory care, the director assured me that Mom was satisfied. People with dementia need regular 'down time.' Over-stimulation can worsen anxiety. She was no longer isolated in the middle of her piles of 'stuff' and many of her old fears disappeared. She gained a few pounds but the new doctor who examined her at memory care was not concerned. Her medications were working.

Mom's two remaining brothers and a sister and their spouses visited monthly as did my cousins. Mom remembered her siblings' names and was surprised and happy to see them. They drove forty miles and loved visiting with Mom. My aunts always called me afterwards, pleased that she seemed happy, and all agreed that she was in a good place.

I still spent many hours thinking about Mom and felt guilty that I was no longer visiting daily or doing more for her. I wanted to find a way to make her upcoming ninetieth birthday special. In truth, I worried that her ninetieth year may be her last.

My cousin, Steve, volunteered to host a birthday luncheon at his house and invited her siblings. By then, I was certain that enough time had passed that I could safely drive Mom back to her hometown without worrying that she would plead to go to her house. The only issue that concerned me was that Mom was becoming incontinent and would have to wear adult diapers. The aides were accustomed to dealing with the accidents, but I was not.

I was spoiled by the ease of visiting Mom without worrying about the details of her care, changing or bathing her, washing her clothes, or any other chore. I focused on her and was her daughter, not her nurse. I often wondered what she was thinking or feeling, she never complained. Physically, she was safe, clean, fed, given her medications, stimulated by her interactions with the kind aides, and given time to rest. It became apparent that she was content. But I missed my loving, caring, mom who always listened to my problems .

When I hugged her and said goodbye, she always asked when I would return. My answer never changed, "I'll see you tomorrow, Mom." I sometimes knew that it may be several days until my next visit but she never scolded me for my absence.

I thought about my good fortune in the way things worked out. The memories of living each day on desperation road, racing to care for and please Mom, lingered. Each time that an aide opened the door and I walked out into the sunshine, I rejoiced. Mom and I highly valued freedom. That darned disease! How dare it rob her of her most important rights and abilities!

The Party

Steve opened his lovely home, cooked lunch, and handled all of the details. My only responsibility was to bring Mom. His round dining table was set with beautiful china, matching serving dishes, and fresh flowers adorned the center. The house was comfortable and inviting. If only his mother, Aunt Edith, Mom's oldest sister, Aunt Mary, and her brother, Kenneth, could have been there.

When we walked in the door everyone yelled, "Surprise, Happy Birthday."

"Oh my. It is my birthday, isn't it?"

We laughed, hugged, and Mom enjoyed being there. Lunch was delicious and the birthday cake was scrumptious. She opened her gifts and thanked everyone.

After lunch, we sat in the living room and talked. That is, everyone talked except Mom. She was quiet and if asked a question, she paused before giving a simple response, yes, no, or I don't know. There was a distant look in her eyes.

She asked to go to the ladies room and I helped her. Her diaper was wet and I changed her. She could not remember the steps that were necessary to accomplish that task. Before we returned to the others, she quietly asked, "Who are those people?"

Tears filled my eyes and I quickly turned away and calmly recited their names.

"Oh, yes. That's right. Who is that man who lives here?"

"He is your nephew, Steve, Aunt Edith's son."

"He is nice, isn't he?"

"The very best, Mom."

Everyone wished Mom Happy Birthday again and left by three o'clock. Mom looked at me and asked, "How old am I?"

"This is your ninetieth birthday."

In the past, she often asserted, "I am not," after she asked that question. But instead, she nodded her agreement.

I again thanked and hugged Steve, as did Mom. I wanted to leave before the afternoon rush hour traffic so that Mom could return to memory care before dinner was served. I crossed my fingers that she would not realize she was leaving the city where she spent most of her life. What would I say if she wanted to go home at least drive by it?

She was tired and said little as we journeyed west.

"Did you enjoy your birthday party, Mom?"

"Oh yes."

Sweet Excursions

After the birthday party, most of our outings were mid-afternoon visits to the donut or ice cream shops. Our last lunch at the cafeteria was stressful. Mom wanted to sit at a table while I went through the cafeteria line and selected our food. "You know what I like."

As I transferred the plates from the tray to the table, Mom's face radiated horror and disgust as she stared at her meal.

"There are bugs all over my plate!"

Oh no, delusions! "That is just seasoning, Mom."

"No! Don't you see them moving?"

"I will take your plate and get another."

My explanation of Mom's imagination to the manager quickly produced a new plate with fresh food.

When I sat it before her, she smiled and said, "My favorite."

Mom always wanted to leave the cafeteria with extra food in a take-out carton. If I persuaded her not to, she hid something in her pocket when I was not looking. I learned from the aides that Mom saved some of the food she was served in the dining room. They frequently found spoiled food that she stashed in her closet or in her bed. Snacks appeared between the sheets every time the linens were changed. Her hoarding behaviors and fears of scarcity were still intact in her brain.

She never asked to go out. I was the initiator of all excursions. Her participation in activities and games dwindled. Most afternoons, I found her snoozing in her comfortable chair and I sat quietly until she awoke.

One day, out of the blue, she said, "Guess who came by to see me."

"Who, Mom?"

"R. O."

She always referred to my Dad by his initials, but his sisters called him "Brud," their shortened version of brother.

"He did? Well. I would love to see him!"

"You will."

That was the first and last time that she mentioned his name. Most of her comments and questions were about her parents and her childhood.

"Have you seen Mom lately?"

"No, not recently. Have you?"

"Yes, she had to go somewhere and do something. I forgot."

"Well, I am certain that she will return later."

Thank You, Stranger

On most days, Stuart visited Claudia in the mornings. He usually walked her to the dining room to eat lunch before he left. After he seated her on a chair at her table, he sat beside her. He looked into her eyes and hoped that she if she gazed at his face, she would recognize him.

A resident loomed over him, paced back and forth, and demanded, "You are in my chair!"

"You know, you are right! I am in your chair and I am sorry. Here let me hold it for you."

He smiled. "Whatever they say, you just agree and play along with it. The other day two men were sitting together talking babble. They weren't using words, just sounds that I didn't understand. One would talk and then the other and they seemed to understand each other.

"Does Claudia know you, Stuart?

"She has no clue who I am. The other day I took her some new clothes and she said, 'Thank you, sir.' I always take her candy or cookies and she smiles and tolerates me. I guess that I am the nice man who brings her treats. One day, she called me by her father's name and on another day, her brother's name. Sometimes when I arrive the aides tell her that her husband is walking down the hall. Then, she might call me husband but not Stuart."

"Do you think that she is OK there?

"Oh, yes. She is getting to know the people and the routines. The aides and the residents like her. She is definitely satisfied."

Stuart's face was relaxed and rested. He smiled and was eager to talk about Claudia. Placing Claudia in memory care removed gigantic strains that he had been under for a long time. Claudia's refusal to cooperate with him had taken a toll on his happy disposition, but he was beginning to smile again.

"I don't go everyday. She has her routines and schedules and sometimes when I am there she says nothing, walks away, and goes wherever she wants. The aides take good care of her. I am confident of that."

The support group laughed as he told of unsuccessfully searching for an hour for her lower denture. He finally advised the aides, "If you see teeth laying around, they are Claudia's." The staff soon located them.

The group praised him for his courage over the last few months.

"Placing her there was the hardest thing, but the best thing for both of us. It was a terrible load that I was carrying. I have had one heart attack and I knew that my body was talking to me. Oh, I miss my wife. That is, I miss the loving Claudia, the person I knew before the disease consumed her. When I look at old pictures, I see the vibrant, quick witted, and funny Claudia. But when I look in her eyes now, that person is gone. Her look is hollow, vacant. I have to accept reality."

"I still feel guilty that I put her there. I am no longer in control and that is difficult after caring for her for years. But feeling that way is my problem, not hers or theirs. Those feelings are inevitable and I am learning how to deal with them."

Ann's Quandary

Mom's body sat in her comfortable chair but her mind was in the past. The memories of her childhood that remained deep in her brain for most of her life were precious jewels that engaged and enthralled her. It was all that she had left and I played along and encouraged her journeys back in time.

Fortunately, or unfortunately depending on my mood at the time, my body and mind were very much in the present. My confusion and uncertainty about my own future remained. Those nagging questions that plagued me were still unanswered. What do I do now? Who am I? What CAN I do? What do I WANT to do?

Dale fulfilled his promise and we began an addition to and renovation of our lake house. Much of my time involved planning the design and overseeing the workers. I loved creating beautiful spaces but I could not make building our house last forever.

Too many years had separated me from my

academic career that was at one time my goal in life. I remembered the exhilarating rush that I received when I stood before a class of young minds and devised ways to open and expand their worlds. But did I have the fortitude and time to return to that life? I was too old and it was too late. An academician cannot step away from daily emersion in new information and ideas and expect to jump back in without spending years absorbing all that she missed.

You must do something else! What? Rational Ann asked, *what do you want to do when you grow up? You can do anything. You demonstrated that ability many times in the past!* Emotional Ann laughed and then cried. *You are lost! You are just as lost as your mother!*

Rational Ann disagreed. *Don't listen to that nonsense! The activity you love most is your weekly support group. Ten years of focusing on and dealing with dementia enables you to empathize with and educate people who become desperate when they step into the taxing role of caring for someone with dementia. Don't stop. Keep helping. They need you.*

A Looming, Gigantic Task

I ignored a huge problem that sat, unattended, in the neighborhood where I grew up. Since Mom moved to memory care, I avoided going to her house except for quick stops to make sure that everything was still there and still locked. My brief moments in Mom's house were painful and the minute that I relocked the door and drove away I redirected my thoughts elsewhere. Mom admonished me each time I touched her treasures.

Although I accepted that she would never go back there, disturbing her things was the final, irrefutable affirmation that I was slowly losing her.

When you have no direction and no clue about WHAT to do, you flounder. Rational Ann advised, *focus on first things first and take care of unwanted, but necessary, tasks.* The more I thought about it, the more formidable the problem became. The dust, dirt, and the sheer volume that must be sifted through piece by piece, was daunting.

As always in my life, when I began thinking seriously about something important that needed my attention, resources and solutions materialized. My phone rang. It was cousin Steve.

"I am retired now and have been volunteering at the food pantry one day each week and that is very rewarding. I have been thinking about you and know that you are facing a gigantic task. I will help you. You cannot do it by yourself. I have my truck and trailer and am willing."

One Day At A Time

The first day, we arrived with industrial trash bags and went from room to room clearing out everything of absolutely no value, trash. We removed grocery bags that Mom had stuffed full of used paper towels and tissues. Empty wrappers, boxes, and hundreds of empty cans, cartons, jars, and bottles were sitting around in various places all over the house. We piled newspapers, junk mail, and other recyclables into the trunk of my car. At the end of the day, Steve's trailer was loaded with forty or fifty garbage bags and we made our first trip to the landfill.

I collapsed in bed that night, thankful and determined. The task would take months, possibly years. I should purchase a big supply of allergy medications. But thanks to Steve's organizational skills, we had a plan. We started early one or two days each week with specific daily goals in mind.

We needed room to work. The second day, our mission was to round up and evaluate piles of clothing scattered around and hanging on every door. Mom never discarded anything. Most of her clothes were no longer wearable, obviously too big, too little, full of holes, faded, or out of date. We loaded our vehicles with donations but several more days were needed just to handle clothing. Some of the closets around the perimeter of the attic were packed with clothing from the 1950's, 60's, 70's, and 80's. The students who loved vintage clothing had a field day at the Goodwill.

I no longer had time to contemplate my future. My hands were full and very dirty. It was hard, gut-wrenching work. I found Dad's robe and slippers and was immediately transported back in time to magical Christmas mornings. Much to Steve's chagrin, I became an urban archeologist and carefully examined everything. I was lost in the past as I touched and evaluated each treasure and sought its existence in my long-term memory. Ah-ha! That was what Mom had been doing all of those years alone inside her house!

My initial reaction was to take some of the mementos to share with Mom. But rational Ann, the analyzer, intervened. *Wait a minute! Think about it. What if she asks where you found them. How will you explain your possession of these items to her? She has always been intuitive. Does that ability remain? Will she know what you have been doing?* Emotional Ann was constantly by my side. *Don't be a coward! She will love seeing them. You may be able to share memories and connect in ways that have been impossible!* Rational Ann disagreed. *You cannot predict how she will react. You may end up causing her unnecessary pain.*

"Are you going to take all day just going through that one little drawer?"

"Sorry, Steve, I was lost in the past. I will try to be more task oriented."

"Here is a box. Put everything that you want to inspect in it and I will load it in your car. You can take it home and spend all the time you want thinking about those things, later.

"My kind cousin resolved one problem. Unfortunately, my persistent cousin added fuel to another, fast-growing problem. Many boxes went into my car and then into my house, but 'all the time that I want' never came. Boxes of my precious memories were stacked in my basement and other nooks and crannies.

The courage that I needed to share artifacts from our past with Mom never appeared. Every time that I was tempted, her words, "I don't want you messing in my things," reverberated in my head. Was I kind, saving her from unnecessary turmoil, or self-centered, unwilling to risk losing her trust? When I look back, I regret not trying to stimulate her memories. Guilt remains.

Middle of the Night Emergencies

The weeks and months flew by. Mom was on a plateau with little or no further mental decline. I visited her in the afternoons and occasionally suggested that we go for a ride in my car. She loved ice cream and donuts and never refused my suggestion that we treat ourselves to a cup of decaf and something sweet. She was easily tired and soon ready to return to her room to rest before dinner.

Mom's roommates changed, but Barbara carefully selected pleasant, agreeable ladies. Mom never complained. The aides loved her and there were never issues with other residents. Occasionally, I had issues with a resident. One day when I entered her room, a man was lying on Mom's bed. "What is he doing in here?" Mom did not respond and the aides immediately redirected him to his room and explained that Henry did not remember where his room was.

Just when things seemed to be flowing along with no problems, they began. My phone rang in the middle of the night. It was the night nurse.

"Ann, we had to send Roberta to the emergency room in an ambulance. She fell. We don't think that anything was broken, but our management requires that we have her checked by doctors. Can you meet her there now?

Mom was lying on a gurney in an examining room, confused, and complained of pain every few minutes.. Regardless of where the doctor touched her, she winced.

"Do you hurt here, Roberta?" He squeezed her upper arm.

"Oh!"

"How about here?"

"Oh!

He repeated the procedure on her leg and a few other places. Finally, several hours later, x-rays indicated that nothing was broken. She was discharged with a prescription for a mild pain medication.

"You will be sore for a while, Roberta. You had a nasty fall."

She was tired. "I did NOT fall!" I took her back to memory care in my car.

Why Are Those People Looking in my Window?

The minute that I walked into Mom's room, my smile faded. Her face was distorted with a horrible expression. She starred at the window.

"Who are all those people looking in my window?"

I gazed out the window, but no one was in sight. It was a sunny day and birds flitted in and out of the feeder.

"You are upset Mom."

"I don't want them staring at me! They have no business out there!"

"I will talk with the manager and she will handle the problem."

Barbara was in her office with the door open. She frowned. "Roberta's hallucinations have returned and seem to be getting worse. The doctor will be here in a day or two. If you want to talk with him, I will let you know the time that he is coming as soon as they notify me. Her medicines may need to be increased or changed."

"Thank you. I will be here."

"For now I will have our handyman go out there,

wave his arms, and tell them to leave."

It worked. Mom was satisfied when she saw the handyman cross back and forth by her window. I suggested we walk to the dining room and have juice or decaf coffee. The warm beverage was good and she smiled. When we returned, she settled in her chair and was content.

The doctor hesitated to change or increase her medicines. He did not want make her drowsy or risk other side effects. Instead, he requested an increase in fluid intake and had his nurse collect a urine specimen.

"Sitting most of the day and low intake of fluids can cause dehydration and urinary tract infections that will affect her mentally. One way that we identify urinary infections in elderly people is that they make unusual, for the lack of a better word, 'crazy' comments. Let's check this first and then, if she still has hallucinations, we will try something else."

There was an infection and a round of antibiotics were prescribed. Everything was fine for a few months. Then, I was again summoned to the emergency room in the middle of the night. It was the same as before, she fell in her room but had no major injuries, just bruises. She returned to memory care and was sore for a few days.

I was concerned that the falls were due to TIA'S, minor strokes. The doctor could not say for certain, but it was possible. Even though the night aides made regular rounds, accidents happen. My guess was that she was awakened by a dream or felt the urge to urinate and became dizzy as she tried to stand and fell forward. There was a buzzer to call an aide attached to her bed but she did not remember that it was there even though she was reminded nightly.

What could be done? Unless someone was sitting

in the room with her throughout the night, it was unlikely that these middle-of-the-night falls could be prevented. Unfortunately, I did not realize that the situation was a ticking time bomb.

Boom!

At five one morning, my phone rang. "Ann, Roberta fell forward and hit her head. The ambulance just left. One of the aides is riding to the hospital with her. We don't know how bad it is but there was blood and you need to hurry."

Oh no, no, no! I jumped into my clothes and ran out of the door. The eastern sky was turning from gray to pink. Just as I turned into the hospital parking lot, I received another call.

"Ann, this is Barbara. Roberta has a neck injury and the emergency doctor sent her in an ambulance to Wake Forest Medical Center. Don't bother going inside. Our hospital is not equipped to handle neck injuries. Go quickly, but be careful. Please let me know how she is as soon as you can."

I was shocked. My heart raced. I was numb. I was nauseated. Aaarrgh!

Why Oh Why?

I was horrified. "A broken neck?"

"She must have fallen forward from a standing position. There is a huge cut and significant swelling of her forehead. The rebound of hitting her head on the hard floor probably caused the upper spinal fracture. If she were younger and did not have dementia, we could operate and after a few months of wearing a brace and neck collar, she would be fine. Unfortunately, at ninety-one, I am afraid she would never make it through surgery. If she did, she would not be able to stand the misery of wearing a surgical collar. They are very uncomfortable."

I was stunned but managed to ask, "So, what can be done?"

"We think it best to send her to the palliative care floor, keep her comfortable, give it a few days, and see how she responds. She will be going there soon. You can go with her."

When I saw her, I nearly fainted. Her eye was black and her forehead bandaged and swollen. She stirred.

"I'm here, Mom." I took her hand. "I will not leave you."

Time. Where Did You Go?

At first, the doctors, nurses, and I thought that she would rally. After a couple of days, I convinced her to eat soup and green beans. She could not get up and if her head was raised, she was in pain. I went home late each night and returned early. Everything outside of that hospital room was frozen in time. I did not even think about other things.

Then, Mom stopped eating. I sat by her side, rubbed her hand and face, and talked to her. Her eyes were open and she knew that I was there but she said little. She was not hungry and refused all food.

As I sat watching her sleep, it occurred to me that she had regressed to infancy. She could not walk, did not talk, and barely sipped liquids. She traveled backwards from a functioning adult to lying there, a baby. Where could she go? How could she move any further backward? I shuddered.

The doctors recommended Hospice and two Hospice nurses came in and introduced themselves. After examining Mom, everyone agreed. Mom was ready for Hospice.

Mom's end of life directives popped into my mind. She did not want to be kept alive if there was no hope. *Thank you, Mom. I don't know if I would have the grit and gumption to make that decision for you.* Hospice was what she would have wanted.

Hospice

The big window in her room framed green grass and tall trees beyond a well-manicured garden. Clear Carolina blue skies crowned the idyllic late spring setting. Birds chirped as they searched for bugs and worms to feed their newborn babies.

Mom's room was calm, quiet and comfortable. The doctors and nurses spoke with kind, caring voices. The female doctor that greeted Mom promised to make certain that she could rest and be free of pain. Mom smiled weakly and softly said, "That's good."

As she slept I sat beside of her bed thinking. Mom, ever since Dad died you tried to be strong and self-sufficient. You wanted to stay in your home forever. Your fears of not being able to do that, not having the things you needed and having to depend on other people drove you. How sad and ironic that the things you feared most are with you at the end of your life.

Mom's brothers, sister, their spouses, nieces and nephews came. Alex was by her Gang's side. She drifted in and out of sleep and was not in pain. She was tired.

I squeezed her hand. "It's OK to go, Mom. Dad is waiting and he will not leave you. I love you dearly and I will miss you but I will be all right. You need to go be with Daddy."

Epilogue One

Two days after Mom turned 92, she was gone. It was a glorious, early summer morning, much like the one when she was born. The birds sang and her suffering was over.

The wooden pews were filled with family, friends, neighbors, church members and customers. Her dear nephew, Richard, spoke of the life of his kindhearted, fun-loving Aunt Bert. The pianist played the Battle Hymn of the Republic as her strong nephews rolled and then carried her casket to the cemetery. I walked close behind, holding onto Dale. Alex followed and Alana's Dad carried her with one arm and held Alex with the other. Alana's eyes were wide with wonder. She was too young to realize the gravity of the moment or understand the fragility of life, but she saw us crying and understood that something sad was happening.

Mom's body was placed beside Dad's in the beautiful, green cemetery of the church she attended all of her life until dementia closed her world. On the top of her casket was a plaque engraved with "The Hardware Lady."

After the final prayer everyone hugged, aunts, uncles, cousins, and friends. Church members served lunch and family shared their fond memories of Roberta. Old photographs of Mom when she was young, with Dad when they were dating, and with family and friends were flashed on a big screen at the end of the fellowship hall.

I was one of the last to leave and as I sat down in the car I realized that I left my jacket in the church. "I'll get it, I remember where I left it." As I stood by the car, I paused, turned, looked at Alex and said, "Don't Leave Me!

Epilogue Two

Rational Ann insisted, "Come on! We are going to be late for the support meeting."

Emotional Ann countered, "You don't need me! You are the rational decision maker! Go without me."

Rational Ann admonished, "I cannot do this without you! Dementia is the only disease that cannot be cured! People need us! They pour their hearts out, feel sadness, outrage, confusion, doubt, fear, and to stay sane, they must laugh occasionally. Thanks to our journey with Mom, we can listen, understand, and let them know that they are not alone. Rational decisions have to be made but not without emotions!"

Emotional Ann did not budge.

Rational Ann was exasperated. "Sit there if you must but I am leaving." The door slammed.

Emotional Ann jumped up. "Wait! Do you have my tissues? What about my cookies? Don't leave me!"

Advice for the Road

Desperation leads to hopelessness and frantic, irrational thinking. A desperate person cannot function well or make good decisions. It is impossible to provide the care a loved one needs when exhausted, frustrated, and desperate. The anxiety and depression of constantly living with those feelings has been linked to higher risks of health problems and diseases.

Do not travel down desperation road alone. Anguish, anxiety, and depression cannot be managed without help. Make it your mission to seek out helpers, friends, information, and community resources. Find and join a support group conducted by professionals. Coping skills and mental health are improved when we talk and tell our stories. One person's honesty and openness encourages others to think about and expose their own emotions. When you realize that you are not in this alone, understanding and healing can occur.

Seek help within your community. Resources vary across communities, cities, and states. Search online or open your yellow pages. Finding one resource often opens doors to others, and many are free. Pick up your phone and ask.

There is a nationally available program called Powerful Tools for Caregivers (PTC) that offers six, free, weekly workshops to help caregivers cope. The course is usually offered through local non-profit agencies and senior services.

A Plea

Please don't turn away from people suffering from dementia or those trying to care for them. Don't worry about what to say, just hug them and let them know you care. Your presence communicates more than words. Ask what they need from the store, mow their yard, or offer a cup of coffee and a few minutes of your time. For those of you who have traveled the road, you are more qualified than anyone to help your friend by sitting with his or her loved one for a few hours.

After the Journey, don't let your desperate days extinguish your spirit. Use the calm after the storm to recharge, re-energize, and move forward into your changed life. Shine your light on the treacherous road and help others find their way. One thing is certain. At the end of every road, we need each other.

Acknowledgements

I am thankful for every day and every person who has come my way. First, my mother, Roberta, and my father, R. O. Jr., blessed me with many attributes and gave me their unconditional love. My family, friends, neighbors, teachers, students, and many others enriched my days and made my life joyful.

At times, I wonder if I could have made it through the last ten years of my mother's life if it were not for Jean Small's love and wisdom. Jean was the former Director of the Tad Williams Adult Daycare Center in Winston-Salem, North Carolina. The staff and the current director, Kathy Long, are phenomenal. The caregivers that I met along the way became my friends and family. It is impossible to travel along Desperation Road alone. Each caregiver needs love, understanding, acceptance and assistance from those around him or her.

To the caring people who encouraged me to write the stories and who shared their thoughts and emotions, without your love and trust this book could never have been written. A special thanks to Mary Frances and Steve who edited, questioned, and encouraged. For my family and friends, what would life be without you? I love you.

About the Author

Ann Renigar Hiatt holds a Ph.D. degree from the University of North Carolina at Greensboro in Human Development and Family Studies. Her graduate research focused on identifying and understanding time-use behaviors and strategies of employed, married women with families. She was an assistant professor in the Department of Human Services at UNC Charlotte before living and traveling in Asia and Europe. In Singapore, she interviewed Philippine women who left their families and worked as nannies and housekeepers to earn money to send home for their children.

After returning, she became immersed in a stressful but necessary journey with her widowed mother who was diagnosed with vascular dementia. For the last twenty years, Ann has interviewed, documented, and written about the physical and emotional highs and lows of kind, caring people called caregivers. Her conflict-driven stories are crafted to entertain and educate readers and, hopefully, promote widespread awareness of tragic, mental degenerative diseases.

Ann and her husband live on Lake Norman in North Carolina. Detour Down Desperation Road is her first non-fiction book of stories. You may contact her at www.annhiatt.com.

45197826R00174

Made in the USA
Middletown, DE
27 June 2017